What's Your Business?

What's Your Business?

Corporate Design Strategy Concepts and Processes

CLAIRE T. TOMLINS

Routledge
Taylor & Francis Group

LONDON AND NEW YORK

First published 2014 by Gower Publishing

2 Park Square, Milton Park, Abingdon, Oxfordshire OX14 4RN
52 Vanderbilt Avenue, New York, NY 10017

Routledge is an imprint of the Taylor & Francis Group, an informa business

First issued in paperback 2019

Gower Applied Business Research
Our programme provides leaders, practitioners, scholars and researchers with thought provoking, cutting edge books that combine conceptual insights, interdisciplinary rigour and practical relevance in key areas of business and management.

British Library Cataloguing in Publication Data
A catalogue record for this book is available from the British Library

Library of Congress Cataloging-in-Publication Data
Tomlins, Claire T.
    What's your business? : corporate design strategy concepts and processes / by
    Claire T. Tomlins.
        pages cm
    Includes bibliographical references and index.
    ISBN 978-1-4724-1746-6 (hardback : alk. paper) -- ISBN 978-1-4724-1747-3 (ebook) --
    ISBN 978-1-4724-1748-0 (epub)
        1. Corporate image--Design. 2. Industrial design coordination. 3. Web sites--Design.
    4. Strategic planning. I. Title.
    HD59.2.T66 2014
    659.20285'4678--dc23
                                                                                2014000114

ISBN 13: 978-1-4724-1746-6 (hbk)
ISBN 13: 978-0-367-87918-1 (pbk)

Contents

List of Figures

List of Tables

List of Plates

Preface

Whilst working in a wide range of businesses and considering their strategies, operations and business processes, it became increasingly apparent to me that design was a crucial input often considered irrelevant. As the internet and new media began to impact these businesses, how they were designed was likely to have a significant impact on their activities and success in the rapidly changing business world.

Throughout time businesses and organisations have operated within complex environments relative to their era, geographical location and technological expertise. Today, the pace and extent of their operations have changed dramatically. A local market trader may buy a van, promote his business on a blackboard and proclaim the daily special offers. Another business may have a computer, design a website and use social media to communicate with potentially global clients. Both have a key component when someone asks: 'What's your business?' – the business idea and the development of its distinctive existence in the marketplace.

The aim of this book is to provide understanding of corporate design strategy, concepts and processes across traditional and digital media and their relationship and interlinkages with business strategy. This subject area also includes a wide array of art and design practitioners who, through their particular skills, knowledge and media, produce the tangible outcomes of the strategic story.

The book encapsulates key strategic components and concepts in creating a business, whether this is in the real world or online. To maintain this practicality, a subsidiary thread of questions and answers are placed at the beginning and end of each chapter to facilitate the development of the reader's new business project.

What's Your Business? provides a comprehensive pathway through this subject in five sections:

1. By examining how the terms *corporate identity, image, branding, communication* and *reputation* evolved and art and design's contribution to the subject;

2. Then recognising an identity based on a story, to spark the corporate and design strategy that positions the business in its selected marketplace, and surveying necessary business and creative skillsets;

3. Critical design management and intellectual property law topics are provided, as well as measures of design success;

4. The creation of symbolic elements that aesthetically place the business in its market through visual identity elements, organisational behaviour and environmental context are described;

5. Finally, exploration of the impact of developing digital technology and social networking media relevant to corporate design strategy.

Who Should Read this Book?

What's Your Business? has been written for people who wish to understand how design can be of benefit to their business by providing that extra added value. CEOs, senior managers, design and marketing professionals of SMEs or large corporate enterprises will find this book directly relevant to their work. Here they will recognise their roles in contributing to a corporate strategy and design strategy with explanations of corporate design necessities and processes. Professional design practitioners can also recognise where their skills can be applied, enabling them to concentrate resources on fruitful projects.

Academically the book updates concepts and definitions to include digital media applications. By capturing all the key inputs, it will enable business students to understand why design is important and where it can be applied; and design students can see where their skills are required within the corporate environment.

Acknowledgements

There are many contributors to this book across business and academia through my experience over many years working with clients, colleagues and educators. Through projects, presentations, discussions and writing, my interests in a wide range of subjects have been developed, tried and tested in the real world. As the internet developed, this opened a new page and another set of colleagues as this work merges with the real world.

For this book I would particularly like to thank staff at UAL (CSM and LCC) and UCA who developed my interest in design in recent years, in particular Martin Woolley, Lizabeth Goodman, Teal Triggs, Ian Barraclough, Nick Gorse and Kathy Best. I also thank Michael Wolff for an insightful interview, and Carmel Allen of Heal's for providing a useful and interesting case study for the book.

Additionally I thank my consultancy colleagues across a wide sphere, including Roger and Gill Cooper who introduced and developed my management consulting skills in a range of manufacturing companies, where I realised the importance of design across many applications.

Most of all, I would like to thank my husband Richard and family for their encouragement and forbearance whilst writing this book.

List of Abbreviations

3D	Three dimensional
AC²ID	Actual, Communicated, Conceived, Ideal, Desired
.bmp	Bitmap image file
CD	Compact disc
CEO	Chief executive officer
CIM	Corporate identity management
CMYK	Cyan, magenta, yellow, black
CRT	Cathode ray tube
CSR	Corporate social responsibility
CSS	Cascading style sheets
CVIS	Corporate visual identity system
DDA	Disability Discrimination Act 1995
DEAR	Decisions are evaluated against reputations
DHTML	Dynamic hypertext mark-up language
EPO	European Patent Office
EU	European Union
EUCD	European Union and Copyright Directive
FTSE	Financial Times and London Stock Exchange
.gif	Graphic interchange format
HCI	Human–computer interaction
HTML	Hypertext mark-up language
ICANN	Internet Corporation for Assigned Names and Numbers
iPod	Portable media player
.jpeg	Joint photographic experts group
LCD	Liquid crystal display
LLP	Limited liability partnerships
OB	Organisational behaviour
PC	Personal computers
PDA	Personal data appliance
PEARL	Process and experiment automation real-time language
PEEST	Political, economic, environmental, sociological, technological
.png	Portable network graphic

RGB	Red, green, blue
SMART	Specific, measurable, attainable, relevant, timebound
STEEP	Sociological, technological, economic, environmental, political
SWOT	Strengths, weaknesses, opportunities, threats
.tiff	Tagged image file format
UK	United Kingdom
UKIPO	UK Intellectual Property Office
US	United States
USP	Unique selling proposition
W3C	World Wide Web Consortium
WCT	WIPO Copyright Treaty
WIPO	World Intellectual Property Organization
WPPT	WIPO Performance and Phonogram Treaty

Part I

Ground Base – How Corporate Design Started and Evolved

Corporate design concepts and terms progress an idea through to its physical manifestation as a business or other type of organisation. This subject has been in existence since the first commercial barter transaction – a person or organisation with an identity and appearance who communicated what they were selling or doing. Throughout the centuries, monarchies, military, religions and trade guilds have recognised the relevance of corporate design and applied its concepts to the creation and use of regalia, uniforms, structures, stories, behaviour, signs and rituals, and this still continues today worldwide.

It was not until the mid 1950s that the subject gained business and academic recognition. Part I of this book considers the terms in their academic origins. Many books today emphasise the practice and the academic, with academic taking second place. However, unless we take time to observe our surroundings, consider what is happening and argue the relevant pros and cons for progression, mistakes can be made. All societies survive and evolve through a wide range of occurrences and cogitations; it is only by formulating goals, structures, policies and laws that they can survive.

In practice, corporate design is applied to the design of academic institutions, the business environment, towns, cities, countries, continents and everything in between to communicate their ethos, way of working and what they stand for. This is communicated through a multitude of communication channels and media.

Part I starts the book by introducing the subject and its key terms and how they were recognised and developed across traditional print media, TV and film. By starting here, the appearance of digital media becomes part of the subject's evolution as well as digital media technology itself and where changes in emphasis and definitions of key terms evolved.

Essentially identity and image are inherent in everything, communicating an organisation's existence to the outside world. This may be a one-man or woman small to medium size enterprise which has a business idea, sets up a stall, prints pamphlets, or designs a one-page website to advertise what it is selling. On the other hand, it could be a global corporation with a clearly defined corporate identity strategy or website branding strategy and complex management systems. Both businesses have an identity and project an image that communicates a message by corporate design approaches.

The following three chapters will explain how the subject of corporate and branding design developed through three interrelated subjects:

Chapter 1   Corporate Identity and Image Development

Chapter 2   Corporate Identity and Branding Debate

Chapter 3   New Media, Communication and Reputation

Chapter 1

Corporate Identity and Image Development

Where do businesses come from?

Introduction

In this chapter, a potted history of how corporate identity and branding developed during the 1950s, 1970s and 1990s is discussed, establishing the modern business through recognition of the terms *identity* and *image*.

Corporate design has been in existence for millennia across the world, as anyone starting an organisation or business communicates an identity and image straight away. Here the journey will start in the 1950s when Pierre Martineau (1958) established the subject and coined the term *corporate identity* which was portrayed through images. At this time graphic designers were the practitioners of the subject as they synthesised information to create an image and message that a business required. F.H.K. Henrion, a British graphic designer, then produced *house styles* for the UK and European markets, firmly establishing the subject within the business environment. Further development occurred in the US, reinforcing the term *corporate identity* through graphic design and visual identity systems (Balmer and Greyser, 2003). Worldwide each country and its organisations have an identity and project an image. This is developed independently according to their geographical location, mores and traditions.

1.1 Early Recognition of Corporate Identity

Walter Marguiles (1977) and Wally Olins (1978) continued advancing the subject during the 1970s, as it gained popularity in the business world. Corporate identity during this period related business image creation as a necessity in establishing and enhancing a company's reputation in the marketplace. Marguiles (1977) suggested that a positive image, created from the business's identity and its initial occurrence and evolution over time, impacted its reputation. Hence a company had to manage the way its image was presented to audiences. Communication and reputation will be discussed in Chapter 3.

There is no clear definition of corporate identity. This is reflected in the business world where executives once had little knowledge of the subject, its strategic implication or management (Melewar and Smith, 2003). Even today, when corporate identity or branding is mentioned, most people consider it only to be visual identity. Over time definitions subtly changed as each term's relevance and purpose became more apparent. Wally Olins has mentioned that it takes time for the corporate identity notion to be accepted and understood. He provided the premise upon which traditional corporate identity is based, which can still be transferred to the digital world and branding, commenting that: '[Corporate identity] can project four things: who you are, what you do, how you do it and where you want to go' (Olins, 1995). The 'who you are' and 'what you do' determine who the company is, whereas 'how you do it' defines what the company is like personally, its personality. This approach served the business requirement on traditional media communication by directing the creation of an identity for the organisation and image to be distributed to the world outside the organisation. Further definitions of corporate identity will be given in Chapter 2. Here it suffices to say that the subject's late recognition and development encouraged not only isolationism but also creativity and innovation that formed around distinct national and disciplinary schools of thought.

The 1970s and 1980s saw corporate identity, design and public relations merge as they began to use communication and behavioural techniques to establish how an organisation communicates externally and internally. The subject gaining popularity as organisational behaviour became recognised as part of an organisation's cultural identity, this being added to visual identity as part of the image creative process consolidating the *symbolic* nature of corporate design. Hence recognition of the corporate design notion took time for people to understand, even though it is a constant feature of daily life.

Another important factor in corporate identity development was that, until the late 1980s, corporate image communication for the majority of UK businesses was fairly local or national in approach. Only international companies had to consider socio-political and legal requirements in other countries. They could control the imagery and its distribution. Historically, these companies formed around products, after the Industrial Revolution. In the modern era, the 1980s internationalist approach defined product branding as principally the process of attaching the name and a reputation to something or someone. Hence these companies created their own symbols to emphasise the company's market position in the selected local or national markets, thereby controlling audience perception of the company and its products by imagery.

Traditional media corporate identity literature in the UK reached academic maturity in the late 1990s. At this time, seven terms had been recognised: *corporate identity*; *branding*; *image*; *corporate communication*; *reputation*; *symbolic visual identity*; and *symbolic organisational behaviour*. The subject is now part of corporate level marketing (Balmer, 2002) where the company philosophy, management and processes receive attention. The identity–image–reputation communication interfaces are of strategic importance, being inherently multidisciplinary in nature (Balmer, 2002; Van Riel and Balmer, 1997) with many skillsets employed and applied to various media which communicate the message.

1.2 New Media and the Internet

The early 1990s introduced the internet's potential as an additional marketing communication channel through which to convey corporate image. The key difference between traditional media and web technology was that at this time website visitors *pulled* information from a computer screen, which could be located anywhere in the world and updated and accessed anytime. Conventionally this same information had to be *pushed* or distributed into the marketplace as detailed above. More subjects and concepts were now being added to corporate identity, as corporate strategists, designers, researchers and website visitors grappled with the digital medium's possibilities and necessities.

Conclusion

To sum up, in the second half of the twentieth century corporate identity terminology developed in the UK, European and US markets from its initial corporate image created by graphic designers under the academic heading of symbolic visual identity. Then the 1980s recognised organisational behaviour, portrayed through attitudes and rituals, which was added to the symbolic subject area. As corporate identity and the created image on traditional media was reaching maturity in the 1990s, web technology began to open up new possibilities. Terms applied in traditional contexts were transferring to web technology, with continual debates as it developed and transformed business.

To answer the practical question – where do businesses come from?

Businesses and organisations start with one person or group having an idea, defining a market *niche* – its position – where they think the product or service will thrive, then advertising the business and its products and/or services by distributing leaflets and putting displays on notice boards and websites, including word of mouth and social media. The manner by which the business is conducted – its rituals – will determine how the business establishes itself in the marketplace. If customers like the business and its products, then they will buy. Thereafter the business's reputation starts to form.

Chapter 2
Corporate Identity and Branding Debate

Am I marketing a concept, product or service?

Introduction

Often there is no clear difference made between *corporate identity* and *corporate brand*, yet the terms are conceptually different with specific definition, purpose and usage. This chapter will provide a more detailed definition of corporate identity and branding theory, explaining how the terms developed, where the confusion has arisen, and their current usage today as branding appears more regularly in academic and business literature.

2.1 Twentieth-Century Corporate Identity Definitions

In the twentieth century corporate identity was seen as difficult, with the consensus being that the term had been narrowly conceived (Van Riel, 1995), regardless of whether it was applied to countries, regions, cities, companies or voluntary organisations. Since Martineau's (1958) explanation, there has been an increasing understanding of the subject as new concepts and subjects were recognised; for example, in addition to graphic design and organisational behaviour, the subject is now under the marketing umbrella, contributing to corporate strategy by considering a wide range of information sources from economics, sociology, psychology, communication, semiotics, reputation studies and other growing new media subjects.

In 1995 a group of academics, including John Balmer and Stephen Greyser, prepared the 'Strathclyde Statement' (see Table 2.1) to explain this multidisciplinary subject and its divergence from branding. The key points are that corporate identity forms a business's individuality, differentiating it in the marketplace, whilst communicating the organisation's ethos, personality, vision and activities by coherent imagery and the corporate visual identity system (CVIS). In the 1980s organisational behaviour was recognised based on cultures, stories and rituals built up within an organisation by its activities, stories and staff, across all its media applications.

Table 2.1   The original 'Strathclyde Statement' on corporate identity

---

The Strathclyde Statement

Corporate identity management is concerned with the conception, development, and communication of an organization's mission, philosophy, and ethos.
Its orientation is strategic and is based on a company's
values, cultures, and behaviors.

The management of corporate identity draws on many disciplines, including strategic management, marketing, corporate communications,
organizational behavior, public relations, and design.

It is different from traditional brand marketing directed towards household or business-to-business product/service purchases since it is concerned with
all of an organization's stakeholders and
the multifaceted way in which an organization communicates.

It is dynamic, not static, and is greatly affected by
changes in the external environment.

When well managed, an organization's identity results in loyalty from
its diverse stakeholders.

As such it can positively affect organizational performance,
e.g. its ability to attract and retain customers,
achieve strategic alliances, recruit executives and employees,
be well positioned in financial markets, and strengthen
internal staff identification
with the firm.

(*Source*: John M.T. Balmer and Stephen A. Greyser, 1995)

By strategically managing this image externally, a company can engage a wide range of stakeholders by way of various media channels. The 1995 statement was further developed by Cees B.M. Van Riel and John M.T. Balmer in the 'Strathclyde Statement' of 1997 where they suggest that corporate identity builds commitment and communication between the company and its diverse stakeholders, this being where it differs from branding which is focused on the product and service's bottom line stakeholders. To complete the definitions, two by Michael Wolff are quite specific: 'A corporate identity has personality, a realization and revelation of self in a corporate context'; whereas: 'A corporate brand is how you exist in other people's minds … retrieved from their memory when the name is mentioned' (Michael Wolff, Interview 2006).

2.1.1 CORPORATE IDENTITY SCHOOLS OF THOUGHT

To continue relating the terms with the real world is important as it provides grounding upon which digital events can be debated. Four corporate identity schools of thought were identified by John Balmer in 2003:

1. Strategic school, addressing company philosophy, vision and mission (Olins, 1989, 1995; Van Riel, 1995), connecting corporate strategy with reputation and image (Van Riel, 1995; Fombrun, 1996).

2. Business Structure Identity school, where a company's structure has an impact on its corporate identity and image communication across two dimensions: i) the manner by which the organisation functions; ii) the mechanisms chosen to reflect this functional structure for marketing purposes (Abratt, 1989; Ind, 1998; Marwick and Fill, 1997; Stuart, 1998, 1999; Van Riel, 1995).

3. Visual Identity school, which is communicated by symbolic graphic design and physical expressions. Visual identity by names, logos, house styles, jingles and slogans, and physical expressions by architectural exterior and interior designs and product design (Argenti, 1998; Baker and Balmer, 1997; Melewar, 2001; Melewar, Bassett and Simoes, 2006; Olins, 1995).

4. Organisational Identity school, which looks internally at employee affinity with the organisation rather than its external focus of image, seeking to capture the organisation's essence, distinctive and enduring features over time (Albert and Whetten, 1985; Gioia, Schultz and Corley, 2000).

Figure 2.1 (Corporate Design Triangle 1) illustrates where the relationship and linkages occur between the main grouping, alongside other writers on the subject areas.

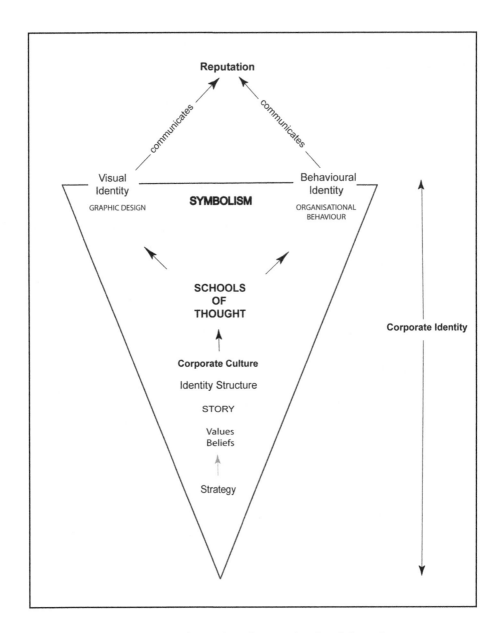

Figure 2.1   Corporate Design Triangle 1 – schools of thought and identity terms

2.2   Corporate Identity Models

2.2.1   BALMER'S AC²ID TEST MODEL

Balmer developed the AC²ID Test (2000) concept to capture the multidisciplinary perspectives in a framework (Balmer and Greyser, 2002), which proposes that, if on initial viewing the user sees one set of messages, whilst the culture or behaviour emits other signals, then there is a misalignment requiring investigation, restructuring and possibly a new image. Companies have multiple identities (see Figure 2.2), but if the message is not coherent on account of a lack of alignment between any two identities, dissonance arises. This can weaken a company. Dissonance can arise at all levels of an organisation, for example, where the *Desired* identity (CEO vision) is at odds with its *Ideal* identity (strategy), or where the *Actual* identity (corporate performance and behaviour) falls short of its *Conceived* identity (key stakeholder groups).

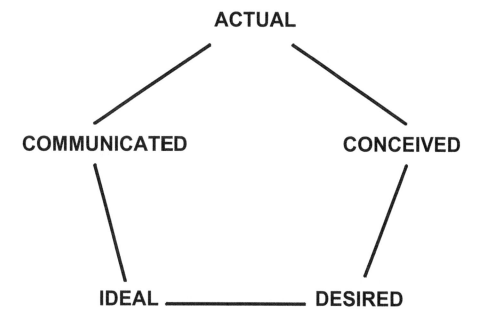

Figure 2.2   Balmer's AC²ID Test Model

Source: John M.T. Balmer and Stephen A. Greyser, "Managing the Multiple Identities of the Corporation", in *California Management Review*, vol. 44, no. 3, Spring 2002. © 2002 by the Regents of the University of California Press.

The following lists the main stakeholders associated within each identity type:

Actual
- those who comprise the company at all its touchpoints
- corporate ownership, leadership style, organisation structure, business and performance, products/service quality

Communicated
- internal marketing communications, marketing partners – communication firms, advertising agencies, media companies
- controllable advertising, public relations and word-of-mouth
- non-controllable social media and spin

Conceived
- external – financial community, government regulatory sector, headquarters, local communities, customers and consumers
- perceptual concepts: image, reputation and branding

Ideal
- internal strategic planning, external financial analysis, regulatory/legislative entities
- optimum market position in a market or markets in a specific timeframe, informed by research and analysis

Desired
- internal CEO and board
- corporate leaders vision for the organisation informed by the CEO personality and ego.

A practical application of this model is presented in Chapter 10.1 (Company Identity Communication and Structure). Two further models provide differing interpretations of corporate identity: Topalian's 'Living' identity and Lambert's Iceberg models.

2.2.2 TOPALIAN'S 'LIVING' IDENTITY MODEL

In 2003 Topalian provided the *living* element of identity, defining how design and technology were changing the digital space. Firstly, a successful corporate identity is *live* and *breathing*, being a tangible reality and representation of the organisation with goals and aspirations changing over time. Ideally changes should be natural progressions; nevertheless disruptive events do occur and have to be carefully resolved. Secondly, a successful corporate identity has to be *lived* by being meaningful and accountable to all stakeholders. Employees adopt the identity, making it alive by working with people on a daily basis, that is, organisational behaviour. External stakeholders then find it easy to recognise the company, get to know and become associated with it.

2.2.3 LAMBERT'S ICEBERG MODEL

Lambert's model views a company's external image and internal identity as closely linked in the business environment. Here accountant's terminology of tangible and intangible elements appear, above and below the line: above the surface, visual elements; and below the surface and view, corporate structure, behaviour and communications, the natural forces of the business all being observed elements of corporate identity.

2.3 Product/Service Brands

Originally brands were built around mass production manufacturing processes aimed at making and selling household products for consumers. Design agencies produced unique styles and looks for these products and services. This look was based on the concept of the *unique selling proposition* (USP), to attract attention to shelf displays and signage to convey attributes and benefits. This enhanced trust and confidence (Dowling, 2004), which increased the company's financial bottom line. Throughout the twentieth century lithographic and technological advances increased advertising possibilities. Adverts appeared in newspapers, magazines and billboards. Wider geographical reach then became possible by way of radio, TV, cinema advertising and corporate entertainment. This increased brand exposure further by distributing corporate image to a wider international audience. Hence designing a unique brand became important to the company's financial existence as a range of brands, each with their brand attributes provided a financial safeguard to the company. To illustrate the difference

**Plate 2.1 Product brand mark: name and
location conveying source and quality**

Source: *Heal's 1810–2010 – 200 Years of Design & Inspiration* (2009), p. 55.
© Heal & Son Ltd. With special thanks to the V&A Archive.

between corporate identity and branding: if a corporate identity is affected, for example, if Virgin's reputation is dented, then it has an impact on all its branded products, including the company. Whereas if one of Ford's marques is discredited, it is only the reputation of that one brand that is affected, not the whole company itself. Olins progresses his thinking on brands (2000, 2003): 'Theoretically, the dividing line between a brand identity and a company or corporate identity is very clear: a brand is a wholly concocted creation that is devised solely to help sell and it has no life of its own' (Olins, 1978).

It can take a long time to build a brand, with many contributors: corporate and design strategists, market and design researchers, design firms, advertising executives, public relations firms and collaborations with a wide range of designers, artists and craftspeople. Once the brand is established, it evolves through commentary from customers, employees, suppliers, business partners, distribution, related financial services and, today with social media, anyone wishing to provide commentary.

2.4   Internet Branding

During the 1990s a disruptive technology appeared: the *internet*. This was the beginning of a new era for branding and corporate design as web technology transformed business models at an even faster pace. In the first instance, Web 1.0 began as an electronic version of established printed media and for many organisations this approach continued until the mid 2010s. Previously a brand was managed according to hard surface printed material and analogue communications. With the advent of digital media, new *corporate brand* opportunities arose and brands such as the Spice Girls conveyed each unit or brand separately to the consumer as an independent product, such as monolithic identity with a consistent story, one name, visual idea and expected behaviour. The internet also required a domain name: *dot.com* companies had arrived. To communicate with the wider world by the internet, it is necessary for a business to have a website with a company, shortened or abstract name. Often this was a one-page advert, regardless of whether it was the local plumber or a FTSE 100 company. The latter was often sceptical of this new media and reluctant to invest in it. IT companies and creative digital artists continued to find new applications, and users began to find the internet a beneficial addition to their lives, for the most part. Websites became a repository of company information for internal, intranet and external usage. These databases became huge; in many instances the digital tree architecture became a forest.

Throughout the late 1990s and early 2000s there was continual debate on definitions of corporate identity and corporate brand: academically: '... unlike classic product brands the corporate brand involves a concern with all the organization's stakeholders and with total corporate communications. The latter is based on the premise that everything an organization says, makes and does will "communicate"' (Baker and Balmer, 1997). Then in the business field: '"Brand" has one further advantage over "corporate identity" in the commercial world, and that is that brands have direct and clear links with money, value and profitability' (Olins, 2003).[1] Yet the clearest differential definition between brand and corporate identity is in section 2.1 above.

Once Web 2.0 and social media appeared, the definition and expectations of a corporate brand changed. So what is branding now? Clearly the internet has added another stage in corporate design strategies, even though this took some time to be recognised. A brand is now defined by what customers consider to be important, created by their individual interpretation and experiences. So companies now have to reflect on how to communicate a favourable brand experience for customers. This has resulted in a seismic shift as website audiences move away from traditional and Web 1.0 technology attributes and benefits, to choices based on the textual and image content on social media platforms such as Facebook, Twitter, YouTube and LinkedIn. Today branding is consumer-centric, the *unique buying state* (UBS) of customers as they browse the websites to select their products or services (Neumeier, 2006), rather than the *unique selling proposition* (USP) of a product that differentiates itself from others in a marketplace, shop and shelf.

Since the beginning of the twenty-first century, companies have been collecting a wide range of data by way of websites and social media on their products and customers. This *big data* creates profiles relating to demographic groups, traffic flow, behaviour patterns and by interest grouping, such as lifestyle brands. One of the key changes with this current technology is that it is not content but flows of information that are important – who is speaking to whom and what about. Keywords are part of one voice on social media channels, and the aggregation of content and audiences are part of the collective mind (D'Orazio, 2013). Where this is leading is difficult to determine. Some say there is too much data and no one knows how to interrogate it effectively, while others think it useful for their brand management. This will be discussed further in Part V.

---

1   From Wally Olins, *On B®and*. © 2003 Wally Olins. Reproduced by kind permission of Thames & Hudson Ltd., London.

2.5   Branding with Art and Design

Art is often considered to have no particular function; this is untrue within corporate design as an artistic object such as a sculpture or picture can communicate an ethos, which otherwise is difficult to convey in words or actions. Design has its own techniques and approaches, which with art and creativity aim to transmit an idea. Design is not art as it has to recognise all the constituent parts that make an object or system function. Art can then be added to provide the requisite aesthetic. Art, on the other hand, is not functional *per se* but it can convey a concept or ethos through cultural values and aesthetic.

The key difference between art and design is that design is not an end object or artefact in itself but an intermediary stage between the maker and the user. Design is equally applied to form and function of particular processes, for example, corporate identity design and hardware and software design. In his book *Art and Industry* (1934), Herbert Read argued that there was a correlation between the artist as research scientist and the designer as industrial chemist and physicist. The former are interested in researching new approaches which are then utilised by the latter to solve practical problems.

Within web technology, digital creative art forms and innovative expressions appear in the 'digital artists' and 'creative technologists' forums that pursue artistic activities, driving the creative digital designs, and often the technology itself, forward. Avant-garde early innovators develop software and digital effects by setting trends and breaking away from traditional approaches. These developments contribute to future websites' corporate design.

The relevance of art and design to corporate design is that for the most part there has been little attention paid to this. In his article 'The artist and the brand', Schroeder (2005) made a number of points. Firstly, marketers were unwilling to use artistic work in branding projects. Secondly, art and business are perceived to be opposite sides of the communication and culture coin, the former high brow and the latter low brow; hence the disparate impact on consumers' and cultural researchers' perceptions. Thirdly, Schroeder suggested that artists such as Andy Warhol, renowned for his branding superstar status by way of his Campbell Soup exhibition, recognised that brand equity, extensions and image were relevant to both artists and business people. Today increasing attention is being paid to artistic output in branding projects as the internet allows artists to show their work and capabilities and, for business people, it provides greater access to artistic portfolios. This results in both parties recognising appropriate artistic styles for their branding projects.

Conclusion

To conclude, through business and academic work, the distinction between corporate identity was defined as 'a realisation and revelation of self in a corporate context' (Michael Wolff, Interview, 2006) that is communicated to a wide range of stakeholders, whereas brands are how other people perceive the person or product. The subject area has gained further recognition as new media technology required further explanations and thought leadership across a wide range of design and behavioural subjects. Various academics have proposed models. Balmer classified corporate identity by four schools of thought, these being strategy, business structure, organisational identity and visual identity. Then it became necessary to clarify identity type and stakeholders such that if dissonance occurred between two groups, the misalignment required attention. Then Lambert provided an accounting approach divided into: i) tangible visual identity; and ii) intangible, these being the remaining organisational aspects. Topalian (2003) recognised the living aspects of identity within the digital sphere.

Branding definitions have moved away from: manufactured products that impact the financial bottom line, to become the key term in defining a business and its products online. This has required further explanations and thought leadership across a wide range of new media technologies and subjects, including applying art and design skills and techniques to differentiate company image and messages online, whereupon the importance and difference between art and design are recognised as the functional and aesthetic online images become important branding tools.

Am I marketing a concept, product or service?

Through corporate identity/brand design, an individual or group of people with a business idea can define: firstly, *who* the business is by its name and formation and *what* it does; secondly, the brand personality, created by communicating the business's existence by advertising online and/or offline. Through time, *how* they conduct their business will develop the brand as customers and stakeholders recognise the product and its service and submit their own commentaries through social media.

Chapter 3
New Media, Communication and Reputation

How do I communicate the business message?

Introduction

In this chapter corporate identity and brand are discussed, along with the impact these have on external factors and stakeholder interests. Firstly, we define the corporate image as the interface between identity/brand and external stakeholders as websites become the first point of contact with consumers. Secondly, we look at how an image creates an impression across a wide range of controlled and uncontrolled media, providing useful input to a business and its operations. Thirdly, we consider how perception varies culturally and the relevance of aesthetics as an image differentiator. Finally, the image impact on reputation and what this contributes to a business.

3.1   Corporate Image Definition

Image has always been a key interface between a company's identity and its stakeholders, conveyed through various media. If this image is blurred then the company is not sufficiently differentiated in the marketplace (Bernstein, 1989) for an audience to appreciate the company, its products and unique identity, which can cause confusion. When someone gets confused between one company and another, or an analyst or a customer associates the company with one product when there is another of greater relevance, this affects business in sales and reputation. The corporate image construct established how companies communicated their identities in the 1950s to 1980s, and today it is still the *popular* definition of corporate identity. Abratt (1989) founded the concept of corporate image management processes (CIM), where he highlighted the identity–image interface and observed that a key factor of image management was to guarantee that a positive image was created from a defined identity, this being consistently conveyed to stakeholders through selected media channels.

As web technology develops, image has significant implications, as conveying a positive impact has wider appeal and repercussions. The audience's perception of that image is important as it travels across diverse geographical, social, economic and political environments. 'Corporate identity and corporate image are still some of the core building blocks of an organization's strategy. Competing in the new economy will not only involve rationalizing the business processes but also evaluating the attributes of the corporate identity and the consumer perception' (Melewar and Navalekar, 2002). On entering a shop or office and inspecting products in the real world, the corporate *look and feel* or *presence* is easily perceived. This is not yet the case online.

3.2   Communicating Corporate Image

The objective of marketing communication, whether on a printed hard surface or communicated through a digital media display screen, is to advertise the company and its products and services. Corporate image has always been important as an impression is made within a few seconds, enabling recognition of the business in the future. This interface shows how people work and behave, impacting business relationships as consumers evaluate the business ethos, products and services. Hence communicating a clear identity and image contributes to a positive competitive advantage; even more so on websites where this interface is the first and often the only point of contact with consumers and clients. As viewers become familiar with a company's image, they begin to select that company's products rather than another company's.

Traditionally two types of communication exist: controlled and uncontrolled. Controlled communication is achieved by an internal marketing communication strategy expressing the company's objectives by advertising, public relations, graphic design and sponsorship, these being applied to various company and stakeholder touchpoints through billboards, pamphlets, reception areas, artefacts, film, TV advertising and early websites. The purpose of these controlled mechanisms is to ensure that the marketing strategy is achieved. Having a CEO who is an exceptional communicator, both externally and internally, is also an asset as they deliver a clear company image and message; for example, Sir Richard Branson of the Virgin Group has evolved with marketing approaches and technology for 40 years, still maintaining his casual image. Taking Rolls-Royce as another example, it sells prestige cars in many countries; its website, company literature and buildings have to reflect the company's brand ethos of design quality, innovation and reliability. Additionally it has a large worldwide market with various cultural differences. 'The company presents the same product with specific values in different ways to meet the demands of different markets' (Melewar, Bassett and Simoes, 2006). Hence coherent communication channels have to be strategically managed to ensure the appropriate message is conveyed to stakeholders (Duncan and Everett, 1993). This is why design communication and all its collaborators are important as their skills and knowledge produce the relevant image that impacts an audience's perception of its products and services.

Originally a company could control its external image distribution on conventional media and early websites, evolving with current fashion, topical trends and technological developments. Today Web 2.0 social media communication and digital devices provide additional routes for uncontrolled communication as it reaches a new zenith. Uncontrolled communication has always existed, both internally and externally to an organisation, for example, by word of mouth, gossip and spin. Today external groups and individuals can use Twitter, Facebook and blogs, acting as advocates for a company's brand, products or services by providing alternative or reinforcing views, in addition to those generated by the company. 'Communication recursively recalls and anticipates further communications, and solely within the network of self-created communications can it produce communications as the operative elements of its own system. In so doing, communication generates a distinct autopoietic system in the strict (not just metaphorical) sense of the term' (Luhmann, 2000). These communications can impact an organisation's reputation, promoting and maintaining its success and financial market confidence, and therefore have to be carefully managed by the company's marketing and communication strategy to ensure that the company, its products and services are well known and recognised in published and unsolicited material.

3.3   The Aesthetic Image

Aesthetics as a philosophical discipline was established in 1750 when the German philosopher Alexander Baumgarten (1735) published the book *Aesthetica*. He defined the subject as the science of how things are cognised by means of the senses. Immanuel Kant then suggested that 'the beauty of objects, artworks and natural phenomena alike, consisted in their ability to stimulate the free play of the cognitive faculties in virtue of their pure forms, both spatial and temporal, and without the mediation of concepts' (Kant in Levinson, 2005, p. 5. By permission of Oxford University Press.) Aesthetics has a direct relationship with corporate design in both its conventional media and website application, where the above aesthetic foci can be recognised in artefacts and graphic designs. For example, pictures and symbols have been a way of communicating with other people throughout time and cultures, such as Stone Age cave paintings, brightly coloured imagery and hieroglyphics in Egyptian tombs, Chinese characters and Indian scripts, all providing illustration of various aspects of life as it existed then by forms, colour and imagination. This beauty or dynamism through perception – being part of image design. Don Norman's (2002) mantra of *attractive works better* is echoed in both dimensions, as the aesthetic appearance of products increases usability.

In the business context, aesthetics is becoming an increasingly important competitive tool for company strategists and CEOs, as they look beyond having a web presence to something that provides an emotional response from the website visitors. An aesthetic image is relevant to both product and communication design to clearly differentiate a business online, as well as selling a unique product: 'if a CEO plans on integrated, strategy-driven efforts to establish global presence, it must involve the building of a presence through a strong corporate identity (Foo et al. 2001) on the internet. In the identity building process, visual aesthetics are critical elements' (Foo, 2006).

Figure 10.1 illustrates the corporate design terms of *position, symbolism* and *coherence*, and their relationship and linkage in the creation, communication and resultant reputation interactions that occur.

3.4   Image Perception

Sight and the brain are the main sources for perceiving difference. Sight can detect size, contrast and colour, whereas the brain makes meaning of the image, for example, emotional reactions, distances, weight and levels of complexity (Neumeier, 2006). Hence when an object is perceived to be beautiful, it is held in a higher aesthetic regard and it is this premium that branding tries to achieve. The perception of images varies over time due to differing interpretations and design trends. Symbols can look old fashioned or associated with an era, for example, retro, 1970s, Edwardian. When this happens, the corporate image has to be continually updated; for example, the Shell company's pecten shell has evolved subtly over time (see www.shell.com). Hence audience and customer perception of communicated images and intended meaning is a complex process, varying temporally, contextually and spatially between individuals, groups and cultures.

An image can overcome language difficulties, but it cannot be taken for granted that a message or image has been communicated in the required manner and that the audience's perception has understood the message. Semiotic studies concentrate on this subject and it is integral to communication design and marketing.

Companies with a clear positive and can-do attitude towards their image are Shell, BP, Virgin and Vodaphone, each one conveying a *world class* image. Their advertising and public relations may differ from country to country but the company image itself is the same throughout, regardless of the amount of money spent on advertising, familiarity again leading to favourability (Fombrun and Van Riel, 1998) as a company's image is clear in your mind on choosing its products.

3.5   Reputation

Reputation can be garnered from websites, social media, business literature, trade magazines, word of mouth and popular magazines. Corporate reputation is a multidimensional structure, comprising corporate identity and its created image relationship with its audience perception (Dowling, 2004). This develops stakeholders' value and confidence in the financial marketplace. A good reputation is the product of orchestrating a clear communication policy to sustain competitive advantage (Fombrun and Van Riel, 1998). It has a great impact on the confidence that financial stakeholders have in the organisation, for example, earnings per share and healthy profit. A good reputation is therefore a way of establishing the business commercial position and continuing success.

3.5.1   DIFFERENTIAL IMAGE AND FAVOURABLE REPUTATION

Key to ensuring a differential image and favourable reputation (Fombrun, 1996), a company has to design its organisation, products, services, character and behaviour to facilitate trust and confidence in the company with customers and stakeholders, so that they support this company over its rivals in a sector, fostering trust and confidence. This ensures that the stakeholders will purchase the company's goods, invest and want to work for it (Balmer, 1995; Dowling,

2004; Van Riel, 1995). This links the perceptual construct of corporate image and the emotional construct of corporate reputation: 'perceived socio-cognitive congruence [exists] between the organization's character (viewed over time), its prescriptive beliefs (values) and individual stakeholder's reactions' (Dowling, 2004). Westcott Allesandri (2001) reinforced these points where image has a knock-on effect, building a reputation initially from the company's mission impacting its identity, which in turn impacts image, all of which is within the firm's control. Hence a strong identity has to underpin the creation of a differential corporate image for its marketplace.

Where there is dissonance between the external reputation, image and internal corporate identity, then the image and identity management processes have to be realigned – see Balmer's AC^{2}ID Test. An image can be changed quickly but when the company has lost its way in the market and is no longer visible, then new ideas have to be considered through restructuring and board changes.

3.5.2   REPUTATION'S CONTRIBUTIONS TO A BUSINESS

Reputation has four important contributions to a business:

1.   Consumers identify capabilities and reliability by *character traits* (Powell, 1990) so that customers are willing to pay premium prices for products and services. For example, Fombrun and Rindova's (2000) study on Shell's reputation management found that it was inextricably linked to the organisation's identity management. Corporate reputations become a stakeholder assessment of the organisation's prestige and describe the social systems within the company's industrial sector.

2.   Investors reward good reputations with higher share prices. Chief executives focus on this as *reputational capital* (Dolphin, 2004). Key intermediary information sources, for example, market analysts, journalists and investors, confirm this reputation through analysis and assessments.

3.   Stakeholders have a deeper sense of trust and commitment when corporate transparency is realised. This trust, built over time, results in expectations on how the organisation will react to a given situation or issue reflecting behaviour through many small decisions (Vergin and Qoronfleh, 1998). When a problem does arise, online stakeholders wish to feel confident that their business is safe

and any dispute is being quickly resolved. Balmer (1998) called this the *decisions are evaluated against reputations* process (DEAR).

4.   Recruitment is easier as people wish to work for the company (Greyser, 1999). Appropriate staff recruitment is critical (Pruzan, 2001). For example, as social media develops, web savvy employees with good writing skills can make a difference by clearly articulating the business ethos in their writing style.

> *Heal's has gained a reputation for its unwavering belief in design quality and innovation.*

A reputation interview survey of 21 communication departments in large UK national or international organisations (Dolphin, 2004) suggests that: firstly, winning companies gain a good reputation when the combined message and media convey an organisation's uniqueness in the marketplace; secondly, reputation is perceived to be a key corporate governance objective, indicating how an organisation sees itself communicating with stakeholders and the wider public, whilst acting as guardians of its reputation; and finally, the difference between reputation and corporate image is still a matter of scholarly debate.

Front-runners in reputation management began communicating their company's image and resultant reputation by storytelling in the 1970s. For example, Dame Anita Roddick of The Bodyshop, created stories around her environmentally based business to be unique in the marketplace. Thereafter she developed an environmentally friendly image for her products and fought to maintain its corporate reputation. At the time she probably did not realise the impact this would have on the company and its future communication strategies, as the internet had not been developed. However, its reputation and storytelling approach found popular appeal and application.

Conclusion

To conclude this chapter, a company's cultural values and business practices provide a starting point for image creation, defining what the company stands for, justifying strategies and interaction with key stakeholders. This creative input, its communication and audience perception of the created aesthetic contributes to a large part of a company's success, both in a marketplace and online, variable over time and geography. The emphasis between controlled and uncontrolled communication has dramatically changed as website and social media activities have gained acceptance. A good reputation facilitates trust and confidence in a company, which in turn ensures that stakeholders will favour that company and its products over another. Further on, recruitment is easier and financial stability is established and maintained.

Image creation and communication is gaining increasing relevance and importance as web technology develops, requiring socio-economic, geographical and political consideration and understanding.

How do I communicate the business message?

The message itself has to have a sound basis sourced on an identity. After that, an image can be created and communicated by relevant media channels being controlled by the business with uncontrolled inputs. Websites require careful attention as the perception of imagery varies culturally throughout the world; this is in addition to the business requirements of communicating a positive image. The business reputation is built from the customer's experience of the organisation both offline and online. This reputation has to be carefully managed so that customers support and wish to work for your business, as opposed to another.

Part I Summary
Ground Base – How Corporate Design Started and Evolved

What Has Happened So Far?

In the latter half of the twentieth century the subject of corporate identity and brand design was increasingly recognised, with contributory subjects such as identity, image, communication, symbolic visual identity and organisational behaviour. Corporate identity was eventually defined as the communication of the corporate self with all its stakeholders. Originally branding was related to manufactured products and the financial bottom line. As companies promoted themselves online, the definition of branding changed to become consumer-centric where customers pulled information from a website and contributed their own commentary through social media. To attract attention online, artistic and design skills increased in demand as creating an engaging online image became important.

What Have We Learnt in this Section?

It only takes one business idea from one person to start one business. As that person progresses through establishing the business organisation and processes, they create a visual identity for their promotional material and by the way they work. Branding relates to how people recognise and contribute to a business and its product development, both financially and by relevant conversations that progress its reputation The business image and message has to be based on a positive identity and communicated by appropriate media channels. Ultimately the identity/brand and image impacts reputation – a critical element in business success.

What Will Part II Encapsulate?

As the main terms and concepts on corporate identity and branding design have been described in Part I, Part II will concentrate on development of both the corporate strategy and corporate design strategy inputs, whilst detailing how storytelling provides a source for identity and design strategy. This is followed by the introduction of the perceptions and perspectives of all stakeholders and their related skillsets.

Part II
Setting the Strategy

What is strategy? Essentially it is identifying a need or requirement in an environment, setting goals and planning how to get there. The requirement may be a service and/or product which people will consume, use or experience, this being paid for through monetary, barter or voluntary contributions.

Historically large organisations such as the military, religions and business people would plan to travel the world to find these new products and provide the required services. Competition was always prevalent, as today.

This competitive environment increased as analogue and digital communications advanced, enabling a faster pace of business development through better advertising, clearer operational structures and regulations. Twenty years ago the internet and digital communication revolutionised and inconceivably changed the business world and the world's daily lives. Business strategies have had to take account of these developments as they were evolving across a number of dimensions.

Again business was venturing into unknown territories. This time the geographical, cultural and legal boundaries were well defined in the real world. However, the internet created a faster pace to transactions sourced from increasingly vast data and information sources, whilst new situations and problems have had to be overcome and legislated for.

So the strategic emphasis now had to consider wider implications relating to its products and services. This combination has brought forward the 'customer experience' concept where a combination of inputs is formulated.

It is within this background that corporate design strategy has evolved and is increasingly becoming an integral part of the corporate strategy team which works with the CEO to define and shape the goals that they wish to achieve. In a highly competitive global market, it is the unique experience that captures the viewer's attention. A website on a digital screen is now the starting point for many purchases, voluntary services, hobbies and life's little problems.

Here the importance of creating a clear identity and story that enables a strong competitive position in the market, created by the corporate and design strategy, is explained through:

Chapter 4   Corporate Strategy

Chapter 5   Storytelling and Identity

Chapter 6   Corporate Design Strategy

Chapter 7   Perception and Perspectives

Chapter 4
Corporate Strategy

How do I start a business?

Introduction

How CEOs and their boards establish their company's strategy, setting the company goals for a period of time in accordance with the corporate vision and mission, is the subject of this chapter. This strategy has to work in three complex and interlinked environments: the business world, design environments and the company's internal organisation. Demands on both companies and CEOs have increased dramatically as digital developments take hold in a world of instantaneous communication and tremendous market possibilities. Here is an explanation of the necessity of a clear, focused plan for all parties to act upon.

4.1   Setting the Goals and Objectives

Setting the strategy's goals and path for a business's development requires foresight, opportunism and adaptability, both in its creation and delivery. Corporate goals have to be well defined and successfully communicated, internally to staff and externally to all stakeholders. This reinforces customer expectations in a manner concurrent to their perception of the organisation's ethos, that is, its culture and values. These goals have to operate within the company's: a) *philosophy*, that is, the idea upon which the business was created, even if this is not initially apparent; b) *vision*, which is where the company/CEO wishes to be; and c) *mission*, that is, undertaking the operation. In addition to a corporate strategy, a company can have tiers and specific functional strategies such as a subsidiary's business strategy and its operational strategy. Each strategy will have project objectives and plans, listing each operation, activity and milestone, and defining when an operational activity should be completed, by whom and who signs off that stage of the project, and then the project completion itself.

1906   Ambrose Heal's vision: *To work with highly skilled designers and craftspeople creating comfortable and beautiful, elegant yet affordable furniture reflecting the ideal of the Arts and Crafts Movement, whilst embracing modernity to show that manufactured goods could be as beautifully crafted and designed as any piece from a workshop.*

Current vision: *We want to inspire people to create beautiful homes.*

The market within which a company operates is continually changing, particularly with digital technology. This has accelerated the rate of business ideas, their manufacture and transaction by faster communication, production and sales channels. Business product lifecycles are shorter as online brand selection means that customers can buy the latest version, if not a customised version, of their mobile phones and trainers. Today these two products change styles and versions as regularly as the clothing fashion industry. Companies experience mergers, acquisitions and divestments more frequently, and expectations of corporate responsibility and sustainability are increasing. These pressures have resulted in corporate strategies having to be more flexible or at least reviewed more frequently and the necessary action taken.

To ensure that the company and its organisation can adapt to market conditions, CEOs have to be aware of the business environment and their organisation, using all their skills, knowledge and research. Design can contribute much to a corporate strategy at specific stages of the company's development and organisational lifecycle. Then, by the CEOs logic, quantifiable and explicit knowledge combined with the designer's qualitative and tacit knowledge, a relevant identity and image for their current branding project can be created and integrated with the corporate strategy. This strategy then provides direction and focus for other divisional and business strategies and operational plans.

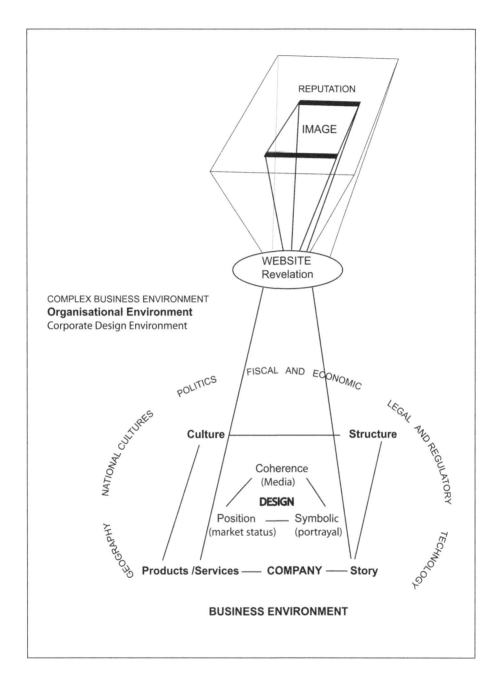

Figure 4.1 Online and offline corporate strategy, corporate design and organisational environments

4.2   Complex Interlinked Environments

Businesses have always worked in complex environments relative to time, technology and socio-economic progress and downturns. Traditional business models find a need in the marketplace; establish the company; make the products or provide a service to fulfil this market requirement. Figure 4.1 illustrates the main components: within the lower circle of the business environment the product or service progresses upwards into the marketplace. In recent years corporate strategy has been influenced by a reputation-down approach, with the introduction of the internet. Here a vision known as the *big idea* (Jones, 2000) is communicated to the market, and then the business environment is encouraged or discovers the product and brand. If the audience likes the brand then the network widens, especially through social media where brand advocates are essentially widening the company's marketing possibilities.

Setting the corporate strategy has always been fraught with difficulty but it is the first stage in establishing, or re-aligning, the organisation within its marketplace. A vast range of topics have to be considered when starting a business or progressing it to the *next step*. Visioning what is going to happen and setting goals in this complex environment is difficult, regardless of whether the business is a small start-up or a global business. At the strategic level two key questions are: What do we want to achieve? How do we get there? Wider and more detailed research can be sourced in relevant information environments, creating the AC^{2}ID Test's *Ideal* state, so that the strategy is firmly based on the current business situation and surrounding circumstances. There are three aspects to this complex environment:

- Business environment

- Corporate design environment

- Organisational identity environment.

4.2.1   BUSINESS ENVIRONMENT – PEEST FACTORS

The business competitive environment has to be evaluated by considering the current political, economic, environmental, sociological and technological climate and situations that the business has to contend with, so that goals can be set, contingencies prepared and scenarios outplayed.

Political

Political issues cross local, regional and national boundaries at an incredible speed with potentially global implications. The impact can occur in much shorter time-spans than previously experienced. Ideologies, wars, political disturbances, new governments and leaders, and new working practices all require relevant information and updates. With social media there is always some information, but what is relevant to the company and its operation has to be carefully selected. Company restructuring, deregulation and privatisation impacts corporate strategy and image, both offline and online. Hence ensuring that the company's business approach is relevant to the market segment is very important. Additionally, legal jurisdictions and frameworks require that regulations, standards and restrictions are consulted and adhered to. On a smaller scale, politics can permit a business to start quickly and easily with access to good advice. Political issues can arise regarding a vast array of subjects that directly or indirectly affect a business, with corporate design implications. These will be discussed later in this section and in Chapter 9.

1932   Heal's economy furniture was introduced during the Depression. Whilst World War 2 continued, Heal's changed from civilian manufacture to military equipment.

Economic

Economically, interest rates, inflation and taxes affect financial strategies and plans that the CEO and board wish to pursue, by the amount of money that is available for projects, including design. The downturn in the financial markets in recent years has had a dramatic impact on many businesses and even countries, as they are bailed out of near and full bankruptcy. It could be said that this is where corporate branding of products and services on the internet has gained momentum, as the potential market is truly phenomenal, even more so with social media communications. On another point, design diversity can have economic implications as the price and value-adding components facilitate product differentiation; for example, mobile phones can be manufactured in many models, shapes, sizes and colours with variable processes to suit market segments and pockets. Furthermore those phones that sell in Europe may not sell in the Far East, as each geographical location often has a different specification for each market and its segments.

Environmental

Environmental requirements have increased in recent years as expectations and legislation are put in place. The problems are industry-specific with varying geographical implications. Hence strategies to alleviate disaster have to be established. The environmental problems likely to occur are diverse, some of the key ones being related to oil, smoke and noise pollution.

Sociological

Sociological barriers and hurdles are often perceived to be the most difficult obstructions to overcome, both in communicating the corporate message and selling products and services to the targeted audience. Understanding people's lifestyles, expectations and requirements is crucial. Marketers and designers have to think about the demographic and cultural groups, age profiles and patterns of behaviour so that a product or website can be appropriately constructed, along with shops and work environments.

Technological

Technology has had the greatest impact on daily life and business in recent years, advancing at a fast pace. Recently boards have had to decide on which social media platforms to network through, allowing access by the website homepage, whilst information on how customers are buying online and offline permits technology strategies to be more specific across hardware, software and communication formats. Other decisions have to be made regarding devices upon which the messages are communicated, from printed matter to smartphones and tablets, as the latter increases in market share and PCs decrease. Lean manufacturing is currently a popular management topic, associated with reduced time to market as design techniques and manufacturing processes are refined and design processes generate new products and services. Now product quality and workmanship examinations have to be conducted to ensure that they adhere to industry and company standards.

Further strategies

Three further corporate and corporate design-related strategies are the subsidiary business, marketing and public relations strategies. The key headings are listed here as they overlap and interlink in both conceptual and operational approaches, corporate identity and image often being included under the marketing umbrella.

Business strategy

A business strategy can be compiled for a subsidiary of a corporation and will include: a competitive market analysis; a product or service strategy including design aspects; a business model defining likely demand and revenue; environmental sustainability reporting; a marketing strategy and plan.

Marketing strategy

The marketing strategy has to have a goal and be specific, measurable, attainable, relevant and timebound (SMART). A clear target market/audience has to be defined with a brand position statement, strategy and plans for product, service or concept branding, distribution, pricing, promotion, post-sales service and necessary resources. Promotion has to consider all essential media touchpoints, such as the website, social media, printed material, TV programmes and any further branding projects such as books, apps and downloads.

Public relations strategy

A public relations strategy requires an objective and timescale clearly defined by establishing what has to be achieved and the necessary audience. This group can be defined by researching what they read, who they converse with (including social media conversations, if they use this communication channel), to whom they listen and which programmes they watch. The key message has to be well written, edited and approved, and an appropriate communication platform selected.

4.2.2 CORPORATE DESIGN ENVIRONMENT – STEEP FACTORS

Corporate design strategy considers the business environment from an alternative angle but the subject matter has the same elements – sociological, technological, environmental, economic and political, with the emphasis orientated towards people and processes within the corporate strategy. This is not to say that finance is unimportant in design; it is. Still, design has to solve a problem or create something that is useful to people. This article has to have a form and function and increasingly a clear aesthetic, which essentially means producing an effective and attractive product or service. Corporate design requires commitment from the top of the organisation, that is, the CEO or business owner. Then by information research found in written and oral histories, the company history, culture, structure and current business activities can be considered.

The corporate design strategy for a business then has to think about four aspects:

1.   *Positioning* the business to differentiate the company in its selected market – for example, will it be a market leader in its sector? – using the latest innovations and technology for its products and marketing. Or will it take a middle position that ensures quality and cost effectiveness for the selected product?

2.   *Brand personality* to be portrayed, this being the company, product or services ethos, spirit and attitude, with staff working with and sharing the same standards.

3.   *Attractive design*s and website content that engages audiences across working environments and website platforms.

4.   *Coherence* across all communications, conveying the essential messages by visual and behavioural means.

This subject is discussed further in Chapter 6, being essentially the style necessary for the business image creation through all communication channels in the physical and digital environment, encompassing:

•   Working environment

•   Visual identity elements – name logo, fonts, colours and straplines

•   Organisational behaviour – staff attitude, rituals and routines.

Company strategies are always evolving; for example, the website Amazon launched its online business in 1995 determined to capture the online book market and its distribution. It did take time for this business to become established and many people considered that it would never reach financial stability. Amazon also had to overcome buyers' reluctance to use a website when the technology was still in its infancy and customers preferred published hardback or paperback books in bookshops. Technology developed and customers became familiar with websites. Electronic books appeared and could be read on an Amazon device called a Kindle, whilst a sample of the book could be viewed online. Then the business expanded into selling a wide range of products with loyalty cards, to the extent that it has almost become the online high street. Hence by focusing on the customers and its various stakeholders' needs and ensuring that the design of its advertising and communication with customers is effective, Amazon has captured and maintained its hold on its selected market position. Yet it still has to continually assess its corporate strategy in the light of current events to ensure that its products and services are relevant. Of course this occurs through a clear image and message that communicates and displays its products and services effectively on a website with an appropriate aesthetic style, functionality and effective navigation that leads to a purchase.

4.2.3   ORGANISATIONAL ENVIRONMENT – SWOT ANALYSIS

The third analysis to consider is the organisational identity, this being the business's internal organisation: Who is the leader? Will he or she be able to present the appropriate image for the business? How does the business operate? What equipment does it possess? What skills and talents are available? What type of culture and rituals do you wish to develop – friendly and approachable or strict and hierarchical, with the appropriate structures of hierarchy, matrix or free-flowing format? This is covered in business topics on:

- Organisational leadership

- Business structure

- Operating culture

- Intellectual capital, products, services and experiences.

A SWOT analysis allows the managing director of the company, or a subsidiary company, to consider its present situation by addressing the internal *strengths* and *weaknesses*, whilst the external *opportunities* and *threats* can be identified.

This consists of the management structure and personnel, operations and activities, risk management, financial planning, capital requirements such as plant and machinery and internet strategy, whilst the organisational environment and its identity considers its culture, local situation and values that exist within all the internal and local stakeholders. The organisation then changes itself or part of its business and or manufacturing processes by creating a business or organisation strategy that identifies the planning and managing operations necessary for the business to be successful.

4.2.4 BUSINESS PLANS

There are varying attitudes to business plans – should they be one page or a detailed 100-page tome? Essentially this is the business owner and their bank's decision. Often a business plan requires consideration of the PEEST, STEEP and SWOT elements and analyses, so that relevant and potentially critical events can be acknowledged. If a technology such as social media is introduced to the market and is accepted as a useful business tool, then writing a detailed plan, reviewed annually, would mean little. However, a quarterly plan and review would be more realistic. Alternatively if this is part of a corporate business plan, then this budget item would be one amongst a list of others. It would be included but with few details, hence the necessity of good management information and quality systems. Figure 4.2 illustrates the main terms presented in this chapter to show how they develop through time and interlink. At the end of the book, Figure 16.2 illustrates how all of the corporate strategy, design strategy and organisation topics interrelate with one another.

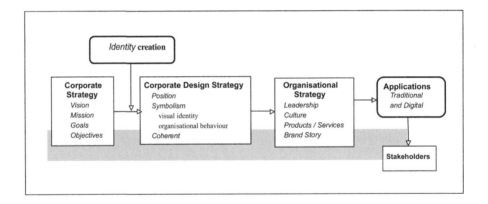

Figure 4.2   Corporate and design strategy flowchart

Strategic change and corporate design interventions

Corporate identity and brand design occurs when:

- A new business or company is formed, where a unique image has to be created to establish the business in the marketplace. This is considered to be the most effective application of corporate design, requiring a *from scratch* approach to research and conceptual design. Designers have a blank sheet of paper upon which to be truly creative and apply innovative technological solutions within the brief and budget limits set by the business owner.

> *1810 John Harris Heal starts a feather dressing business – bedding and bedroom furniture.*

- A takeover, merger or company spin-off occurs. On buying a company, the corporate identity management (CIM), its character, size and identity, inspires confidence and attracts buyers and therefore a financial implication. Negotiations occur for the takeover and then the new CEOs determine the organisation's strategic direction, whilst the former identities and companies struggle with one another, at all levels of the organisation, until they find a bond that provides the nexus for the newly combined company's identity – a *new personality* with a different identity formation (Balmer and Wilson, 1998) and a new heart that will change the corporate *face* (Melewar and Harold, 1999).

> *In 1983 Heal's sold its business to Terence Conran's Design Group, becoming part of a larger company with a branded identity within the Storehouse group.*

See Plate 4.1

- New trends with new fashions require a new direction or brand update. Some sectors are more prone to this than others; for example, IT and telecommunications companies change their designs frequently, with each technological advance increasing the business's personality and identity, the largest factor in consumer choice. Fashion, particularly teenage fashion, has a fast turnover rate, often with four new-season catwalk shows each year. So each season has a new design and image to communicate and maintain its market sector status.

> *1951 Festival of Britain: 'a sense of recovery' after World War 2.*
> *1978 The Buzz furniture range for the younger, more cost-conscious client.*

See Plate 4.2

"HEAL'S, LIKE SO MANY COMPANIES, TURNED
FROM THE MANUFACTURE OF GOODS FOR
CIVILIAN CONSUMPTION IN PEACETIME,
TO PRODUCING THE MILITARY EQUIPMENT
NEEDED FOR BRITAIN'S VERY SURVIVAL "
JAMES TAYLOR, IMPERIAL WAR MUSEUM

**Plate 4.1   1940s: Heal & Son manufacture
realignment from civilian products to military**

Source: *Heal's 1810–2010 – 200 Years of Design & Inspiration* (2009), p. 73
© Heal & Son Ltd. With special thanks to the V&A Archive.

**FESTIVAL
OF BRITAIN
1951**

**Plate 4.2   1951: The Festival of Britain –
'a tonic for the nation'**

Source: *Heal's 1810–2010 – 200 Years of Design & Inspiration* (2009), p. 88.
© Heal & Son Ltd. With special thanks to the V&A Archive.

- Socio-economic and political events define an era, whether this be Victoriana, a world war, Beatlemania or the Olympics, each having a memorable identity and image that readily springs to mind.

During these changes, numerous events and activities are occurring in a flurry of excitement and trepidation as to what the final outcome will be. It is important that the CEOs/business owners and design strategists concentrate on the corporate design. This includes *positioning* the company in its marketplace through the corporate visual identity system (CVIS) creation and organisation behaviour practices. These can then be applied to offline and online touchpoints such as websites, stationery, uniforms, products, presentations, sales points, buildings and equipment, where stakeholders such as customers, government and local authority departments, business partners and employees are likely to come in touch with the organisation. If these points are attended to within a timely and relevant corporate design strategy and design management system, the results will be more efficient and effective, enabling:

- The necessary changes to business processes to be rapidly implemented within the organisation

- Everyone within the organisation to come to understand and inform others about what the company stands for, what they do, how they do it and how the company's activities relate to each other

- A coherent message to be spread across all selected media applications through a carefully chosen style which will allow the corporate image to express its market position and impact across all communications

- Stakeholder trust to be gained as the company's reputation and reality coincide.

Conclusion

To conclude, setting the company's goals and path for business development requires foresight. These strategies have to operate within the company philosophy, vision and mission, and have to be clearly defined and successfully communicated to all stakeholders. Further business strategies and operational strategies can be created. All strategies will have project objectives and plans listing each operation, activity and milestone. CEOs need to access information across the business and organisational environments so that the strategy is based on sound PEEST and SWOT factors, whilst the corporate design strategist considers the STEEP factors. Business plans ought to be prepared. For a new business, these can vary in length but the objective is to ensure that all aspects of the business's activities are listed and costed with relevant funding. Company strategy can change unexpectedly and a new approach be taken when: a takeover or merger happens; a new fashion or technological event occurs; or in the event of socio-economic and political events that require the business to be repositioned in the market.

How do I start a business?

A strategy has to be clearly thought out, based on thorough research and understanding of the marketplace. From the prospective business owner or CEO's viewpoint, this includes undertaking two projects: firstly, a SWOT analysis of the resources currently available for the business; secondly, an analysis of any likely political, economic, environmental, sociological and technological (PEEST) events and occurrences that could impact the business. Then they should prepare a business plan listing all the project's costs, budget and projections with commentary and explanations. If funding is required, the bank manger is the next step.

Chapter 5
Storytelling and Identity

How does a good story differentiate a business?

Introduction

To achieve the CEO's strategic goals, a visionary design strategy has to be created. This chapter shows how a distinctive identity and its story initiates this strategy by focusing attention on a unique concept. The chapter begins with an explanation of identity across geographical areas and the impact this has on a business. It then progresses to storytelling and how this provides design research, a rich source of stories and material upon which a business identity and conceptual design can be formed for the company or branded product.

5.1 Identity: The Gap Between Strategy and Creativity

As business becomes more competitive on websites and in real life, the ability to recognise an identity/brand that clearly differentiates a business is crucial to its success. 'At the corporate level the discussion of strategy, reputation, image and communication become difficult, if not futile, unless identity is brought into the equation. As Gioia mused, the concept is fundamental to the conceptualization of the corporation' (Balmer and Greyser, 2003). It has been found that a unique identity does progress strategy and enables a unique corporate story to be created (Abratt, 1989; Ackerman, 1988; Marguiles, 1977; Olins, 1990b). This unique identity creates value on the balance sheet, appearing as an intangible in accounting terms, previously known as goodwill and now often called brand value (Knox, Maklan and Thompson, 2000). It is the CEO and company's decision on what identity to reveal (Topalian, 1984; Wolff, 2006), particularly pertinent to websites, as visual cues provide greater significance than their conventional media counterpart.

Anthropologists spend years finding and studying cultures and their identity characteristics, each making their own judgement and postulating theories through their own eyes, as they are not part of that culture, and mindful that they are not part of the groups. Often these sample groups were isolated geographically by distance or inaccessible locations that only the intrepid would venture into. To survive, these groups of people adapted their local environment to their requirements: memorising their group's stories to teach younger members and remind elders; making clothes for everyday wear and artefacts for daily usage, and perhaps some body art to improve their appearance. 'Identity acts as a magnet attracting and repelling through design' (Rowden, 2000). As they advanced, ceremonies to various gods were conducted with rituals and practices. Distinctive decorated robes were designed, made and maintained, thereby employing and increasing their skills and knowledge of their local materials. Rarer materials gained higher importance. Hence jewellery and artefacts were made and buildings became more ornate as the hunter gatherer phase was passed. This isolationism had created an identity.

5.2 Geographical Identity

5.2.1 LOCAL IDENTITY

Local identity used to be a defined unit with clear geographical and physical boundaries and communication restrictions. Each local area had distinct cultural approaches to life, where unique creative artefacts and stories were sourced by anthropological studies. Only certain people within social hierarchies travelled, returning home to recount their adventures by storytelling and conversation, enabling society, education and businesses to develop. As the local identity evolved by its own myths and stories, this became known as vernacular identity, considered to be the true source of corporate identity and its design.

> *Heal's has been a long-established location in Tottenham Court Road since 1818, with six extensions since then.*

Today this clear definition of a local identity is disappearing (Morley, 2000); local identity cannot be so clearly defined in socio-economic, language, decor or physically defined terms: '"identity" is produced simultaneously in many different locales. One's identity where one lives ... is only one social context and perhaps not the most important one in which it is shaped' (Marcus in Morley, 2000, p. 10). George Marcus (ibid.) suggests that in the contemporary world, traditional anthropological notions of community or identity are no longer mapped onto locality. This situation can be seen in London's Elephant and Castle, whose history is in its working-class roots. The name is reputed to be the name of a pub. Today this locality is home to many nationalities. Local physical geography may not have changed much over time but the socio-economic unit has altered exponentially, where the internet has played a part. Hence the local identity on which individuals base their original identities is now subject to these changed parameters. Socio-economic and sometimes technological progress impacts local identity, altering structures during periods of change and crisis – for example, the Industrial Revolution, World War 1, the Irish Potato Famine and the Scottish Highland Clearances – again changing the location's history and identity.

5.2.2 NATIONAL IDENTITY

National identity can be viewed as its brand, having an important part to play in maintaining a national identity and conveying an image to the world stage, both for attracting investment and tourists. Drawing from Held and McGrew (2000), nationalities are seen to be communities occupying defined, bounded territories based on ethnic cores, where the nation's family, class, religion and communities have established myths, values, belief systems, symbols and memories forged by a governing elite and elected government. The educational system, by its ideas, meanings and practices, emphasises this and forms a basis for cultural identity. Common public culture is also instilled by legal rights and duties that have to cross many cultural barriers. Although new communication systems may generate global technologies and languages, they do confront the *situational geography* by which people make sense of their lives. This can be seen by the consistency of national institutions such as monarchies, organisations, newspapers, and local and national radio. A point to note is that the term *national brand* is a term recently applied and it can be controversial. Spain's *Espania* logo, designed by Miro, is an example of a national branding programme.

> *Heal's expansion: 1972 in Guildford, Surrey; 1985 in Croydon, Surrey; 1995 in Kings Road, London; 1999 in Kingston, Surrey; 2003 in Manchester; 2005 in Redbrick Mill, Yorkshire; 2007 in Brighton, Sussex.*

Today Malcolm McLuhan's term 'global village' is highly prevalent where travel and internet communications have enabled better access to remote and isolated places. Yet many countries in the world are inherently multicultural by virtue of political and economic upheavals. Countries like Malaysia have a very diverse cultural mix, as do local areas throughout the UK. All have brought with them their identity and this has merged and remained a part of the local identity. All eat, dress and undertake their daily activities, including trading and business, to survive and add to the local economies within the local environment.

5.2.3   REGIONAL AND GLOBAL IDENTITY

After national identity, the next step is usually global. Nonetheless, on viewing websites, it became apparent that there was an intermediate grouping based on geographical regions or continents, for example, Australasia, China, North and South America. The impact of this is that imagery depicted on websites portrays a broader range of nations and cultures. When placed in the global context, this complexity of social, political and cultural roots adds an important dimension to the region's psychological complexity. These are important considerations on designing the impact of website images and on particular regions and cultures. Burawoy et al. (2000) introduced global ethnography, addressing these aspects and focusing on how globalisation affects cultures. For example, are languages applied to the website? How are they depicted – by text or flags? Do they use language scripts? Hence global ethnography is receiving considerable research interest.

5.2.4   GLOBALISATION

The final geographical identity term is 'globalisation' and it stirs many positive and negative emotions. And yet there is no agreed definition. It is seen by many as a *real and historical development* where topics such as branding can flourish within a global corporate culture (Van Gelder, 2003; Wilson and Dissanayake, 1996), and where the *shrinking world* and *global village* (Fry, 2000) concepts can thrive, instead of travellers taking products or services abroad and in turn being influenced by the countries visited. Today, assuming that there are no STEEP barriers, a consumer can view a product on the website and, if they are within the company's distribution area, have the product delivered. The implication of globalisation and the internet is that socio-economic and political occurrences can have major ramifications.

5.3   Business Identity

A business identity can originate through various occurrences but primarily from two sources: firstly, the personality of a person starting his or her business and providing a product or service where they place their own stamp on a company's character, thus establishing its unique characteristics that differentiate it from others. A sole trader may not be aware that he or she has an identity or that an image is being created by signage, pamphlets, answering the telephone or in the manner they conduct business. Large and small organisations may use the same stationery for years, not realising that their image created has become outdated and is perhaps not attracting the same target age group that they were in the original design specification. Secondly, a business may start online, create a designed website identity, portray the necessary image and deliver the products or service. They will be judged not only by the website aesthetic and functionality but also by the manner in which they communicate with the customers and the reputation they have gained. So this business in a wider sense is based on a reputation; there may be a *big idea* (Jones, 2000) but it has to be carefully thought out to ensure that an identity and image carefully threads its way through all its business activities. This is even more important online as customers view a number of websites, each with its own brand. Comparisons are made on prices, quality, delivery times and any other factors customers are interested in. If the information is not on the website, then social media are at the customer and company's disposal. A question may be asked and the answer is provided by another customer or the company. Here the reliability of the information has to be assessed. Ultimately businesses in both the real world and the online version do have to maintain and update their corporate image with carefully chosen identity characteristics.

If the company diverts from this identity path, there are a number of repercussions:

a)   Customers may not recognise the company, regardless of whether they are online or offline, thereby overlooking the business, its products and services.

b)   Recruiting and retaining staff can be difficult as potential employees may not relate to the new organisation and its change in direction or image characteristics.

c)   Trade journalists may be puzzled about what is happening to the company and not recognise new product and services, and therefore make no commentary. The business is then losing free publicity for the company.

d) Financial investors and other backers providing moral support may pull out and again the company has lost valuable inputs that keep it going.

This being said, social media can rectify these problems very quickly once the situation has been spotted. In the end, having a clear identity aids stakeholder recognition of a business, a key corporate communication performance indicator.

> An identity exists within a confusing and emotional market area. It is vital to create and manage an identities [sic] purpose, strengths and effectiveness. The leap from instinctive and emotional first impressions to logical and consciously reasoned opinion is an unpredictable process. A successful identity succeeds in managing this effectively. A poor identity does not. (Rowden, 2000)

As a business develops, its identity evolves and its organisational structure and employees change; therefore managing the original ethos becomes more complex as history, rituals and behaviour become intertwined. For example, when the original founder dies or retires, a personality deficit happens (Olins, 1978). These people are the driving force and the *go to* person within the business who have forged its identity. They often find it difficult to let go if they have not died. A new chief executive and board may be appointed to act as effectively a surrogate for the founder (Baker and Balmer, 1997) until they establish whether someone else can run with the original identity and image or whether a new corporate design is necessary. In either case, the discussions become the focus of a new corporate strategy as the new CEO establishes him or herself. Hence managing an organisation's identity and communicating an image to the outside world becomes of strategic importance as there are many aspects and competitive environmental factors to consider.

> From 1810 to 1983, a Heal's family member was the company owner/figurehead. In 1983 the company was sold to Terence Conran's Design Group when the direction of the company changed. No direct family member has been the CEO since that time, albeit they have had active roles in the company previously and ensured that the identity evolved rather than changed.

An organisation can also have multiple identities (Albert and Whetten, 1985) as Balmer's (1994) study found that a *cohesive* corporate identity was not achieved easily, despite organisational commitment to the subject. At one time differing ideologies within an organisation could be managed. Indeed railway companies introduced corporate liveries and modes of employee conduct in the nineteenth century, not just to differentiate themselves in the marketplace but to pull employees together into one cohesive group. At that time employees were often uneducated and from various parts of the UK. Overall, maintaining a single *voice* or managing the multiple company voice is a difficult job, increasingly so as social media networks develop. Resulting from these features, a balance has to be maintained between the competing requirements of stakeholders and the organisation itself.

5.4   Clarifying Identity by Storytelling

Often stories relate to how people do things rather than how they see the world. Storytelling has therefore been used throughout history to explain and reinforce cultural identity features by recognising collective history (Shaw, 2000) of beliefs, values, social and cultural patterns, memories, myths, legends and jokes with visual symbols and artefacts, rituals and behaviours. Heal's Heritage webpage (see Plate 5.1) provides access to a wealth of information on the company's history.

When people tell stories and anecdotes, they are engaged in a perceptual activity, organising data into special patterns that represent and explain experience. By way of a story, emotional and sentient details communicate a message. Stories are like software, varying by culture as they focus on different things, such as language, gestures, facial expressions, body language, sound and tones.

An audience is crucial to storytelling as it responds and is captivated by the storyteller and the story, just like a website viewer going through a website or taking part in an online game. The composition of the audience can be particularly relevant: an audience of children will actively listen and respond to the story. Again, if the same story is told to a different audience composition, say a mixed male and female audience, the reactions will be very different.

In the business context, storytelling is an established method of communicating an organisation's business ethos, identity and brand, essentially illustrating how the organisation functions around core ideas, its vision and mission (Mitroff and Kilmann, 1979). Stories can be collected from

Plate 5.1   Heal's Heritage webpage

throughout the organisation, as well as top-down and bottom-up. The top-down information source is the CEO and his or her board, where they attend to the strategic articulation of the organisation's mission and philosophy and provide information on corporate goals that were successfully achieved and those that went astray, and why they were not successful. At this level there are few designers but this situation is changing as the relevance of design to business success is being recognised.

Operational, bottom-up input is from the staff who have gained valuable tacit and explicit knowledge of what does and does not work in their organisation, whilst recognising apt image portrayals of its identity-image on media applications. Furthermore, they know the company's external reputation and can determine how this can be maintained or changed in line with current trends. This enables a business to be positioned, or to maintain its position, in the marketplace. Both top-down and bottom-up approaches can be effectively applied to website design. If the two groups do not agree, then a consensual decision has to be made on what corporate story to reveal.

These stories can serve a range of purposes, such as teaching someone their new role within the organisation. The accompanying anecdotes and stories that employees associate with the role, and possibly previous incumbents, can be recounted. Stories can boost morale and provide lifestyle guidance. Metaphors are often used to explain a particular project, which by association provide an indication of what is expected of the individual or group in a project. Scenarios are a well-regarded strategic role-playing exercise where particular occurrences are acted out to identify likely outcomes and downsides, so that these can be resolved in the likelihood of a similar real-life situation. Finally, the obituaries in many trade magazines and newspapers carry a person's life story and contribution to whichever organisation or activities they supported. Sources of storytelling can now be found on the internet through social media, texts, images and videos. Still, the reliability of these stories has to be checked, as often these can be written from a subjective angle or by someone bearing a grudge, which could ultimately reflect badly on the organisation.

Collecting this data and information can be painstaking; this is even after winning round the gatekeepers. Yet by recording events chronologically and or geographically by direct observation, interview recordings, grey material, images, sketches, photographs, artefacts and produce, patterns can emerge. Collating material on particular topics for analysis or for mind-mapping exercises enables systematic linkages and concepts. This wide range of inspirational stories allows discussions between an organisation and designers in the conceptual design phase, as the creation of an image starts with these corporate stories. A good story, clearly communicated, makes listeners and viewers feel that they can trust the company and its values, bringing them to life and engaging the user at a personal level, whilst a story conveys corporate philosophy by expressing its corporate ethos and business practices to customers and stakeholders: 'Communication will be more effective if organizations rely on the so-called sustainable corporate story as a source of inspiration for all internal and external communication programmes. Stories are hard to imitate and they promote consistency in all corporate messages' (Van Riel, 2000). Perceptions can be enhanced or changed by these recorded events and issues, eventually impacting reputation, market capitalisation and profitability. As the amount of data and information stored in computer format increases, there is also a strong likelihood that this could skew the real-life situation, resulting in an unwelcomed outcome. It becomes clearly apparent that decisions have to be made on the specific type and quantity of information that staff within and outside the company put online and that this is carefully policed, otherwise the brand identity could become compromised.

Van Riel (1995) suggested two reasons why corporate stories are applied in business today: firstly, there is a global trend where company transparency is a basic requirement, as the internet gains increasing usage amongst all company stakeholders; and secondly, legal constraints and increased media interest in what is happening in the world are both based on stories. In a similar vein, Chajet (1989) suggests that increased frequency of business news through all media and by digital TV broadcast has significantly increased storytelling since the 1990s. Complex meanings can be expressed across cultural and language barriers, in a manner that would otherwise sound blunt.

Conclusion

Today identity sources are geographically and culturally variable. At one time identities were distinct units, but as travel and communications advanced, the boundaries of defined units became blurred. Chajet (1989) indicates that, if the modern *problem of identity* was how to construct an identity and keep it solid and stable, the postmodern *problem of identity* is primarily how to avoid fixation and keep the options open. In this vein, identity is a mask that can be changed according to context or whim. This is a particularly apt point of view regarding website design, as audiovisual elements can be changed to meet market requirements.

To conclude storytelling, an organisation's image is created by its history, stories and anecdotes of particular occurrences, crises, issues and ethical conduct that form its identity. This determines a source of constructive currency binding an organisation together, as stakeholders recognise that the story relates to a particular organisation: 'Stakeholders must know that the story indeed pertains to the "distinctive" and "enduring" characteristics of the Organisation as a whole' (Van Riel, 2000). This allows complex situations and problems to be explained, such as total quality management where consequential stories of good and bad behaviours are narrated. Stories aid learning and understanding so that, if the situation should arise, the appropriate *software story* downloads from the brain, allowing the person to respond appropriately, and adding meaning, significance and empathy through two-way communication (Grunig, 1992).

How does a good story differentiate a business?

An identity story is sourced from the collective history that exists within any organisation or company. Events from the list of corporate stories recounted orally or textually can be selected. In a business context, stories: communicate business philosophy and mission, establishing how the organisation functions; provide a means of learning by explanations; and, by scenario playing, identify potentially disastrous situations and possible solutions. Crucially, stories are a source of a business's image. Through one anecdote, occurrence or crisis, an identity story can be formed, around which the designer can create the corporate or brand image. Observers, on viewing the image, recognise the company and *download* their impression of the brand story from their memory.

Chapter 6
Corporate Design Strategy

How do I position my business

in the marketplace?

Introduction

A clear vision is a key component of corporate strategy, but a corporate design strategy requires design knowledge and capabilities for the emerging, new and unexpected, each strategy drawing upon the other in design-oriented organisations. The real-world and digital environments within which design has to operate have seen rapid change in the last 20 years as the internet and communication networks impact design strategies, working practices and measures of success. This chapter draws on theoretical and practical explanations of corporate design, highlighting the key corporate design terms of *position*, *symbolism* and *coherence*. Regardless of whether the terms *corporate identity* or *image* are applied, these three terms serve the same purpose, as will be explained later. The chapter progresses through business identity structures relevant to design and organisational practices, then looks at the four key design strategy and operational terms and design project considerations. Thereafter diagrams will illustrate key points and applications in the real world and online.

6.1 Corporate Design Links with Corporate Strategy

In any corporate strategy, whether a new business, product or service, differentiation is key. Corporate design facilitates differentiation by using designer perceptive skills and creative abilities to provide an image that is acceptable in the CEO's selected market position. There is a value exchange occurring where marketing and designers create *messages and meanings* into products and services, these being targeted to specific audiences and groups within market sectors and segments, who *want* to buy the product. Where the branding of this product is *positioned* in the market is a critical combined decision made by the CEO, marketing and the design strategist. Realistically there is also a wide range of other factors to consider in valuations, but design increasingly plays a greater part as aesthetics become a differentiating competitive tool that can add value to the business and its products.

Whereas corporate strategy addresses the sustaining and functional services and systems that produce products and services, a key input is design. Designed aspects include: the working environment and communication structures; marketing material, website presentation and multi-media production; customer service operations, staff training, uniforms and rituals that reinforce the effective and expected levels of service. All of this provides an initial impression of a business, regardless of budgets and funding.

6.2   Corporate Design Strategy

Once the CEO and design strategists have established the market *position*, design strategy establishes how a selected identity story portrays the message in the marketplace through the corporate identity mix, which occurs by *symbolically* conveying a corporate story by means of visual identity and organisational behaviour techniques, to communicate the created image *coherently* across all media applications to its audiences (Melewar and Karaosmanoglu, 2006). A corporate design strategy and process is important as it ultimately impacts on the company's reputation (Fombrun, 1996) and the financial market's confidence in the company. Figure 6.1 illustrates the linkages between corporate strategy and corporate design strategy: at which point the *position* is decided, when *symbolism* is created through visual identity and organisational behaviour and how *coherent* messages are communicated across all media. Each of these concepts and terms are described in sections 6.3 and 6.4. Through this aesthetic, all stakeholders can gain an impression of the company, its products and services, thereby signifying the organisation's key qualities, reliability and approach to innovation. The main question now is: how is this achieved?

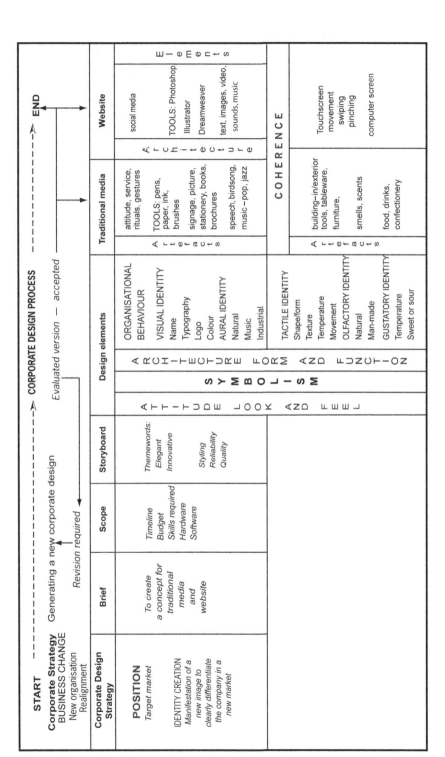

Figure 6.1   Corporate design strategy and processes on traditional media applications and websites

6.2.1   CORPORATE DESIGN ELEMENTS

Position

A new market *position* in the marketplace is necessary on four occurrences:

- A new business venture

- To reinforce a reputation in the sector

- A takeover or merger placement

- Trying a new sector to enhance reputation or resulting from STEEP changes.

A CEO *positions* a concept, product or service in the marketplace where it is most likely to thrive, that is, the CEO's *Desired* identity in the marketplace (Balmer, 2000, 2002) which is considered to be the best market location over a period of time. Further research and analysis may define the *Ideal* identity, but there is also an element of tacit knowledge and *gut feeling* that defies reason. The organisation's board and strategic planners consider a range of factors within the marketplace, for example, the organisation's general business and competitive capabilities – subject to external political, economic, environmental, sociological and technological (PEEST) factors.

Corporate design then articulates the selected identity concept by strategically positioning the company in a market, often revisiting the same sociological, technological, environmental, economic and political (STEEP) factors, but seen through a designer's eye. The corporate design consultant should work with the CEO or business owner to ensure clarity in creating the relevant image/brand personality. Then, through symbolism of imagery and behaviour, in a specific design style, they can convey a corporate message coherently across all its media channels (Van Riel, 1995). For example, is the *position* to be:

- Expensive or budget

- Established or alternative

- Craft or fine art

- High tech or traditional.

If two airlines are considered: Easyjet does not appear to spend much on designing its brand or image, apart from its orange corporate colour, whereas British Airways has a number of design initiatives, from the controversial tailfins of the 1990s to lifestyle photographs in aircraft cabins and interior designed business waiting lounges. Easyjet and British Airways have *positioned* their businesses in different market segments, the former in the lower price range and the latter in the higher price range.

Symbolism

Symbolism is achieved by appropriate selection of visual graphics and behaviours – a particular style of typography, colour, shape and layout in conjunction with organisational ritual and way of doing things that people associate with that market position and industrial sector. This is important as ideally stereotyping should be avoided, so that the company's corporate personality shines through. There are various design techniques to accomplish this, by being non-specific or leaving the design open to interpretation and perception, such as *The Economist* billboard advert's red hue, with its specific tone that is recognised across most of the Western world. Logos and images can cross language and cultural barriers; for example, the Red Cross and Red Crescent – both humanitarian organisations use the colour red in their logo, although the sign is different. Yet again, Switzerland's flag is a colour reverse of the Red Cross emblem.

Coherence

At this strategic level, decisions have to be made to ensure that *coherence* of the corporate design style and associated messages are applicable across all its media applications. Operationally colours and size have to be transmitted and scaled to fit billboards, letterheads, computer screens and reception area information desks. Style manuals, templates and style sheets are usually available for this work. This consistency may have to be adapted to adhere to conservation area requirements; for example, McDonalds adheres to local planning regulations by selecting a suitable style through changing typographic colour and shop frontage style. Some businesses have to adapt to new mediums: Jaguar racing green colour had to be changed to a more recognisable shade on TV. Online strategies have to be put in place to ensure that content not only communicates the relevant message but is instantaneously attractive and engaging. The message can be the same whilst the design style defines the brand image. The following identity groupings explain how this occurs.

6.3   Identity Groupings

The study of identity has become a subject in itself, incorporating many disciplines, addressing the management of countries, companies, products and services. Both corporate identity and branding authors have recognised three identity structures applied across marketing functions and organisational structures.

6.3.1   MONOLITHIC IDENTITY

Monolithic identity is built around a consistent story, one name, theme and visual identity, applied to everything the organisation does. Barclays Bank applies the same name; financial sector technology and user friendly banking theme; spread eagle logo and turquoise colour on all its buildings, products and services. Virgin applies a variation on their visual identity: the same shade of red is used and the font is often the same, but some subsidiaries apply different font styles appropriate to their market sector. Business threats can arise when monolithic identity is employed – for example, if a crisis occurs such as a bad train crash in one subsidiary, which can have implications for the group of companies as a whole. A further detraction for monolithic identities is that innovation can be stifled lest it detracts from the corporate image (Ind, 1992).

6.3.2   ENDORSED IDENTITY

Endorsed identity is part of a visible parent company, with subsidiary companies and brands each with their own style; for example, Nestle products have brand names appearing under their own names, such as Kit Kat biscuits and Walnut Whip chocolate. The strength is that brand equity is created and maintained by the brand, which has financial advantages. Weakness occurs as each brand has to be considered to ensure that a balance is maintained in communicating each brand's identity and image. Today each brand can have its own website and social media, almost appearing as commercial entities in their own right, although still under an umbrella company which itself has a corporate brand.

6.3.3   BRANDED IDENTITY

Branded identity conveys each unit or brand separately to the consumer as an independent product. In reality it is owned by an entity that manages, controls, markets and distributes the products; for example, Diageo distributes Guinness, Johnnie Walker, Baileys, Smirnoff, Pimms and Tanqueray drinks.

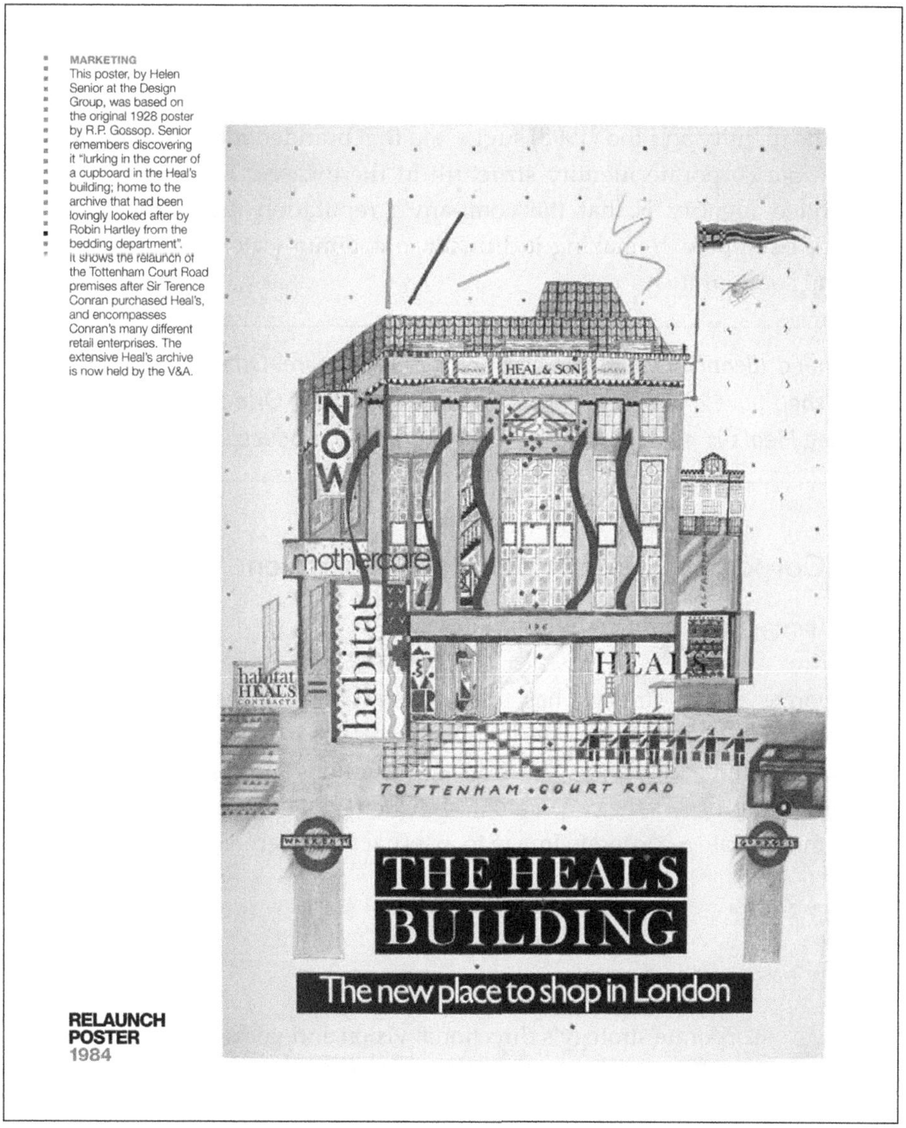

Plate 6.1   The relaunch after Terence Conran purchased Heal's, depicting the Design Group's diverse brands

Source: *Heal's 1810–2010 – 200 Years of Design & Inspiration* (2009), p. 138.
© Heal & Son Ltd. With special thanks to the V&A Archive.

Branded products often appear on the home page as a list or scroll; from these icons the product and service websites can be accessed. Van Riel (1995) noted that complex organisational structures often have difficulty in communicating corporate identity and Ind (1998) suggested that branded identity was the most appropriate corporate identity structure in these cases. The main weakness of branded identity is that the company's reputation may suffer from its fragmented approach, making it difficult to communicate its strengths to the financial community.

> *Branded Identity: Heal's is a high-end furniture store. Other brands sold in the shop have a similar clientele: Ercol, Original BTC, Orla Kiely, Alessi, Ligne Roset. Heal's is now returning to its own branded products.*

6.4   Corporate Design Strategy and Operation

6.4.1   FOUR KEY CONTRIBUTIONS

A corporate design strategy has four different strands that contribute to its creation and implementation. The following chapters in Parts II and IV provide a structure around which the multifarious contributions and considerations can be grouped and progress the corporate design strategy and operational necessities that communicate a corporate image to external and internal stakeholders.

Strategy

Strategy has two components:

1.   Corporate strategy's directional vision and goals establish where the business wants to be, that is, the desired position in the marketplace.

2.   Corporate design strategy *positions* the company images for the chosen market through sentient and behavioural means.

Perspectives

Perspectives relate to people and skills contributions. The designed product and the process of achieving this require many skills, knowledge and talents through a wide group of stakeholders. A list of these is included in Chapter 7, but this is not exhaustive. Essentially with any design project the essential skills need to be recognised and the appropriate person contacted for availability. Then their time and charges can be factored into the budget

PRODUCT
The Buzz range was launched to appeal to a younger clientele with less money to spend. The aim was to entice them away from lower-priced high-street newcomers, such as The Reject Shop and Habitat. It closed in 1983, when Sir Terence Conran bought Heal's.

CREATING
A BUZZ AT
HEAL'S
1978

Plate 6.2   The 1978 Buzz range, appealing to a
younger clientele with less money to spend

Source: *Heal's 1810–2010 – 200 Years of Design & Inspiration* (2009), p. 131.
© Heal & Son Ltd. With special thanks to the V&A Archive.

and work plan. Other perspectives include customers, regulatory bodies, financial services, government and peer groups who through social media can now have an impact on the company and its products and process.

Design style and elements

Design style and elements considers the development of *symbolic* visual identity elements and organisational behaviour used to create the designed aesthetic (see Chapters 11 and 12).

Design evolution and applications

Design evolution and applications address the impact that technology, sociological factors, economics and politics have on the design process, communication channels and audience acceptance. Arising from situations that have arisen in each of these STEEP factors, legislation, regulations and standards are formulated.

6.4.2   DESIGN PROJECT CONSIDERATIONS

In discussion with the CEO, a design strategist has to recognise the business requirements and confirm the corporate goals. Before a design concept can be created, a designer has to understand the company that he or she is working with. Most companies are design followers, only allowing step changes to occur, whereas companies that are design leaders accept that there are risks with possible financial losses (Oakley, 2001). To progress and design projects, there are a number of topics to discuss with the CEO:

Company-related considerations

a)   What is the company's outlook on design, for example, is it actively encouraged or generally ignored?

b)   Has the company seen or had any discussions on what design could achieve for the business?

c)   How often are new design products and services put into the marketplace?

d)   Is there a research and development or other department within the organisation itself where *silent design* could be occurring?

e)   Do the business processes, management structures and information systems target a particular market position or segment?

f)   Is there an efficient accounting and IT system, including internet services?

g)   Are all statutory legal and regulatory requirements carried out and agreed?

Project-related considerations

h)   Does the company wish the project to be a design leader or follower?

i)   Is there someone within the company who can champion the project and persuade anyone who has reservations?

j)   Is the project's success totally dependent on the new designs?

k)   What design skills, knowledge and expertise are essential?

l)   How will the work be undertaken: internally, one-stop shop or by collaborative teamwork?

m)   How will project staff be reassigned from the company workforce or selected from external sources?

n)   Has a design budget been approved that realistically allows the corporate goal and design management objectives to be achieved?

o)   Does the company operate to current industry and design standards, as they provide useful guidelines in production and marketing matters?

p)   Does the company own or lease key equipment and software, with all the necessary licences, certificates and warranties?

Offline the ambience, visual styling and staff behaviour emit messages by which a customer perceives the business's products and service quality and reliability, that is, the strategic articulation. Online this is still developing but in recent years there has been a vast improvement. The following diagrams provide an illustration of real-world and website environments, structures, artefacts and systems, all being part of the creative process and therefore designed.

6.5   Traditional Media Artefacts and Skillsets

Each company and its business organisation has different design requirements, but key to all is that they comply with the business ethos and attitude by

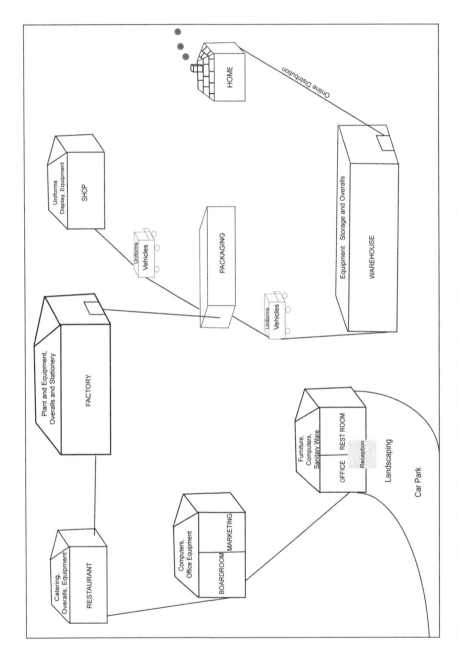

Figure 6.2 Manufacturing, retail and distribution environments and processes

material, decoration, finish, staff attire and behaviour throughout their operations. Within any activity, design occurs; even whilst reading this book, look around and observe all the *design* that has occurred, so that you can sit on a chair, with your feet on the floor, on a stool, with papers strewn on a desk with a PC, or reading on a tablet; or whilst walking through the office corridor, to the car park and your car. In this short period you have travelled across three environments: environmental, products and information.

Design is about people and processes set in motion to achieve goals, set in a strategy, with planned operations and management to ensure that one step and/or activity follows on one to another until the goal is reached. Sometimes refinements are necessary when the original concepts or plans do not function effectively, but most projects do reach completion. Figure 6.2 illustrates where these components interrelate in a real-world setting:

- Communications

- Product, services and experience creation

- Working environment.

The combination of these three components has to *coherently* convey the aesthetic and atmosphere that create or emulate the business's strategic *position* in the marketplace, this being achieved through *symbolic* visual identity elements of names, logos, typography and colour, and organisational behaviour undertaken by induction on how the business operates, expected behaviour, rituals and attire, reinforced by training. The design management of these components is discussed in Chapter 8, with Chapters 10, 11 and 12 addressing symbolism, the visual identity creative process and organisational behaviour respectively.

A schematic of a website homepage is included in Figure 6.3 to illustrate the online experience. Further discussion of this occurs in Chapters 13, 14 and 15 with content on digital branding strategy, digital content and social business.

Today each of these components – communication, products, services and working environments – can be in different countries, with suppliers having a completely different working ethos, and information communication being transmitted across vast distances by the internet and other communication systems.

Table 6.1 lists aspects to be considered in corporate design projects, as each design project is bespoke and there are always additions and variations defined by the required vision and goals.

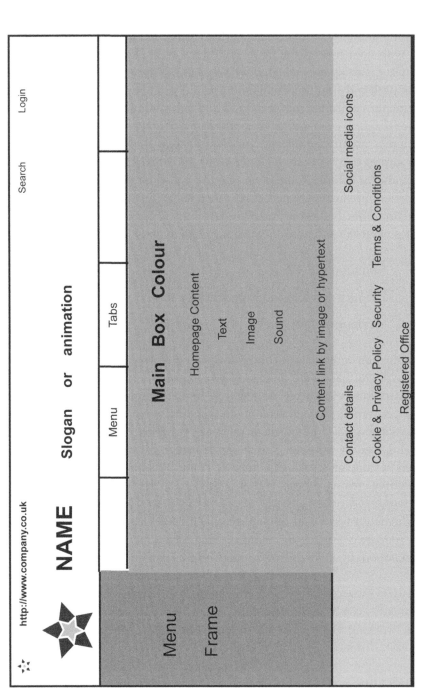

Figure 6.3 Online environment – website homepage

Table 6.1   Designed working environments

Information communication:

Packaging – product covering, cups, food wrapping with special requirements, garden product boxes

Signs – various styles to perform specific functions

Stationery – labels, headed paper, compliment slips and business cards

Websites

Electronic displays

Uniforms – specific job-related requirements: catering, security, receptionists, gardeners, laboratory and maintenance overalls

Manufacture of a wide range of products requiring:

Machinery and tools – to make and repair artefacts

Raw materials – fabrics, metals, nuts and bolts, threads, plastics, wood

Warehouse, picking machinery and delivery to machinery floor, quality checks

Package design and wrapping process

Protective clothing

Food preparation:

Recipes and ingredient sources

Machinery and tools – to make food and package

Distribution process:

Loading and unloading areas, suitable vehicles and containers to transport products

Retail process:

Shop fronts and displays, storerooms, changing rooms

Merchandise and packaging/boxes, coat hangers

Working environment:

Buildings – a vital part of organisational identity where architecture provides a first impression to visitors

Styles range from high-tech design constructed with expensive materials to organic building development made from 'make-do' or cheaper local building material

Interior design – sentient design creates ambience by colour, finishes and furnishing internally

Office space, washrooms, medical areas, waste disposal

Research and development laboratories, workrooms

Catering – kitchen: preparation and cooking areas, wet and dry kitchen equipment, sinks, cookers, work surfaces, food sources, recipes and displays

Restaurant – serving hatches and containers, dining room furniture, tableware and cutlery

Sculptures, paintings, photographs, cartoons and displays – internal and external

Vehicles:

Vans, cars, lorries, trailers, carts of variable sizes; parking and cleaning areas

Landscaping:

Ambience created by the selection and spacing of internal/external plants and floral decoration

Internal floral displays and plants; external trees, shrubs and plants

Gardens and pathways – pathway plans and necessary material; screening, plants, shrubs, trees

Parking area, access roads for various business vehicles – clients/customers.

Uniforms:

Safety equipment, spectacles, visors, safety pins and name tags

6.5.1   CORPORATE DESIGN IN DAILY LIFE

So what does all this mean to a business and its customers, visitors or clients? On entering a shop, you may wish to buy a dress or suit. On going to an entertainment park, you may want to ride the highest rollercoaster. Visiting a garden, you may wish to see which plants are growing and the garden's approach to growing methods and display. Throughout there are websites to look at on your mobile phone, tablet and kiosks. Alternatively there are various styles of signs and pamphlets providing directions to different locations that display information on topics and future events. There is a reception and payment booth ...

> Front and back offices with desks, noticeboards, computers ...
> Staff uniforms for all the various functional roles and restroom facilities ...
> Restaurant and catering facilities, furniture, tableware, utensils, food display and serving ...
> Publications, annual reports, packaging, promotions, advertising, pop-up shops, and the list goes on ...
> As corporate designers say, look around you and observe ...

This is not so different from a pre-twenty-first-century day–trip, but the combination of real-world, mobile and online can make the visit more enjoyable by providing pre-visit information, entertainment and facilities for pre-purchase browsing so that selections can be previewed before buying in a real-world shop or on the company's e-commerce website. Today we look towards a source of information as an experience from the first point of typing a website URL and then by the visiting experience, which can be in a real-world or digital environment. We then encounter the service experience – should the real-world and digital environments be the same? – then the purchasing experience, again possible in a real-world or digital environment. All of this has to be strategically and operationally designed for the required market position.

Each of these requires specific skillsets and knowledge to ensure that the ethos and imagery is in place and can be recognised and understood within both the organisational and the wider business environment. Eventually the *BRAND* is recognised by way of its products, service and overall experience. Then when someone mentions the name, you immediately have an impression of this entity, what it stands for and how you feel about it.

... Leading to a BRAND

How do I position my business in the marketplace?

A good idea, and the decision to go ahead with it, initiates the whole corporate design process. The combination of a designer and business owner allows this idea to be manifested in the real world and/or online. Obviously: a) having a business plan helps to define the financial and business process framework; and b) the business idea is developed as the business owner and designer focus and refine, continually asking each other and others questions ... and finding answers, until it becomes clear where the business and or product *niche* lies in the marketplace, this being its *position*. Themewords and styles are proposed for the creation of the CVIS which is the symbols used to evoke the business's unique features in the market, these being applied to all the working environment artefacts. Ultimately the objective is to convey the organisation's function, aesthetic and atmosphere for the business's marketplace position, this being created by a designer's ability to manifest an idea into reality.

Chapter 7
Perception and Perspectives

*How do people recognise my business
and who are the stakeholders?*

Introduction

Design would be unable to exist without two key aspects: the perception of the viewer and the perspective of all those designing a product, each influencing the other. First key aspects of perception are explained and then the differing approaches to the same problem that can occur by a designer and the CEO. Following this, the perspective section takes a role approach, itemising and grouping related roles and contributions, with a short summary to illustrate the wide range of contributors and expertise necessary in corporate design projects. Many of these roles are often overlooked once a project is completed but their skills have to be maintained for other projects.

7.1   Perception

How one person perceives an image may be perceived differently by another. Yet the person in the image knows what they were thinking and viewing as they walked through the shop. Between our full consciousness of an object and our senses, an elaborate mental process takes place converting the sensory patterns into perceptions of the world as we individually know it. This perception can vary according to age, culture, nationality and many other life experiences.

All communication is sentient, transmitted through movement shapes, sound, colour, spatial location, text and texture received through the five senses: sight, hearing, touch, smell and sometimes taste. Ruth Finnegan's book on communication (2002) discusses these aspects in detail. Each of our senses is used in communication design:

- Sight allows us to identify shapes, colour, movement, size and distance. This occurs by finely tuned eye movements assimilating patterns of light and colour on the retina which the mind translates into a coherent world. Colour forms a very distinctive part of our visual sense where our eyes react to colour and their intensity at varying speeds.

- Hearing allows us to distinguish sound that has travelled distances and round corners, where visibility is impossible. Whereas there can be many pictures on a computer screen, there can only be one dominant sound occurring in sequence. Sound recognition has many properties – volume, pitch, rhythm, intensity, speed, tone, cadence or timbre – which the ear can differentiate: natural sounds of birdsong and animals; vehicular traffic sounds; musical instruments and sound in all its forms, as well as sounds we make ourselves, such as footsteps, sighing, sneezing and so on.

- Touch is a direct communication sense that often empathises with other senses, such as hearing a vibration, and undulating movement and noise through feeling. Touch facilitates our identification of shapes, texture, temperature and movement. Increasingly touch and hand movements are used in human–computer interaction (HCI), such as swiping, pinching and scrolling on tablets.

- Smell can swiftly take us back to a specific situation or event.

- Taste has its associations with culture and lifestyle. It has a wide range of gustatory sensations, such as sweet, sour, dry, spicy, hot to cool, bland, bitter, in liquid to solid forms.

Referring back to Figure 6.2 (Manufacturing, retail and distribution environments and processes), visualise walking through this environment and all the senses that you use in understanding the business, its operations and the message the company is communicating. Consider the spatial arrangement and dimensions; sounds – natural or man-made, music, machine rhythms; colours and associations – warm or cool, positive or negative; imagery through the general aesthetic of the environment and the static pictures and videos; language used, fonts, symbols and textual content; numbers – time, associations, lists in serial or sequences, analyses and logic of why and when these appear.

Websites and digital media can be construed as a basic level of communication. This is part of our practical consciousness, the practical skill and knowledge that people utilise in their behaviour; knowing what to say and do one moment to another – essentially what is acceptable and appropriate, whilst the discursive consciousness brings out our common sense on what is acceptable within our own cultures and experiences (Gardener, 1983). Consciousness also provides a means of accessing our memories, to develop whichever aspect we wish to pursue into knowledge, or as a distractive entertainment medium.

There is an overriding perceptive paradox in using digital media – we use technology for information, purchases and entertainment, but at the same time our approaches to the tasks and resultant actions have already been mediated, tailored by operational design of the device and communication platforms. Hence the information we receive from computers can be wrong or not quite specific enough. Currently, we do have the knowledge and experience to question the results, if something does not appear to be correct online. As the saying goes: 'we make our tools and then our tools make us.' This is an important point: as computers record all our words and actions digitally.

7.2   Designer Versus Business Outlook

In many corporate design projects, business and design consultants work together, even though their working cultures differ, each having their own way of thinking – generally designers display divergent thinking and business executives convergent thinking. Specialists observing the two groups have found differences relating to perception, and physiological and psychological make-up. Hence fruition of a corporate design project requires continual discussion and iterative working between both parties to ensure that corporate goals are achieved. The following shows the differing approaches but also explains why it is important to speak with as many people within the client organisation and with the project's specialist designers, so that everyone understands what has to be achieved.

DESIGNER	CEO
Who are we? What are we like?	Corporate personality
What do we do?	Capabilities and know-how
How do we accomplish this?	Making products/services and marketing them
Where do we want to go in the future?	Vision and mission statements

In practice both parties benefit from having knowledge of each other's working environments and the sectors in which they operate. A business executive requires detailed knowledge of his or her sector to maintain competitive edge, and increasingly many are becoming design-aware. On the other hand, designers have to be able to tap into the business executive's expertise and then compare this knowledge with previous projects they have worked on, including those in their current project sector. The fact that designers often run their own business is overlooked. This fact alone makes it possible for them to relate to business problems.

7.3   Perspective – Strategists

Perspective represents the internal and external stakeholder viewpoint and skill contributions necessary in creating corporate and brand designs, these being apart from the CEO and design strategist: staff, design specialists, customers, clients, financial institutions and regulatory bodies. Each of these stakeholder groups can contribute a wide range of knowledge, skill and experience.

7.3.1   CHIEF EXECUTIVE OFFICER (CEO)

The key contributor and decision-maker is the CEO, who sets the tone of the organisation and has business responsibility and legal authority invested in him or her with the job title. Many corporate design contributors reinforce that direction has to come from the top of the organisation and is seen to be of primary importance (Marguiles, 1977; Michael Wolff, Interview, 2006). A new board may be necessary when the company is going in a new direction, as the CEO has to have the necessary experience to understand the environments that the business will be working in. CEOs cannot delegate their responsibility for corporate communications both to all internal stakeholders and to external stakeholders, as the message communicated is just as important as earnings per share. The CEO has to know and develop what the company stands for – its philosophy and culture, history and structure, including the vision and mission statements so popular on corporate noticeboards. Once all of this has been clearly defined, it allows greater clarity for the design strategist's input to the symbolic communication.

As CEOs are goal-oriented, they are likely to be design-conscious but often require persuasion to go ahead with a potentially adventurous, if not financially risky, project. Often design can solve or resolve some of the problems that the organisation is encountering (Turner, 2013). CEOs have to know sufficient detail about their organisation, its functional departments, and individuals – but not all the detail. Hence often they are the best to initiate new design projects, with their tacit knowledge and experience. Ultimately the CEO's aims are: a) to achieve and maintain a positive corporate image in the marketplace with little business risk; and b) to maintain a good reputation and confidence in the financial markets. A good corporate design strategist can help him or her achieve these goals.

A Heal's family member has been head of the company continuously for 170 years, often being designers themselves.

7.3.2   CORPORATE DESIGN STRATEGIST

The corporate design strategist works with the CEO, initiating and developing a design concept from his or her holistic and intuitive expertise that creates the image for the new market position. If a new direction is essential for the company, a new CEO and board may be necessary to lead the company in achieving this goal. The corporate design strategist uses his or her expertise, gained through numerous design projects, by listening and speaking with people throughout the organisation and observing how the organisation operates. This emphasises the importance of dealing with and persuading the CEO level when developing identity and brands, to ensure that the project has all the necessary authority. The CEO cannot delegate communication responsibilities as he/she has to initiate and articulate what the company stands for, its raison d'être, both internally and externally. There may be a mission and vision for a set period of time but the company's philosophy and corporate values are infinite.

Both CEOs and design strategists have to be aware of developing technologies and their impact on traditional approaches. Digital – including website – technology has impacted all aspects of both the aesthetic and functional aspects of corporate design, this being increasingly important as web technology progresses and image becomes a corporate asset:

> *The future CEO should be one who is, through his or her deep appreciation of the aesthetics, able to create if not structure or better still foster a distinctive, identifiable visually aesthetic environment. If that happens the corporate world of the future including manufacturing environments can become aesthetically more pleasing ... Moreover CEOs as leaders ought, through aesthetics, better shape a corporate identity.* (Foo, 2006)

7.3.3 OTHER BOARD MEMBERS

When there are other more important business issues to attend to, getting other directors to accept that design can positively contribute to resolving some of these takes time and patience. Often a *design champion* is essential to convince the board of a design project, as they have to accept the business and design proposal. When a new business is being launched, this is not difficult as both are working from a blank sheet of paper. This is thought to be the best way to approach a corporate design, whether on traditional media and/or a website, but is rarely the case. The scenarios are likely to be a merger or takeover; re-positioning the company; a new product or service in a new sector resulting from PEEST environmental situations. When this is the backdrop to a design project, it can be difficult to get all the board members to agree, as they feel that 'important issues' ought to be to discussed. But perseverance is necessary, as often design can overcome an obstacle – through design thinking and discussion – that a business person has overlooked or not understood. Three directors can be instrumental in contributing to and achieving the goals of the CEO and design strategist:

Marketing director

The marketing director defines the marketing strategy for the company's products and services, establishing the target market/audience and positioning them in the market where they are likely to sell well, in a similar manner to the CEO and design strategist's approach to positioning the company and its products. He/she also defines how the goals of the marketing strategy are to be achieved, ensuring that each service or product's goals are SMART, that is, specific, measurable, attainable, relevant and timebound. A branding strategy for each product or service may be necessary if the market is particularly competitive or the product or service is to be sold online. This will also include promotional material and pricing. Distribution and after-sales services may be necessary, together with any further resources.

Creative director

The creative director oversees aesthetic strategy by applying both art and design techniques and processes, this being conducted within the company's policies which are the articulation of the strategy related to a specific project. Policies provide the reference points upon which the design implementation should progress.

Design director

In the past, most companyies were reluctant to have designers on the board, but this has been changing as the importance of corporate branding online has provided a channel for designers to explain the importance and relevance of design to organisations. A creative director has a wider brief than a design director.

7.4 Working with Designers

The characteristics appertaining to a designer cannot be automated; they have a *designer intelligence* unique to each individual designer, generally regarded as *flair*. This flair becomes recognised by others, establishing the designer's style where they often work with a few selected media. Through the British Library Oral History Archive, it is possible to hear testimony of designers explaining how their skills and knowledge of their subjects were developed and about the roles and projects they worked on within companies who employed them.

Designers need to be culturally aware, understand markets and people and have good research skills and facilities. In Michael Wolff's assessment, designers, through their assimilation of knowledge, will produce a design based 99 per cent on looking, listening, hunches and how the business operates and 1 per cent on research about the company. Keeping up to date on their

CORONATION
MEMORABILIA
1953

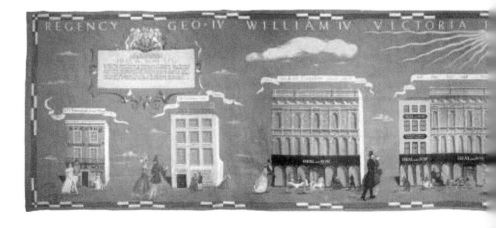

(*bottom*) Plate 11.1   Heal's local expansion in Tottenham Court
Road, serving national and international markets

Source: *Heal's 1810–2010 – 200 Years of Design & Inspiration* (2009), pp. 92–93.
© Heal & Son Ltd. With special thanks to the V&A Archive.

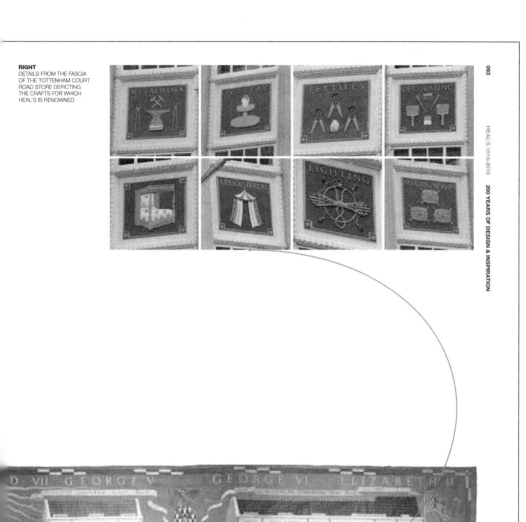

RIGHT
DETAILS FROM THE FASCIA OF THE TOTTENHAM COURT ROAD STORE DEPICTING THE CRAFTS FOR WHICH HEAL'S IS RENOWNED

(*top*) Plate 7.1   Tottenham Court Road building fascia,
depicting the crafts for which Heal's is renowned

Source: *Heal's 1810–2010 – 200 Years of Design & Inspiration* (2009), p. 93.
© Heal & Son Ltd. With special thanks to the V&A Archive.

recognised subject is crucial. Ideas for design projects are omnipresent and designers have to be able to recognise where and when the idea can be applied. Continual development of their technical skills is another requirement as, regardless of whether this is a traditional or digital skillset, it impacts, creating a unique concept with innovative execution that satisfies the client's brief. In other words, a designer is a complex character who absorbs multifarious sentient data and information from many situations and organisations to create effective designs.

Locating a design specialist with the requisite knowledge and skills is difficult and therefore a wide-ranging designer network, both in traditional and digital art and design skills, facilitates a smooth running of the design process. Most artists and designers are self-employed freelancers, whilst others work in partnerships and companies. Those within companies tend to be design and marketing managers who have been allocated a project and need art and design skills to complete the work. Plate 7.1 illustrates Heal's designed and made products, along with maker's tools.

7.4.1 INFORMATION ENVIRONMENT DESIGNERS

The original creators of visual identity were graphic designers. As their skills gained importance across conventional media in the 1970s, their skills were transferred to digital media in the 1990s. Web technology opened new avenues for skills and media development as innovative devices continually appeared with updated versions. Old working practices have disappeared or been adapted to new technology. Users' expectations also changed as they adapted or grew up with these new developments. Graphic design education has seen much discussion on the applicability of traditional skills as the modern world tilts to digital media. Many have seen this as a loss in quality but this argument has decreased as the finesse of the technology creates better definition for artistic endeavour. The argument that learning by doing develops hand skills and intuitive perceptions still stands; for example, this skill facilitates a clearer expression of *letter* creation as the eye becomes more observant of the refinements, making possible the recognition of what is good or bad design. Information environment designers create images that are functional and aesthetically pleasing to communicate a corporate image and message. Many people connect this with visual identity where they create names, fonts, logos, colours and slogans.

The following job titles are artists in their respective fields and it is through their efforts and collaboration that a corporate design brief is achieved.

Graphic designers

Graphic designers apply a hierarchy of formats, layouts, images and letters of various sizes and styles. They select and combine elements to facilitate a composed image that communicates the necessary message to a specific audience. Graphic designers were the first to recognise the importance of their subject in promoting a business through advertising. Today a huge database of imagery and typographic libraries can be accessed whilst other graphic designers create their own bespoke elements. There was some concern regarding how graphic design was going to develop on digital media, yet once its potential for visual communication and its interactive possibilities were realised, it has opened up more opportunities.

Lettering – typography, fonts and calligraphy

Typographers introduced structure and practices to print with title pages, cataloguing schemes, copyright and modern authorship. They usually have a wide knowledge of communication theory, semiotics, linguistics and information environments (Jury, 1999). Calligraphy shows an individuality that does not occur in print type or digital fonts. Both letters and text have seen dramatic changes from hand-formed calligraphy letters to metal type, and now digital capabilities have further widened selection sources. Both provide information on paper and screens by individually designed typeface/font letters that convey character and purpose in themselves, and by the manner in which they are grouped together as a composition (Spiekermann and Ginger, 2003; Lupton, 2004).

Logo designers

Logo designers have seen a resurgence in their work as logos became a necessity for websites as well as on traditional media. Logo designers have to be able to synthesise a message and express this visually in small dimensions. Often the same logo is applied, but a company can have multiple logos for differing projects' websites within their organisation. Hence a hierarchy of logos for different types of work or function can be in place. Scalability is also a requirement as the same logo may be applied on a number of media and artefacts.

Colourists

Colourists use the four dimensions of colour – hue, temperature, intensity and value – in their various combinations for particular design projects.

Often designers, architects and artists create their own combinations that become part of their style (Feisner, 2014). Colour wheels are made use of to visually show how colour is generated through red, green, blue light (RGB) or by cyan, magenta, yellow and black pigment (CMYK) for print.

Photographers

Photography encompassesa wide range of styles. For example, commercial, portrait, lifestyle and wildlife. Photography has seen rapid change as it found applications within digital media on smartphones and tablets with in-built cameras. This has meant that anyone with a mobile phone can take a photograph and upload this on to the internet.

Animators/cartoonists

Animations and cartoons are used for short film-making, now being applied on websites through text, videos and longer cartoons as digital technology allows greater flexibility in design. Animators employ artistic and graphic design skills to convey a story. This is a much longer process than filming but the results can engage an audience as the novelty factor and spectacle are slightly removed from real life. Animations now include avatars, essentially 3D cartoons.

Video and film-makers

Films have existed since the early twentieth century as a specialist role. Today anyone can take a video on their smartphone and upload it to YouTube. Currently videos are the *need to have* website content element as costs have decreased with better digital technology and definition.

Music/jingles

Musical jingles have been a commercial musician's role since radio and filming began and, as with video, the clarity of the music/jingle has improved as their composition has become more refined. The talent in this role is selecting or creating the relevant jingle for a product or experience.

7.4.2   DIGITAL MEDIA AND WEBSITE DESIGNERS

The main digital design grouping is:

Structural designers

Structural designers facilitate information architecture similar to engineering design that looks at the structure and functional aspects of a product.

Cognitive designers

Cognitive designers apply human–computer interaction that links attention, behaviour and the interface, similar to an industrial designer who thinks about customer usage, appearance and styling, for example, look and feel. They also apply current and developing software to unique effect.

Experience designers

Experience designers design the customer journey from the first click on a website to the final exit after purchasing a product or service, or leaving a real-world shop or location.

Developing roles

A number of website-related roles have appeared in recent years such as *Chief Knowledge, Information* or *Data Officer*. This person releases the company website online and needs to understand the implications of a corporate identity-image gestalt and aesthetic apart from and including the website content. Other roles are: *digital strategists* who specify digital solutions; *head of digital strategy* who works within strategic change management and the complex stakeholder environment with its multiple channels and disciplines; *head of digital marketing and e-commerce*; *video directors* for online platforms; and *multimedia producers.*

Creative innovation technologists and digital media artists

Digital creative art forms and innovative digital expressions are initially found in the creative underground (Engholm, 2002a) where new ideas are discussed and thrashed out by continual trial and error. Digital artists and creative technologists pursue their artistic activities, driving the creative digital designs forward and often the technology itself. Avant-garde early adopters develop software and digital effects, setting new digital style trends that break away from the current fashions – ever evolving with each generation of digital artists and website design.

Textual content

Writers create the initial website textual content which can include blogs and other social media.

Editors ensure that the requisite tone and corporate voice is applied to all communications, and where necessary they restructure or rewrite content.

7.4.3 PRODUCTS AND SERVICES

Product and service designers are and were the originators of many key manufacturing and production artefacts. Their role may now have a greater digital input but the skillset and insight are still required.

Product designers

Form and function are the product designer's key criteria to satisfy a particular people or system requirement.

2005   Heal's Discovers brings the freshest design talent to the shop floor.

2009   Heal's ReDiscovers campaign

Industrial designers

Industrial designers provide the aesthetics on a manufactured product to make it more appealing in the market sector or to increase the product standing from *standard* to *bespoke*.

Packaging designers

Packaging designers design product wrapping that includes the CVIS elements, product and legal requirements.

7.4.4 WORKING ENVIRONMENTS

Architects

Architects design buildings, their external and internal layout and building plans providing the first, mostly digitally created, images of what a new building will look like in a chosen setting. With 3D software the viewer can now *digitally* walk through their new office, working environment or home. Architects also control all of the legal and regulatory requirements of any building programme, ensuring that the practical construction is in agreement with plans, local and national building laws and regulations.

Facility engineers and service designers

Service designers and facility engineers attend to utilities within a building, ranging from electrical and computer cabling to telephone systems and plumbing. All of this has to be designed, constructed, maintained and tested on a regular basis. This is one of the original collaborative design projects.

Interior designers

There are interior designers specialising in every conceivable design style, with directories, literature and websites devoted to their work, which concentrates on the internal colouring, furnishing and finishes. Key here is ensuring that the most appropriate style is selected and executed within time and budgetary constraints.

Landscape designers

Capability Brown is a well-known historical stately home garden designer, so the relevance of landscaping in creating an impression and image is well tested. Today this is an integral part of any working environment, whether this be large or small, as landscape designs convey the first impression as a visitor approaches the working environment and its buildings.

Fine artists

Art is another dimension often thought by many to have no particular function. In corporate design, an artistic object such as a sculpture or picture can communicate an ethos that is difficult to convey in words or actions. Often fine artists and graphic designers with unique styles create iconic works for a company or organisation that conveys the corporate message or ethos effectively. For example, London Underground has posters designed by: Mabel Lucie Attwell, *Country Fair* (1912); Alfred Leete, *The Lure of the Underground* (1927); Edward Bawden, *City* (1952); Tom Eckersley, *The London Transport Collection* (1975); David Booth, *Tate Gallery by Tube* (1986). Plate 7.2 illustrates that *modern painting* has been relevant to commercial operations for a long time.

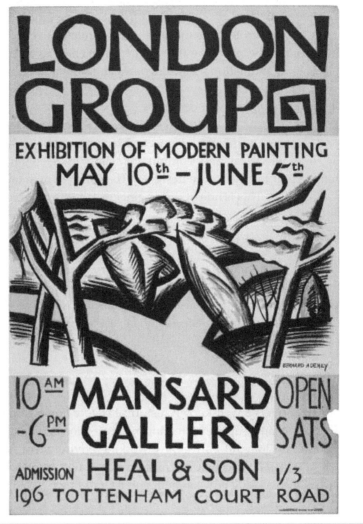

Plate 7.2   Heal & Son 1920s–1930s
Mansard Gallery contemporary art scene

Source: *Heal's 1810–2010 – 200 Years of Design & Inspiration* (2009), p. 48.
© Heal & Son Ltd. With special thanks to the V&A Archive.

Crafts

Craft work can be applied to anything handmade from an extensive range of materials and fabrics which are used to create a wide variety of artefacts. This work provides texture, process or period effects. Sometimes a company will require craftwork, such as Innocent's campaign to knit woollen hats for their fruit drink bottles to raise the public's awareness for Age Concern, a senior citizen charity.

7.4.5   OTHER STAKEHOLDERS

There is a wide range of stakeholders whose perspectives and perceptions have to be considered: investors and shareholders; local authorities; regulatory authorities; suppliers; employees; customers; and the wider public. With social media, all of these groups have a voice and therefore are becoming increasingly relevant as they input commentary on a wide range of occurrences and situations.

Conclusion

To concludes, perception and perspectives are crucial inputs to a design project, being the viewpoint of all the contributors and stakeholders, whilst incorporating the wider public understanding of a design. Perception is related to sentient communication and consciousness. Often there is a friction between designers and managers but once each one's perception and perspective is recognised and considered, then problems can be resolved. In this chapter, perspective takes a role approach, emphasising the tacit knowledge and skillsets required in corporate design projects. There is a wide array of designers crossing the information environment, websites, buildings, facilities, products, services and experiences. Not all of these skillsets are required. In any one project those that are required will be set out in the business case for the design project or within the design specification.

How do people recognise my business
and who are the stakeholders?

On walking around or viewing websites, we are always making judgements according to our own perceptive understanding of a situation or artefact.

What is perceived has to be created and it is through a wide range of designers' perspectives that this is achieved. In any project it is the selection and management of designers across a wide spectrum that defines whether the image they create is perceived in the required manner.

Part II Summary
Setting the Strategy

What Has Happened So Far?

Up to this point, how corporate identity and image developed with branded products and services has been discussed, followed by the importance and impact of image on a company's reputation and financial stability.

In Part II we have concentrated on the strategic approaches. Chapter 4 explained how a CEO and the board determine the company's goals and objectives, these being defined after considering their company's competitive market position in their business sector through a range of business techniques: business environment PEEST factors; design environment STEEP factors; and the organisational environment's SWOT factors. Then in Chapter 5 we considered the organisation's identity through storytelling, as identity bridges the gap between strategy and creativity. Further explanations of identity were explained encompassing local, national, regional and global implications and the business's identity within these environments. Next Chapter 6 concentrated on corporate design strategy and how it links with corporate strategy and then develops the business's market position through a coherent CVIS and organisational behaviour. Here organisational structure often impacts the visual aesthetic and hierarchy, used to reflect the organisation's functional structure for marketing purposes, categorised as monolithic, endorsed and branded identity. This chapter progressed by looking at operational aspects and design project environments. Finally in Chapter 7, through the combination of perception and perspectives, we progressed on to the extensive range of corporate and design skillsets required and stakeholders involved in the creation of a corporate design.

What Have We Learnt in this Section?

Corporate strategies are formulated for a wide range of business occurrences which constitute the business development path to achieving the company's goals. This requires *positioning* the business in a new marketplace resulting from a new venture, a takeover/merger or a new product, in which case the existing CVIS will probably require a new design or alteration. The CEO and corporate strategist, through their intuition, foresight and previous knowledge and understanding of the marketplace, will determine the best market *position* for the business, that is, Balmer's AC^{2}ID Test *Desired* market position. In addition, PEEST, SWOT and STEEP analyses will be undertaken by others to confirm the company's *Ideal* location where they consider success is more likely to occur. When both are in agreement, then the company's market position is likely to be more successful. To create a new CVIS image, research has to be undertaken into the identity features that already exist, sourced in anecdotes and various occurrences that would allow a story to be created. Stories bind people together, teaching them what to do if the same situation arises again or at least how to approach the problem according to the business's ethos and way of doing things. The CEO and designer focus and refine the required theme and style to be created and convey the new entity's market position. Then the design brief is written and the required skillsets located to create this symbolic image.

What Will Part III Encapsulate?

Part III will address the management and legal requirements when establishing a business, preparing the corporate and design strategy and progressing and maintaining the design and creative operations. Management of design input, with controls and measurement of design activity, is crucial to the success of any design project. Here the key necessities are discussed and lists provided for key processes. The legal requirements in a corporate design project are covered by: business ethics; the creation and running of a business and/or project; intellectual property rights; and internet-related laws and regulations. Building and employment law are not included here as there are many topics to cover and plenty of other sources available.

Part III
Cohesive Design Management

Ensuring that a cohesive message is communicated through services and products is no mean task. There has to be a clearly defined approach as each design project is bespoke by definition, catering for the requirements of the business, its people and processes.

Design management enables a product to be made by defining all the stages in the process. It addresses all the internal and external resources, functions, environments, legal and financial requirements. By providing this structure and a checklist, it facilitates efficient and effective operational and managerial operations.

Legally the subject area covers many topics, each legal subject interlinked with another. Some of the legislation is of long standing with updates to ensure current relevance in areas such as business formation, ethics, contracts and traditional industrial property law. In recent years internet-related subjects, including domain names, intellectual property and various treaties, have been introduced.

The following two chapters provide a summary of the key areas related to corporate design. It is by no means exhaustive but provides a starting point for your own detailed research. Part III addresses:

Chapter 8   Cohesive Design Management

Chapter 9   Business and Intellectual Property Law

Chapter 8
Cohesive Design Management

What design management has to be in place?

Introduction

In this chapter the management that arises between the board's strategic objective and the creative execution is discussed. This is specifically called design management. As the subject has a wide remit, here it has been called *cohesive* design management to ensure that the strategy and practicalities are well organised, executed and recorded. The main topics will be presented with a précis of requirements. There are a number of books that directly relate to the subject (Best, 2006, 2010; Cooper, Junginger and Lockwood, 2011). The chapter starts by considering how design and corporate strategy objectives are measured by a *balanced scorecard* and its reporting system. Then the design policy that articulates the strategy and its implementation. This is followed by the design audit to gather and evaluate information, which then establishes the project design management process, comprising project goal, designer activities and working practices. Subsequently there are the creative stages with design briefs and standards, the business case and detailed design stages. Finally we consider the resolving of designer–manager conflict and the design financial measurements of success.

8.1   Measuring Strategic Vision

Design objectives have to be established and agreed with the CEO, board and management, then timelines created on *what* needs to be achieved *by when* and *by whom.* CEOs have a number of goals and metrics that they work with. A useful tool that pulls all of these necessary activities and metrics together is the balanced scorecard. Although there is a standard approach, this can be tailored to specific business or organisational requirements. A list of business drivers has to be defined to establish how the company and business subsidiaries are to progress operations across all their sustaining and value-adding functions. Often the same question can be asked in a design context but this time the objectives and drivers can cut across functional silos. By this latter approach, a better product, routine or refinement may emerge to the organisation's advantage.

Managing the corporate strategy by a balanced scorecard (Kaplan and Norton, 1996), key management reporting systems can feed into the relevant scorecard perspectives. For example, a financial strategic perspective may be to make a profit rather than break even. So objectives are set, metrics established, targets set and initiatives defined. If the goal is achieved, then the company gains stakeholder trust and commitment, leading to a better reputation and market capitalisation by an increased share price. A basic scorecard usually has four perspectives related to vision and strategy, these being:

- The financial situation is defined as revenue plus cost reductions and by identifying value-adding and non-value-adding activities, plus the cost of human and technological asset utilisation.

- The customer's viewpoint addresses the brand vision and value through product attributes, plus image and customer relationships. Included in this is the breadth of the offering, with an error-free service that is convenient and responsive.

- The internal business process driver adds value to the customer's experience of the company and ensures that their requirements are met. Here innovative, operative processes and after-sales services require thought and attention.

- The organisation's innovation and collaborations looks at learning and growth through information and communication technology (ICT) and employee capabilities that impact motivation and empowerment.

Each of these considerations can have a key performance indicator (KPI) metric for outcome and performance.

This exercise can take time but, by considering all the necessary points and a traffic light system, perhaps monthly or quarterly, indicating where problems are arising in red, possible problems in amber and all going well in green, it is possible to make a quick review on how the strategy is progressing both in output and financially.

8.1.1   DESIGN POLICY

Design policies endorse design as a formal activity at board and senior management level, articulating the corporate strategy. Needs are identified that complement the organisation's goals, customer satisfaction and trends. Mark Oakley considered this to be understanding the constraining and enabling features in the particular design context so that work progresses systematically. This makes sure that all contributors appreciate what is necessary and allows coherent communication of production, marketing and sales requirements to all internal and external stakeholders.

Gorb and Dumas (1987) suggested three points relating to design policy:

- A design policy cannot be purchased off the peg; it must be bespoke.

- Do not expect a design policy to be effective if a structure does not exist to implement it.

- Do not expect designers to understand the company if the company does not develop methods to implement designs.

An example of the types of design policy questions to be answered for a website are:

- What will the website contribute towards the corporate goals?

- Will the website be a design leader or follower?

- How long will the website's lifecycle be?

- What aspects of the website's design are important to the organisation?

- Should the design be undertaken internally or externally?

8.1.2   DESIGN AUDITS

Design audits provide a useful information-gathering and assessment exercise between strategic objectives and the daily operational practicalities by:

- Establishing how often design is used within the organisation.

- Showing how design standards and regulations are adhered to.

- Recognising where improvements can be made.

- Identifying competent people, equipment and media.

- Recognising skillset shortfalls and beneficial outside collaborations.

A design audit focuses a designer's mind on what is important for the project by considering:

a) Current business financial status, leadership and reputation.

b) What is the organisational structure, products, services?

c) History, vision, principles, values and ethical stance.

d) Current strategy, marketplace position and niche markets.

e) Branding policies and brand equity.

f) Customer perceptions, loyalty and credibility.

g) Where is the business located? Are there multiple locations? Where are they?

h) Who are the people in the organisation? What do they do and how do they present themselves at work? What is their attitude towards the business?

i) Are there communities of practice or other communication networks, so that it is possible to spot who speaks to whom and when?

j) What communication systems are used to connect with customers, clients, suppliers and other stakeholders?

k) Where would the company like to be in the future?

l) What enhancements would allow them to achieve this?

A post-project audit will include:

a)   How satisfactorily has the result achieved the brief?

b)   How satisfactorily has the design solution achieved the strategic objectives of the organisation commissioning it?

c)   How satisfactorily has the work been completed?

d)   To what extent has shareholder value been optimised by its deployment?

8.2   Design Management and Process Stages

The daily practical link between strategic objectives and the daily operational activities (Oakley, 1984) encompasses many skillsets, equipment and media applications and therefore a key skill is design management to ensure that the necessary products and services are made to set standards, or if not, that explanations are made available. This role manages the constant crafting and refinement of artefacts. Hence there is a steady stream of questions whilst the making and review stages are underway, from the start to the final product completion. As many projects require regular communication and information between staff and designers, having a branded project name and intranet website can be effective. Website design offers another dimension to product design management. Designed elements can be inserted into the website architecture homepage and content pages, for example, text, photographs, animations, videos, legal statements and social media communication. This encourages efficient communication and cohesive grouping for project information and ultimate knowledge base.

8.2.1   PROJECT GOALS

Project goals have to be specific, measurable, attainable, relevant and timebound, that is, SMART. To achieve goals, a number of key features have been recognised by Mike Press and Rachel Cooper:

- A suitable collaborative team structure has to be put in place, with crowdsourcing considered (Press, 2011).

- The right people with the right skills have to be recognised and found, particularly in rapidly developing digital technology.

- These skills have to be kept updated by training.

- Good communications from the beginning to the end of the project are necessary.

- Reliable and efficient management information has to be available.

- There has to be mutual commitment to resolve any problems.

8.2.2   BUILDING THE BUSINESS CASE AND PROJECT PROPOSAL

a)   Scope – timeline, budget and objective to be achieved.

b)   Conceptual design – pulling all the ideas together and proving that the project is viable. Many discussions happen at this stage as the project has to be sold to clients.

c)   Developing prototypes – these are the physical manifestation of the design concept. Today they can be in a physical format created by carefully constructed models: a *plastic* 3D CAD model, or a digital 3, 4 or 5D model which rotates and, where appropriate, provides walkthroughs.

d)   The cost of developing the design, inclusive of conventional media and websites, can range from a few pounds to multi-million-pound projects, but there is no direct correlation with company size, the budget essentially being allocated according to the company's attitude towards its corporate image and design.

Refinements occur often through presentations and discussions. This is usually fine tuning. Then again, the project can be scrapped or further iterations become necessary.

8.2.3   DESIGNER ACTIVITIES AND WORKING PRACTICES

Designers

Designers use aesthetic methods to tap into customer emotions to create imagery and sell products. To achieve the requisite aesthetic, a designer requires a good working knowledge of design processes and practices across multifarious techniques and media applications, whilst ensuring that the necessary quality is maintained. This is important as creating a pertinent concept in an innovative manner can make or break a campaign. They have to understand, recognise and continually develop their technical skills, regardless of whether this is a traditional skill and materials or innovative technological developments that impact their skillset.

Collaborative working

Collaborative working has always been in existence within art and design projects as many people have a specific skill essential at a particular stage of a project. The design process itself can be complicated, with numerous collaborative skills and media applications being necessary: for example, interior designers, painters, sculptors, landscapers, photographers and website designers – the list is endless.

Currently collaborative working is used by many businesses as each project is bespoke, requiring a different skillset at various stages and on different projects. Social media facilitate companies to present projects online, and artists and designers to bid for the work or be approached to undertake work. Alternatively many artists and designers can display their work online through their website, whereupon companies can approach them directly. These operations still have to be carefully managed internally – sometimes called the integrated marketing team – but it does mean that the brand knowledge stays within the company. The design director or manager becomes an orchestra conductor, directing and managing a wide range of talents and skills, some experienced, some newly skilled on the latest technology, each artist, designer or craftsperson adding their expertise to the project and final aesthetic. Here branding is considered to be a continuous network activity controlled within the company.

Frequently two other networking methods arise (Neumeier, 2006). These tend to be twentieth-century approaches, but it is worthwhile mentioning them:

- One-stop shop – when the corporate communication was created by an advertising agency. They would: carry out research; devise strategy; create campaigns; and assess results. One person in the company was obliged to direct or manage the brand's development. Today one-stop shops have expanded and can be a firm specialising in one type of design skill or a holding company with a cluster of specialist firms.

- Brand agency – here the company works with a lead agency, which pulls together a team of the best or most appropriate specialists to work on the brand development. The brand agency leads the project as a contractor and the specialists are sub-contractors. Here a cohesive corporate message is easier to achieve. On the other hand the project management is more with the brand agency than with the company.

8.3   Creative Stages

8.3.1   DESIGN BRIEF

The design process starts with a design brief, following the corporate design strategy approval process. Design briefs can take the form of just a few words and images up to a large booklet. In essence they are essential for the design specification (Johnson, 2005). When a design brief is given to a designer, the company has decided that their image has to be redesigned. Two issues then have to be considered:

1.   The reason why the corporate identity, image or brand is being redesigned.

2.   The corporate outlook/images to be applied and key characteristics to be represented.

Often designers have their own design agendas, without understanding or realising the organisation's goals or target audience. On the other hand, organisations fail to recognise or understand what a designer's input is and can be to a project. Hence it is important that the design brief and standards are explained and understood at the outset, and, if a website is necessary, a map constructed to show the different aspects to be displayed.

8.3.2   DESIGN STANDARDS

Once the design objectives are set, showing what needs to be achieved, then the design standards show how results are obtained. Generally speaking, design effectiveness is achieved by attitudes, beliefs and standards, not rules and regulations. Design standards show *how* results are obtained. Standards should have boundaries or levels showing where results should be. For example, to maintain a leading edge in technology, negotiations and compromise are necessary to maintain an impressive and forward-looking brand. Design standards fall into three categories:

- National and international standards – advisory or mandatory including advertising and safety standards

- Company standards

- Style manuals for: CVIS house styles, colours, shapes, typefaces and logos, audio and environmental.

Other standards can relate to:

- Aesthetic features associated with the organisation; perhaps trends aimed at certain markets.

- Website functionality and aesthetics, including specifications for local parts of the organisation. The website design may have one approach but the sub-sites or pages have another for products and services. Nonetheless design managers have to ensure that the output fits with the organisation's image.

8.3.3   DESIGN RESEARCH

A project may begin with design research: photographing, sketching and topical information recorded in a sketchbook for future consideration on topics such as:

- What already exists within the organisation

- What already exists in the marketplace

- What has worked previously and what has not

- Essential technical competencies.

8.3.4   CONCEPTUAL DESIGN

When the project is live, each creative idea has to be encouraged, explained, shared and accepted by all concerned. These sketches are *firmed up* by further iterations, interventions and updates, whereupon a design begins to appear in the designer's *mind's eye*. Design themes and styles are used to convey characteristics relevant to the brand or corporate image. Designers compile relevant visual elements and media applications in print and digital *storyboards* to facilitate different designs and usages to be assessed.

8.3.5   DETAIL THE DESIGN PROCESS STAGES

All artists and designers prepare sketches which are previewed by the creative director and team to ensure that the image is acceptable. Thereafter the design is *firmed up* and applied to the relevant media, either by traditional skills, tools and methods or by digital software and hardware skills and methods.

Silent design can happen when employees and interested parties make contributions to the design process without realising that what they are saying is actually design, as they perceive it to be part of another process within their own work area (Gorb and Dumas, 1987). To overcome this, employees are encouraged to be active in design tasks, contribute to the design process and frequently work alongside professionally trained designers, so that design is suffused throughout the business. Designers across disciplines share a culture based on the creation of new systems and the management of existing ones. Essentially the design process occurs from the beginning to the end through many activities, from graphic design to software and hardware creation, engineering, architecture and interior design (Johnson, 2005).

The final design is chosen from a selection of designs which then forms the *style manual* necessary for future reproduction and design stages. This can be kept in a printed, website or electronic book format. An electronic book allows texts, images (stills and videos), sound backgrounds and music, and links for future information to be added.

Designing a website is a separate process that can be integrated into the corporate design process as one of the selected media applications. The style can be the same as the printed format or have a separate style to attract a different market sector or segment.

8.3.6   CHECKS

Once created, the design will have to satisfy cultural and media implications, although these should have been considered previously. Is there anything in the drawing that could cause offence? Will the logo design communicate the relevant message? Will the scale be clearly seen on a mug, website or billboard? And will the material specification be durable?

In 1999 the Design Council suggested seven design factors for success: ensuring that the product is reliable through good performance; that it is ergonomically simple and straightforward to use; that it is aesthetically pleasing; that it is easy to maintain and service; that it is safe; that it is easy to manufacture; and that it is good value for money.

> *1915 Ambrose Heal, with other manufacturers, retailers and designers, founded the Design and Industry Association, a predecessor of the Design Council.*

8.3.7   RESOLVING DESIGNER–MANAGEMENT CONFLICTS

Designing for companies is not without problems, but designers are problem-solvers who achieve results by being focused, well organised and customer-led. They have to be ahead of their client, anticipating change in a similar manner to the marketing director and board anticipating changes in the business environment. This focused approach can be in conflict with corporate culture and management activities, so being aware of these likely occurrences is vital (Black, 1975). To overcome any possible issues, it is important to have constant communications and operational conversations, as many design projects require input from various functions in the organisation. Political and professional boundaries may have to be crossed to accomplish the design objectives, which can cause ripples. All of this is part of the continuous design cycle, influenced by external issues and internal imperatives that communicate the corporate message by its services and products. A design cycle has to be in place, with clear communication feedback loops for developments that need attention. Work schedules can help.

8.4   Measuring Design

As mentioned at the start, balanced scorecards can be a useful tool to establish how projects are progressing. A traffic light system acts as an aide memoire and visual mechanism for the board to recognise successful projects and activities and those requiring further improvement. Feeding into this, any number of hard copy or online social media commentaries can be collated within the contributory reporting systems. Many of these projects have budgets, with conceptual design, construction, commissioning, production and maintenance cost centres, and periodic – usually monthly – reporting systems. Each of these headings is further subdivided into various cost categories. So timesheets and invoices matter as they are the starting point for the whole reporting system that impacts on the profitability of the company. Much like the design process, each step is dependent on the next. If this is clearly accounted for, then the financial markets have confidence that the company and its new design project are a success.

Raymond Turner (2013) suggested four ratios that CEOs and designers recognise as being pertinent to ther projects. Detailed explanations can be found in most business and financial books, but this explanation leans to the designer's viewpoint:

$$Gross\ Margin\ (\%) = \frac{Sales\ Revenue\ less\ Cost\ of\ Goods\ Sold}{Sales\ Revenue}$$

Gross Margin is often a critical measure of trading performance for retailers. It does not include administration costs, borrowings or distribution costs. Margins are similar in the same sector, varying between sectors. This is sometimes known as *gross profit* or *gross profit margin*.

- Industrial and product designers can increase sales revenue by providing a larger market.

- Cost of Goods can be reduced by decreasing production costs.

$$Net\ Margin\ (\%) = \frac{Net\ Profit}{Sales\ Revenue}$$

Net Margin expresses in percentage how much of each pound (£) paid is profit. That is what remains after administration, sales and promotion. Net margins vary across companies and sectors, from less than 5 per cent to over 20 per cent, ultimately impacting share prices. This is sometimes known as *net profit* or *net profit margin*.

- Design impact can be dramatic here, especially when communication costs are analysed as reductions can impact the financial bottom line.

$$Return\ on\ Investment\ (\%) = \frac{Gain\ from\ Investment}{Cost\ of\ Investment}$$
$$(ROI)$$

Return on Investment is the return in fixed and current assets of investing in people, premises and machinery of all types and their related costs. This can be applied by product development, departments or by the whole organisation being dependent on what is included as returns and costs. This is sometimes known as *Return on Capital Employed (ROCE)*.

- Focused design activity, when measured using this criteria, can dramatically impact efficiency and returns.

Operating costs, also known as *overheads*, are daily fixed and variable administration costs across research and development, manufacturing, administration, distribution and selling. Fixed costs remain the same throughout and vary depending on the number of units manufactured.

- Design can impact on a range of aspects, such as: making one component to replace two; thinking of the long-term cost of a more expensive product than the cheaper version; workflow and people movement; space planning.

Brand asset or *brand equity* is the added value that the branding exercise achieves beyond the object's functional purpose.

These business processes do require regular review, particularly as technology and working practices change. It is at this point that identifying where value is being added, and which is sustaining the company, ensures that business profitability is maintained or improved. The non-value-adding areas can be removed. This said, the non-value-adding and indeed the sustaining areas can be subjective and this is where collaborative working is constructive. Some products/services may be *standard* production and others *specials*, that is, bespoke. In each of the conceptual design, industrial/website design, production and distribution stages, there are events and activities that may be considered to be of no value. This is where extra care ought to be taken and opinions solicited from suppliers, tradespeople, craftsmen, artists and website designers. What can appear to be of no value may actually have some relatively unnoticed importance which, when removed, could prove vital to the final product. This was noticeable within management structures in the 1980s and 1990s when redundancies in middle management lost tacit knowledge as it walked out of the door. Technology has moved on and social media allows information to be garnered, as social media advocates contribute to product creation, purchase and post-purchase servicing. But the ultimate design features, production, reporting and the bottom line are the organisation's responsibility.

Conclusion

Each design is bespoke, as no two branding strategies have the same goal or context. Policies endorse and articulate the corporate strategy. Then establishing how the strategic objectives will be achieved within an operational framework requires good management, control and measurement. Many aspects have to be considered operationally which ultimately feed into the director's balanced scorecard across four dimensions: i. financial; ii. customer viewpoint; iii. internal business processes and innovation; iv. learning and collaboration. As each project is bespoke, careful selection of the management, design and creative teams has to be considered, hence the necessity of ensuring that clear communication lines are in place to avoid designer–manager conflicts. This can be alleviated by having a communication focus such as a branded website. Crucial to any project are the financial controls and measures; many of these are the same for both designers and management, but the emphasis can be different. Overall, by establishing a good system at the start, with periodic reviews comprising both financial outcomes and explanations, the project can meet deadlines within budget.

What design management has to be in place?

Design objectives have to be set and a plan established, with resources, budgets and deadlines. A bespoke balanced scorecard attends to the key strategic vision aspects for the CEO or business owner. Design policy explains the strategy, ensuring that everyone knows what has to be achieved across production, marketing and sales. The policy must be bespoke and the organisation's structure capable of implementing suggestions. Design audits gather information and make evaluations about the organisation and its attitude towards design, also providing background information for the design project and building the business case. The project's management progresses by setting goals, activities and working practices. The creative stage starts with the design brief and ends with the finished product. The final assessment occurs by establishing how satisfactorily the project has been completed across all design management and balanced scorecard metrics.

Chapter 9

Business and Intellectual Property Law

What legal requirements are necessary?

Introduction

This chapter takes a look at business and intellectual property law. Corporate design includes a large number of legal matters, starting with the types of business formation; the ethical basis upon which it is to operate; the legalities relating to business transactions; and intellectual property law. A new body of legislation has now appeared relating to the internet with domain names, content and online transactions. So there are many points to understand relating to business and design; it is wise therefore to consult a lawyer to ensure that everything is correctly established and to refer to if problems do arise. The following summarises the key necessities but is not exhaustive.

9.1 Business Formations

When forming a business, it is wise to have all the legal requirements and checks undertaken. Subsequently, when funds are required or new directors added to the board, the mechanisms are established.

- Sole traders are responsible for running the business as self-employed and are responsible for all the business debts personally.

- Limited liability partnership (LLP) – this is a separate legal entity where profits are shared, the term *limited* provides limitations to liabilities, and the tax situation is different to a limited company.

- Limited company – this is an independent legal entity with an identity separate from those who own and manage the business. There has to be at least one director or a company board of directors. Various forms and fees have to be paid and once the company is registered at Companies House, a certificate of incorporation is issued. Company secretaries take care of all the legal requirements such as filings and shareholder requirements. Articles of association govern how the company works internally and will include procedures to deal with various situations.

- Public limited company – similar to the above but, in addition to the owners and board, external shareholders provide the equity by buying shares in the company. The implications and communications are much wider in geographical extent and diversity of interests. Annual shareholder meetings are held where the CEO and board have to explain the company annual financial statements and operations. Shareholders have voting rights whereby they can decide whether to keep the CEO and/or board each year.

9.2 Business Ethics

Ethical businesses have been in operation within the UK for the last 25 years. Ethical practices are voluntary considerations taken by a company, firstly when there is no law in place and secondly where interpretations differ. In the European Union, value underpins everything, being more important than rules. Alternatively, in the United States compliance is through rules and if there are no rules, then more laws are made.

Ethics are also important in business today as we live in a multicultural society, where values and notions of what are right and wrong vary. We cannot assume that everyone's personal values are the same or that everyone will pick up the same message, as their cultures may have varying interpretations. Hence ethical policies have to be established within the business environment. Among the FTSE 100 companies, 95 per cent have an ethical policy, Whereas in small to medium enterprises (SME) it depends on how relevant they regard an ethical policy to be in their business activities. A useful equation provided by the Institute of Business Ethics is that:

$$\text{Identity} = \text{Culture} + \text{Values} + \text{Ethics} + \text{Conduct}$$

In designing a corporate image, dilemmas may arise between audience value, professional values governed by codes of conduct and corporate values. A designer, in creating an image from the above identity characteristics, has to conceive an appropriate message. He or she will have their own personal values and it is difficult for designers not to invest part of themselves in any design, as this is their unique style recognised by audiences. Another website-related consideration is whether a design is compatible with the company's values and does the website promote these values proactively. This may not be paramount or necessary but it provides a good indication of the values that the business holds in its ethical approach. On completion of a new image, comparison with the company's strategy and values is important, including monitoring audience impressions to safeguard the company's reputation.

Corporate social responsibility (CSR) policies can be full of *projects*, but their corporate values can be dreadful. A range of issues can arise through conflict of interest and mixed messages. A company can have ethical values; for example, ethical guidelines regarding safety and security may look after staff better than the basic health and safety requirements.

9.3   Business Transactions

Legal debates on new technologies have a delayed reaction, to determine how the technology is developing and how it is affecting the society within which it is being used. Digital media has had a tremendous impact on daily and business life globally, within regions and legal jurisdictions. Legal authorities have to establish what is useful and acceptable behaviour, with relevant facts and evidence to further define a case. This includes economic value to society through business models. Although the internet is perceived to be worldwide, in reality many countries have firewalls preventing websites from being accessed.

Sole traders and partnerships may build their own websites and design the business image through default or intention. Public limited companies and private limited companies may employ design consultants and website developers using the latest technology. Resulting from this there are a wide range of legal formalities.

9.3.1   BUSINESS CONTRACTS

Contracts are clear evidence that parties have reached agreement on a particular part of the business's operations, such as selling products and services or employing people, and therefore provide legal protection. Organisations usually have written contracts but oral contracts can also exist, for example, in craftwork. Other written agreements with consumers provide greater statutory protection. If the transaction is business-to-business, it is up to you to provide protection. Laws that are in place are:

- Unfair Contract Terms 1977

- Consumer Credit Act 1974 for sole traders and unincorporated businesses. The Director General of Fair Trading administers this Act, which protects consumers by licensing and other controls of moneylenders, pawnbrokers and hire purchase traders who provide credit, hire purchase and their transaction.

- Sale of Goods Act – a sales description stating: business name; place of business registration; business address; registered office; postal address; price valid until date …; 14 days cooling-off period; terms and conditions for your business; guarantees; franchise agreements; trading terms – shipping duty formalities, import and export rules; exchange rate; insurance – governing law and legal jurisdiction. Retain the rights to expensive items until they are paid for. Specify after sales rights and rights to terminate. Remember that consumers cannot sign away their rights but a business can.

9.3.2   OTHER BUSINESS ACTS

- Health and Safety at Work 1974 – health, safety and welfare of persons at work for protecting others against risk to health or safety in connection with a person at work.

- Environmental Protection Act 1990 – an Act to improve pollution control arising from specific industrial and other processes. This also re-enacts the provision of the Control of Pollution Act 1974 which relates to land waste and the collection and disposal of waste.

9.4   Intellectual Property Law

Intellectual property law relates to the commercial rights of using your intellect and skills to create a design. As technology has progressed, two intellectual property categories have been instigated. The first concerns traditional industrial property law and the second artists and writers.

Traditional industrial property law has evolved with technological developments and today increasingly addresses the internet. The following are product related:

- Trademarks

- Patents for inventions

- Industrial design forms

- Confidential information

- Data protection

- Internet domain names.

9.4.1 TRADEMARKS

The trademark symbol ™ is used for logos and distinctive signs and can become valuable over time, adding to the balance sheet valuation of the company. The Red Bass Triangle, registered in 1876, was the first recognisable trademark. Yet cattle herders have been using branding irons to mark their cattle for centuries. Protection of these logos and trademarks is by registration or use by the proprietor of the mark. The *sign* has to be distinctive and can include words, logos, colours, straplines, two- or three-dimensional shapes, sounds and gestures.

The benefits of registration are that: it permits the *sign* to be licensed and assigned; action can be taken for infringement against third parties, with the case being stronger than passing off, and it can act as a deterrent. Under current registration processes:

- The region has to be defined; that is, UK, EU or US.

- The class has to be defined, for example, computer program.

- The sign has to be registered graphically.

- It has to be established that it is a monopoly right.

- Registration has to be of ten years' duration; perpetually renewable – but it must be renewed.

With the internet, there is a wide range of factors that have to be considered to ensure that trademarks are acceptable in other countries and cultures.

9.4.2   PATENTS FOR INVENTIONS

Unique new product inventions, including logos and branding, protect that individual design; for example, Apple Macs have distinctive hardware and software designs that are protected by patents. Technical innovations, manufacture, design and business methods, hardware and software can be patented. This legislation confers on an inventor an exclusive and absolute right to exploit the product covered by the patent. A patent can be registered through the UK Intellectual Property Office (UKIPO) or the European Patent Office (EPO).This is for a period of 20 years which has to be renewed every five years.

There is a very precise procedure to be followed in filing patents regarding searches, to ensure that there are no identical patents registered. It is advisable to check relevant websites and the Patent Office to ensure that current procedure is being followed. It is important not to reveal your invention before filing as it can become difficult to prove that you invented the product. Even trivial ideas can produce valuable patents.

As regards software, the European Directive of Software Patentability aimed to preserve the status quo in patents across Europe. In the UK the technical definition is *first to register*, whereas the US system differs, being *everything under the sun* and *first to invent* registration. What is patentable? Hardware; software with technical effect; internet applications; and business methods US, UK or EU.

9.4.3   DESIGN RIGHTS – APPEARANCE

- Design rights

- Registered designs

- Topography rights

9.4.4 COPYRIGHT LAW

The second intellectual property category is copyright law which includes:

- Literary and artistic work, for example, film music, images and scripts

- Novels, text and images

- Drawings

- Paintings

- Photographs

- Architectural designs

- Sculptures.

Legal and commercial rights are created by: artists in their performances; producers in their musical and interview recordings; and broadcasters on radio, TV and the internet. For any business, the intellectual property issues are:

a) Who owns the identity design and design processes:
 - Company, as employer or instigator
 - Designer as contractor
 - Employee as designer.

b) The protection of the intellectual property design:
 - Patent, trademark, copyright
 - Software patent

c) How additional income/goodwill can be obtained by licensing:
 - Sole or exclusive
 - Non-exclusive.

Authors' moral rights

Moral rights are concerned with protecting the personality and reputation of authors, rather than the economic rights of intellectual property law. Moral rights provide authors of literary, dramatic, musical and artistic works and film directors with the right: firstly, to be identified as the author of the work, or director of a film in specific circumstances; and secondly, to object to derogatory treatment of the work or film which amounts to a distortion or mutilation, or is otherwise prejudicial to the honour or reputation of the author or director.

9.4.5 CONFIDENTIAL INFORMATION

Confidentiality – avoid novelty-destroying disclosures; have a policy on journal articles' confidentiality agreements; beware of informal chats.

9.4.6 DATA PROTECTION

The Data Protection Act 1998 is the regulation of processing information relating to individuals, and the holding, use or disclosure of that information.

The practical implications of these issues to a company are that they demarcate and defend its market position where it can sue for infringement or establish a licence for financial gain, with classification by use or geographical area. Or the design can be used to raise finance; to sell or assign rights for a loan security; or to gain access to capital markets. Further benefits are:

- Protection by software patent, trademark

- Ownership as an employee, contractor, instigator/employer

- Licensing through non-exclusive licence, sole licence or exclusive licence.

9.5 Internet

9.5.1 INTERNET INTELLECTUAL PROPERTY RIGHTS

Intellectual property rights apply as offline:

a) Domain names – transfers to you; ensure registration payments are made.

b) Website terms and conditions – who owns the software; you get a licence and fees have to be paid.

c) Websites Disability Discrimination Act 1995 (DDA) on Accessibility.

d) Sale of Goods Act 1979 – a sales description, stating business name; place of business registration; business address; registered office; postal address; price valid until date ...; 14 days cooling-off period.

e) Online and Distance Selling Regulation for businesses, in addition to the Sale of Goods Act

– Distance Selling includes: business name and address; goods and services description; prices including taxes; how the customer can pay; delivery arrangements, cost and date; minimum length of the contract; contract termination conditions if longer than one year or open-ended; customers' cancellation rights. After an order is placed, contact the customer in writing and before delivery, providing details on: how the order can be cancelled and who pays for returns; the address for complaints; after sales guarantees and services provided; and again, if the contact is for more than 12 months, you must state how it will be terminated.

– Selling Online includes: a list of steps when a customer is placing an order; electronically acknowledge receipt of order as soon as possible; online contract – all information has to confirmed by email, fax or paper; ensure reasonable steps are taken for customers to correct their mistakes; display languages available to customers; online downloadable terms and conditions clearly stated, with tick box ☑ stating check and tick. It is at this point that the contract is accepted; ensure that customers can save, download and print your terms and conditions; your email address; your VAT number, if registered for VAT; finally provide clear prices and delivery costs.

9.5.2 INTERNET DOMAIN NAMES

Domain names are not regarded as intellectual property under UK law and no legal actions have been instigated for domain name infringement. Instead, the law on passing off and trademarks is applied; all brands and variations are included within this law. All top-level domain names, for example, .com, .org and .net, are the responsibility of the Internet Corporation for Assigned Names and Numbers (ICANN), formed in 1998 as a non-profit private sector policy-making body. ICANN passes the registration of domain names to registrars, each with their own policies and procedures. *Registrant Rights and Responsibilities Under the 2009 Registrar Accreditation Agreement* provides the latest information on this subject. In the case of domain name disputes, ICANN gave powers to the World Intellectual Property Organization (WIPO) to operate a dispute resolution system for transferring domain names, in particular to curb cyber-squatting, that is, when a domain name is registered with the knowledge that someone else will want the name.

If a business's circumstances change and its corporate image is redesigned, locating the correct URL can take time and demand high prices. A company may have been taken over or merged, changing its name and sometimes abbreviation. Larger businesses often adopt the .com suffix as country-specific domain names have already been registered. The difference between country domain suffixes and .com calls for further examination. If a company sets up a domain name that directly relates to their work, in this instance not the owner's name but say a descriptive – for example, www.generator. co.uk – in the UK this can be related to electric generators or a management consultancy. If the same descriptive word is used with .com and users type in the name <www.generator.com> by mistake, then the first impression as the website downloads may be unexpected. Hence when considering using .co.uk and .com, and indeed other country domain suffixes, it is important to know the impact that the website image communicates when it downloads in a particular location. Change generally happens if the name is causing offence in a particular cultural setting, or has negative legal implications. A name may also become dated as markets and technology change – for example, companies targeting young age groups or fast-moving technology rename and rebrand their organisations frequently.

Conclusion

In conclusion, business and design legislation within the UK have a long history but both have had to cater for an increasing number of occurrences that have arisen because of the internet. Business ethics see wider applications as the world is multicultural. Most of the legislation relating to business transaction was passed in the 1970s and 1990s, but again extensions have arisen because of the Sale of Goods Act on the web relating to online and distance selling. Intellectual property law has been revisited and updated as trademarks, patents and industrial form become more relevant as sales expand worldwide through website advertising. Essentially all of the legal aspects have to be addressed; even when using Facebook, the terms and conditions change frequently and have to be read.

What legal requirements are necessary?

Depending on whether the business is an SME or a limited company with a board and shareholders, the legal requirements differ and the respective legislation has to be adhered to. Business ethics exist when no law is in place or interpretations differ. This is important in a multicultural society where there are differing interpretations of right and wrong. Business transactions have a number of contracts ensuring that agreement has been met. Intellectual property law relates to intellect and skills extemporised through trademarks, patents, confidential information and data protection, including domain names. The internet has seen an increasing amount of legislation and regulation. This has included domain name regulation by ICANN and the Sale of Goods Act being adapted to the internet through online and distance selling provisions.

Part III Summary
Cohesive Design Management

What Has Happened So Far?

In Part III two necessary inputs to design projects have been presented together as one often impacts on the other. Chapter 8 looked at strategic vision measurement and design management, and it is called cohesive here to emphasise the necessity of being organised and consistent. This chapter started with design objectives as defined in the corporate strategy and the corporate design strategy, progressing and measuring results through a balanced scorecard. Then the design policy that provides the activation of the strategy was considered, leading to design audits that ratify results or provide input to a new project.

Design management and process stages were addressed through project goals, designer activities, skillsets required, and their methods of working collaboratively. The creative stages of a project were then looked at, beginning with the design brief, the standards that have to be satisfied, the business case and project proposal, design research which can include aspects of a design audit, conceptual design inputs, design process milestones and checks. Then conflict resolution between designers and managers. Finally financial measurements directly related to design through ratios and metrics that feed into the balanced scorecard.

Chapter 9 considered business, intellectual property and internet law. This included types of business formations; a definition of business ethics; business transaction legalities through business contracts; intellectual property law on trademark, patents, design rights, copyright, authors' moral rights, confidential information, data protection and internet domain names. Website terms and conditions, the Disability and Discrimination Act, extensions to the Sale of Goods Act by distance selling and selling online provisions have also been discussed.

What Have We Learnt in this Section?

Design management and legal requirements encompasses many topics where being organised and consistent is relevant and important. By establishing defined processes, a project can be managed more effectively as everyone involved knows what has to be accomplished, when their input starts and finishes and the standard required. Communication between participants can be easier and problems resolved quickly so that the project timeline and milestones are achieved.

Legally standard business and trading requirements exist; however, two key inputs related to design are ethics and the internet. Ethics impacts website and business operations as a consistent business operation is required to ensure cohesive identity and image communication. One ethical approach is that:

Identity = Culture + Values + Ethics + Conduct

Hence in communicating the corporate image, the website design has to be compatible with company values and promote these values proactively.

Websites have had a tremendous impact on societies globally, nationally and locally where each legal jurisdiction acts according to the accepted precepts important to their particular societies. New legal fields have been developing since the 1990s. Legal jurisdictions are based on boundaries, with UK-based businesses adhering to UK law even when websites are hosted elsewhere. Copyright is a major issue, with the UK being directed by the European Union Copyright Directive (EUCD), October 2003. Other regulatory bodies such as the World Intellectual Property Organization (WIPO) have treaties and regulations applicable on the internet: WIPO Copyright Treaty (WCT), December 1996 and WIPO Performance and Phonograms Treaty (WPPT). The World Wide Web Consortium (W3C) determines website design development by legal and technical standards based on website evolutionary process stages and input from designers and large computer organisations.

What Will Part IV Encapsulate?

In Part IV the symbolic aspect of corporate design is presented. This encompasses the corporate visual identity system (CVIS) creation. The visual identity is the aspect that most people consider to be corporate branding. In reality, how the organisation behaves belies its ethos and distinctive existence. Here a more detailed approach to the creation of the elements is conveyed as it provides an indication of the number and depth of skills required in the CVIS creation, which is ultimately communicated by its name, font, logo, colours and strapline, and the recruitment and training of staff.

Part IV
Navigating Symbolic Practice

Now that the market *position* is established and defined through the corporate and design strategies and there is an understanding of design management and legal aspects, Part IV works through the creative inputs to corporate design. Whereas corporate identity management (CIM) defines the communication of a company image through *position, symbolism* and *coherence* – these three terms still apply to branding – the corporate visual identity system (CVIS) considers the aspects that people see, encompassing both visual identity and sometimes organisational behaviour.

Once the design brief is considered by the board and budgetary approval given, then the creative process starts. A range of factors related to creating an appropriate style has to be found which will ultimately be applied across a wide range of environments: buildings, promotional material (both printed and digital), equipment, vehicles and so on. Visual identity is created by graphic design where the creative endeavour produces imagery to clearly differentiate an organisation's functions and existence. Traditional package design, signs, printed stationery and digital media, including websites, require a unique aesthetic. Added to this, in today's marketplace consumers often expect service and an added value experience – this adds to the brand's value and opens further creative opportunities.

Organisational behaviour, first recognised in the mid-1980s, gained increasing importance as the business world became more competitive. Companies began to understand that communication occurred through people and their behaviour and that culture mattered. So, through organisational behaviour techniques, businesses have been redefining their operational structure and formation in order that the company philosophy and ethos should permeate its culture, this being reinforced by recruitment, training, relevant working methods and standards. Part IV considers these aspects through:

Chapter 10   The Symbolic Aesthetic

Chapter 11   The Visual Identity Creative Process

Chapter 12   Symbolism – Organisational Behaviour

Chapter 10
The Symbolic Aesthetic

How do I communicate the business story?

Introduction

An image, and the viewer's recognition of what it communicates, is important within the business marketplace. Visual identity and organisational behaviour are the two mechanisms applied to display the company's market position and ethos through symbolism. In this chapter these two topics are considered as part of the company identity communication and structure by applying John Balmer's AC²ID Test. After that, the relevance of designer selection in creating the aesthetic is addressed. At the end of the chapter the range of media upon which the CVIS and organisational behaviour have an impact is presented, both in text and schematic forms, with an explanation of why *coherence* is necessary.

Graphic designers and marketers realised that a coherent visual message was important in establishing a company in the marketplace. Through visual communication and organisational behaviour traits, the interaction between an image and the viewer's cognitive faculties, however fleeting, registers significance to the image elements, even if the observer is unaware of this, this message being perceived by sensual differentiation, either natural or artificial. Jean Baudrillard (1983) explained that a semiology analysis could reveal a system of signs that permitted users to differentiate between different populations and cultures, thus allowing the recognition of cultural identities. Semiotics has a well-developed literature, based on perception of image, including corporate image (Barthes, 1977b; De Saussure, 1966; Guirand, 1975). The important point here is that to be truly effective a coherent message should be consistently communicated to stakeholders (Bernstein, 1989; Schultz, Tannenbaum and Lauterborn, 1994).

So when you are walking around and looking at a shop or viewing a shopping website, and what you see is unexpected or out of character, in that case dissonance arises as the identity characteristics that you expect to see are not there or happening. If this continues to be the case, when what you expect and what you experience are at odds, you start to shop elsewhere. The business, through your perception of its activities, has lost the characteristics upon which its identity, image or brand is based. This can also result in the company losing its market position. This has been seen in a number of companies where a range of PEEST factors have resulted in perceptions changing. For example, Marks and Spencer lost its way in the 1990s as new specialist shops such as Next captured some of their market. The camera shop Jessops closed as photographers began using digital equipment and they lost their unique market position.

10.1   Company Identity Communication and Structure

To explain this in academic terms, John Balmer devised the AC^{2}ID Test Model proposing that when there was a lack of alignment between two identities, then there was a problem. He suggested five identity terms (see Figure 2.2): the CEO's *Desired* identity for the company strategically; *Ideal* identity created by research and analysis strategically; the organisation's *Actual* identity created by the business structure and activities; its *Communicated* identity by way of controlled and uncontrolled media; and its *Conceived* identity perception of external stakeholders. Taking the example above, when the stakeholders' – in this instance, customers' – *Conceived* identity and the business *Actual* identity are not aligned, then there is dissonance and the CEO and board have to solve the problem. Another situation is when the CEO's vision – that is, the *Desired* identity – is out of alignment with the *Ideal* identity strategy in a set timeframe. The CEO can be right as hunches from his business background can be more in tune with what is happening than reams of analyses. The importance of identity is that it starts the symbolic creative design process forming the corporate image, by *themewords* and *styling*. So it is important that all elements emulate the desired market *position* by careful selection and managed visual identity and organisational behaviour, *coherently* applied and managed throughout the organisation.

One of the key uses of visual identity is to provide an indication of a company's structure, in addition to its branded products. Wally Olins categorised this visual architecture as monolithic, endorsed and branded, while others have also addressed this categorisation as being relevant to behavioural aspects of identity (Ind, 1992; Van Riel, 1995). The link between organisational structure and corporate identity is often applied for marketing purposes (see section 6.3). Stuart (1999) addressed organisational structure, employee identification and corporate identity structure in corporate strategy, where she concluded that the organisation's structural architecture is a key determinant of the organisation's identity and should reflect its system of visual identification. By addressing identity structure, a business can ensure that the corporate message is consistently and coherently applied across all of the organisation's traditional and digital communication channels, in order that the business is instantly recognised.

10.2 Symbolism Through Visual Identity and Organisational Behaviour

Before going any further, corporate identity management (CIM) ought to be mentioned, this being the combination of all the aspects of a business where people come into contact with it – the touchpoints. This generally comprises: the market segment and conditions discussed in Chapter 4; the corporate story to achieve the organisation's goals within a selected market presented in Chapter 5; communication design and designed environment as summarised in Chapters 3 and 6, this being displayed through two symbolic activities: the corporate visual identity system (CVIS) and the organisation's culture and behaviour at all levels. *Symbolism* pervades through all the company's products, services and environment.

10.2.1 TRADITIONAL SYMBOLIC AESTHETIC

Design processes create *symbolism* by visual identity and organisational behaviour to convey the business market *position*. Visual identity is the most popular understanding of corporate identity, now the organisation's culture and structures have an impact. Organisational behaviour and culture is another designed feature based on the organisation's central ethos and essence. Ethos defines what the company stands for by its values, beliefs and attitudes, expressed by its business conduct both internally and externally. The design process is the creative process initially based on the business philosophy and ethos. At first, a business owner would be unaware of its ethos, as it is often described as *the way we do things around here* becoming more apparent as the business develops. Mintzberg (1989) developed a model to show what he called the *essence* of an organisation's structure that he divided into six parts. The sixth part was organisational ideology or culture – its roots, traditions, values and beliefs differentiating

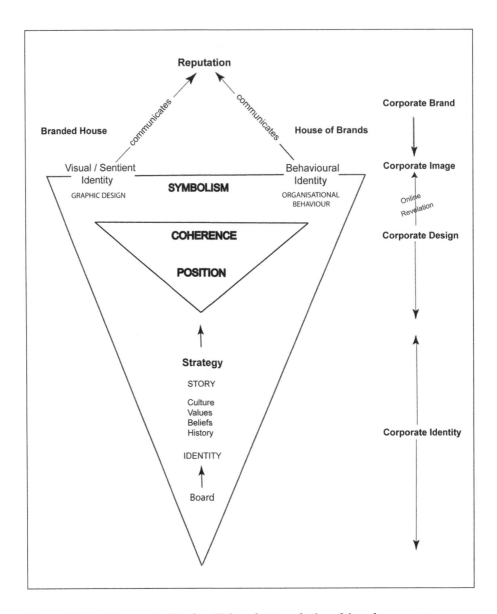

Figure 10.1   Corporate Design Triangle 2 – relationship of corporate
design strategy terms and CVIS process on traditional
media applications and websites

it from others. Figure 10.1 illustrates the corporate design terms of *position*, *symbolism* and *coherence*, and their relationship and linkage in the creation, communication and resultant reputation interactions that occur.

10.2.2   DESIGNER CHOICE

Choosing a designer who can quickly relate to the theme and design around it, utilising their holistic experience and skills to incisively create an image for the organisation, is important creatively and economically. Designers have to think of something that no-one else has conceived, which creates and projects an image for its chosen market. By utilising *stories* and *themewords* and using their holistic intuition in the selection of visual imagery and desired behaviours, they create and project an image for the chosen market (see Figure 10.2). They have to be skilled at rendering images, whilst able to communicate the message in a distinctive manner by catering for all levels of expertise. Hence a designer has a pivotal role in conveying the corporate story in the real world and on websites. Figures 6.2 and 6.3 illustrate the wide range of media applications online and offline where a designer's skills are applied in creating the aesthetic.

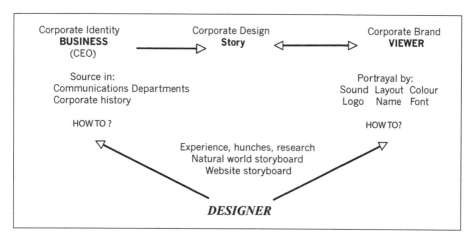

Figure 10.2   The designer's pivotal role in visual storytelling

10.3   Digital Impact on Corporate Design

10.3.1   WEBSITES – A UNIQUE MEDIUM

Websites brought a unique media to corporate design whereby the created image could be viewed globally at any time. Initially, many people were quite excited by this, but as reality set in and the socio-political and legal implications occurred and constraints appeared, websites became information tools with similar design formats and content presented in boxes (Dowdy, 2002). Again on a website design, the company and designer's ability to recognise the business identity and ethos is critical to creating its *emergence* online. Questions arise as to what to reveal and how to achieve this with the current Web 2.0 technology and available finances. Pre-social media, a website viewer from another location, whether this be within London, in Scotland or Japan, only had the designer and organisation's perception of the message conveyed and the viewer's interpretation. With social media this has changed as a multitude of people have an opinion. Digital artists and creative innovators are continually pushing technology's boundaries, producing particular and unique effects that can be applied to create particular aesthetics.

10.3.2 WEBSITE GESTALT

There is a plethora of material on how to design a website but little on the designed identity expression or the corporate image communicated. Initially content was purely textual, with some databases, being operated in the techie designer domain. As generations of websites developed, all the way through the 1990s and early millennium, the technology was advancing to the point where a corporate image could be graphically communicated online. Recent years have seen the graphic interface and communication technology gain increasing application and social acceptance. The images appearing on computer screens have become clearer in displaying corporate visual identity elements, and other textual and image content by way of a clearer gestalt and attractive aesthetic. The ethos of an organisation's behaviour can now be gleaned from the websites functionality and social media communications as the platform's conversations and advocates increase. Terms found in traditional corporate image application are transferring to the web domain.

10.3.3 WEBSITE AESTHETIC

Aesthetics and corporate image are becoming increasingly competitive tools for company strategists and CEOs as they look beyond a web presence (Foo, 2006). Don Norman's (2002) mantra that *attractive works better* is pertinent here, as a unique attractive homepage aids communication. Digital media has developed fast and is still doing so, providing a new dimension for designer skills as design software packages have to be learnt and applied to appropriate messages. Viewers' expectations have changed as they become familiar with the technology, opening up new behavioural and sociological fields; for example, why are viewers more impatient than print readers? Why have shopkeepers become actors for the cameras, reading crib sheets and regurgitating website content rather than working in the real world? There is also much discussion within graphic design education as traditional skills move towards digital media. Many see this as a loss of quality. In theory and historical application, learning by doing develops hand skills, intuitive perception and hand–eye co ordination. This results in a clearer experience of *letter* creation. The eye becomes more observant of refinements, enabling clear recognition of what is good and bad design (Nielsen and Trias, 2000). Overall digital design technology has altered work practices, tools and skills. Printing and publishing processes radically changed, becoming faster and more efficient. Books are now published on demand, to bespoke specifications or mass-produced. This is how nearly all company literature – books, pamphlets and stationery – is printed today.

10.4   Coherent Message Across All Media Applications

Coherence requires that the corporate story and image be consistent across all its media applications by ensuring that the corporate message is consistently applied through all visual and organisational identity applications, with *coherence* in the company voice being a key corporate objective. All media channels communicate messages to all stakeholders, that is, across traditional media touchpoints and websites.

The CVIS should be applied consistently but not necessarily in the same style – for example, Virgin companies are known for their colour shade of *red* and the Virgin logo, but each company and its website has a different style. Yet Virgin is not confused with other organisations as it has sufficiently differentiated itself in the marketplace, both online and offline, by its reputational style, colour and organisational behaviour. Hence the choice of visual identity elements – name, logo, typography and colour – are important. Attention to colour and size is essential so that they can be scaled and put on to a wide range of hard surface materials and digital media such as billboards, letterheads, websites and reception areas. These are defined in style manuals, templates and style sheets. Exceptions to this situation are where companies have to adhere to local conservation regulations; for example, McDonald's shops exist on modern high streets with modern buildings, and also in old market towns within an historic building façade or renovated interior catering for modern requirements. In some businesses the property strategy may entail owning a wide range of period buildings with varying styles – for example, Barclays Bank – with the signage colour and fonts the same as the building style.

A real-world and online identity and brand design may differ but both require a similar *look and feel*. If Waitrose is taken as an example, Ocado is the online shop for Waitrose but their business, name, operations and CVIS differ. Yet the *look and feel* and *voice* are the same across both organisations' operations. Tesco, on the other hand, applies the same CVIS to all its operations including the online shop, to ensure that *look and feel* and *voice* are the same. In the real world music and sounds can be the first sentient expression as sound travels and can be the first impression of an organisation. This can also be designed into a website where sound and visuals become part of the consumer or visitor experience, from the first homepage click to the exit.

Conclusion

To conclude, this chapter has provided an initial insight into the practical design elements and their purpose within the creative design process. Since images register significance in a viewer's mind, if dissonance happens between what they *conceive* an organisation's identity to be and the *actual* business identity – in this case the visual communication is out of alignment – it has to be rectified. To start the creative design process, the business ethos and philosophy provide an indication of the corporate values, beliefs and attitudes exemplified by staff internal and external conduct. Visual identity can provide an indication of organisational structure and products branded accordingly; this can also include the organisational behaviour approach. Websites also have to adhere to the corporate *look and feel* and *voice* as the corporate ethos merges online with the real world. As screen technology develops, the aesthetic image and gestalt become clearer. The topics within this chapter are increasingly important for CEOs, as social media commentary and advocacy increasingly move into the online business world, this being discussed in Part V.

How do I communicate the business story?

By focusing on a business story as an identity source, this facilitates *themeword* selection. Upon these themewords a designer can select or create the business *style* for the selected market sector and position. The combination of *themewords* and *style* must allow a unique message and image to be communicated through its corporate visual identity system (CVIS) and organisational behaviour. Otherwise customers become confused, do not recognise your business amongst others and go elsewhere.

Chapter 11
The Visual Identity Creative Process

What should the business look like?

Introduction

In this chapter the corporate visual identity system (CVIS) is discussed, this being the collective term applied to a business's name, logo, colours, typography and straplines to communicate to the world the company's existence, ethos and personality. This chapter is divided into two parts: Part A concentrates on the business-related topics and strategic inputs relevant to the CVIS's creation, to ensure that the designer has all the necessary information; Part B develops each of the *visual identity* elements: names, domain names, typography, digital fonts, logos and colour, providing- background on each of the elements and how their use and portrayal influence perception of a company, followed by how the design elements are created. Other sentient identity is summarised as this contributes to corporate design in the real world.

PART A   CVIS Business-Related Topics and Strategic Inputs

Background

The original creators of *symbolic* visual identity were graphic designers, their subject having gained importance across traditional media since the 1950s. Now their skills are transferring to digital media. They create the corporate visual identity elements of name, logo, colours, typography and straplines. Balmer (1995) has suggested that within business the understanding of corporate identity is tilted towards visual identity in the popular understanding of the subject. In reality there are further dimensions such as organisational behaviour and the whole working and communication environments. The benefits to be gained from the CVIS are that it promotes trust and reliability by presenting and maintaining the corporate style, advertising its products/ services and conveying a professional image of a cohesive company. This image has an impact on internal stakeholders by providing a sense of community and belonging, whilst externally the marketplace gains an impression of the company and recognises it in any future encounters. This impacts the company's *reputation*, which is of strategic importance. Ultimately image can determine the people who wish to work for the company and influences its confidence in the financial market.

11.1   CVIS Business-Related Topics

11.1.1   WHY IS DESIGNING AND REDESIGNING THE CORPORATE IDENTITY AND IMAGE/BRAND NECESSARY?

There are decision points in corporate strategy when corporate image has to be attended to (see also section 4.2.4): firstly, when the company starts and the design is completely new. This requires greater preparation as there is no pre-determined style guide to be considered in the design process. The business owner or board define the primary identity attributes and the creative media and skills to create them. Secondly, when a new company is created resulting from a takeover, merger, company spin-off or product development. Here the primary attributes are often already in existence. These are adapted for current trends or the new market position. Thirdly, on the occurrence of an evolutionary event such as technology speeding up the design process or having to differentiate market sectors as the technology may only be available to particular groups of people. Other instances are: when legal developments place restrictions on particular images/representations; increased costs; or geographical expansion impacting cultural sensibilities. Often this is thought of as involving different countries and societies; however, in vernacular (local) identity, similar occurrences appear and have an impact on trades and professions.

11.1.2   CORPORATE AND SUBSIDIARY ORGANISATIONAL AND MARKETING IDENTITY STRUCTURES

One of the key uses of visual identity is to provide an indication of a company's structure, in addition to its branded products (see also section

6.3). Other academics have categorised behavioural aspects of identity as relevant to structure (Ind, 1992; Van Riel, 1995). Wally Olins categorised this visual architecture as monolithic, endorsed and branded: monolithic identity structure is the same as the organisational structure; endorsed identity is part of a visible parent company with subsidiary companies and brands; branded identity is where each unit or brand image is designed separately.

> *Heal's endorses brands in the same market segment and new designers by selling their products in the shop.*

The link between organisational structure and corporate identity is often applied for marketing purposes. Stuart (1999) addressed organisational structure, employee identification and corporate identity structure in corporate strategy where she concluded that the organisation's structural architecture is a key determinant of its identity and should reflect its system of visual identification. By addressing these categories, a business can ensure that the corporate message is consistently and coherently applied across all of the organisation's traditional and digital communication channels that make it possible for the business to be instantly recognised.

11.1.3 GEOGRAPHICAL EXTENT

Geographical extent has two purposes: firstly, to determine the locations where businesses have operations and, secondly, the geographical extent of their distribution network. The first considers the points raised in section 5.2 (Geographical Identity): what are the demographics and cultural groupings of the target audience? Is it a defined local, national, world region or global? Will the marketing be in the real world and/or by a website? Have these channels to emit the same message and image or to differ? The geographical reach of a company's operations has to be considered, as the *positioning* in one market may not be the same in another area.

> *Heal's, with its long history, has a wealth of identity stories resulting from events, occurrences and staff activities.*

11.1.4 ACCESS TO RELEVANT CORPORATE STORIES FOR IDENTITY FORMATION

A story reinforces corporate philosophy, values and ethos, through its history, anecdotes and issues, including their resolution. Heal's Heritage webpage (see Plate 5.1) illustrates how a corporate history can become a story and the archive a rich source of material for future branding design exercises. Many of the stories are context-specific with a social and cultural emphasis that facilitates teaching and learning (see Chapter 5). They can add significance and meaning to the designer's understanding of the organisation and can be used in a new brand design. If a new market position is necessary, then a new story can easily be sourced. Similarly, after a merger, both companies' stories can be considered and a composite made of the two for marketing purposes (see Plate 11.1 on pages 84–85).

11.1.5 VISION, MISSION AND POSITION STATEMENTS

Vision and mission

Vision and mission statements have to be clearly expressed by the CEO; that is, where they want the company to be in the market and how they are going to get there (see also section 4.1). This message has to be communicated across all corporate media channels so that internal and external stakeholders understand what is being communicated. The message has to be coherent and consistently recounted so that stakeholders can rely on it. This does not mean that communication has to be the same but the tone of *voice* must run through everything. Sometimes a website will be developed for a separate purpose to the company's main business and have a slightly different way of expressing the same message.

11.1.6 POSITIONING AND RELATED INFORMATION

Background information from the board and other sources is necessary to create the image for the market position, such as:

- The size of the business and its operations and placing in the market sector; this can impact the range of media applications and how the CVIS is created and applied.

- Products and services information relating to product range, sizing, packaging, material and designers.

- Competitors have to be recognised and their design styles examined so that the client company's CVIS is different and clearly differentiates it from others in the same market segment.

11.1.7 COMMUNICATIONS

A well-documented and active communication strategy can be effective in ensuring *coherence* and consistency in the corporate message. Originally content was *controlled* by the company and *pushed* into the public domain by the company. Then web communications advances allowed information to be *pulled* from websites through content management systems. Social communication accessed from websites introduced *uncontrolled* commentary through a myriad of blogs and other platforms, including text, photo and video imagery. Now communications are uncontrolled and have positive and negative impact on a market's confidence in a company.

11.1.8 THEMEWORDS

Themewords are selected by the business executive and designer to convey the new identity or brand's image creation. Themes facilitate creativity and provide the means by which viewers recognise an organisation. Themewords emerge from the stories and become central to the creative endeavour by lending themselves to visual presentation. They are the starting point of creativity and iterations within the boundaries of what fits and summarises the visual identity.

At this point it is useful to revisit Figure 2.2 (Balmer's AC²ID Test and identity alignment) where identities have to be aligned. If the visual identity sends one message whilst the culture or behaviour confirm or refute it, then alignment is correct in the former and incorrect in the latter. This is an important design consideration for the CVIS elements and organisational behaviours. When a local market trader sets up a stall, he will name the stall, have a logo and promote produce by pamphlets and blackboard listings. He may be considered a *friendly character* – that is the *essence* and therefore the organisational behaviour of the business. The combination of the visual identity and organisational identity traits expressed are perceived by the customer's senses. In the above example, the words *friendly character* could be applied as a design themeword. Other examples that communicate a company identity are: strength, aggression, weakness, submission, loud or quiet, which can be conveyed on one image.

In addition to themewords, societal prevailing social attitudes have to be addressed, for example, political correctness, environmental awareness and taboos, so that no one will be offended, otherwise the designs will reflect badly on the business.

Table 11.1   Themewords and sample brands

Themewords	Sample Brands
Ruggedness	Marlboro; Levi; Timberland
Controversial	Benetton; French Connection (FCUK)
Humour/childlike	cBBC
Irony	Ministry of Sound
Organic	Innocent
Elegance	Chanel
Reliable/competent	PwC; American Express
Excitement	Porsche

Table 11.1 illustrates how *themewords* such as 'excitement', 'competent' and 'ruggedness' spark visual imagery and organisational behaviour designs. These *themes* form the strategic articulation and design storyboard which communicate the organisation's ethos, mission and philosophy. This articulation is then developed by the business, artists and designers through specialist image design skills, knowledge and tools applied to traditional media applications and websites.

> *Heal's emphasis on innovation and design demonstrates its style and market position.*

11.1.9   DESIGN STYLE

Style is a key discriminator, where the designed image conveys the market position. *Style* portrays differentiating features and qualities of a business – its personality – through visual, auditory, olfactory or tactile design techniques, making it into a company with personality (Bernstein, 1989). In the real world all the senses are engaged in recognising a company's market position. Online sight and sound are the main sentient mode and therefore a unique engaging homepage has to be specified and rendered. This is key to ensuring that a company is instantly recognised as its website downloads. Various words can be used to describe a *style*, such as traditional or high-tech; expensive or budget; establishment or alternative.

Each artist's style is therefore portrayed, from the minimalist to complex ornamentation. For example, Adolf Loos considered ornamentation to be a crime and advocated *elegance and simplicity* in his work. On websites, a similar approach to style can be seen in <www.joshuadavis.com>. At the other extreme is the postmodern Memphis colourful, *busy and eclectic* style of <www.cartoonnetwork. com>. Another style is *representation*, being the extent to which you wish to represent reality – is the design lifelike? Surrealist artists Saussure and Rene Magritte used *relationship and juxtaposition* of objects to stimulate the imagination, known as the Bewildering Effect, where another concept appears by virtue of the fact that the objects are placed together. Artistic styles have an impact where the degree of detail and artistic skill can place a print or digital image in a class of its own: see <www.presstube.com> for some interesting videos on how this is achieved. Referring to wine labels again, Mouton Rothschild has a wine range for which famous artists design a label each year. Hence it is not just the wine that is being sold but also the print of the artist's work.

There is a wide range of approaches in designing the *visual identity*; for example, if a corporate design brief is given to ten people, the final results can be completely different in execution and the styles portrayed. For example (see Figure 11.1), if a wine label is to be designed for three markets, then the design styles can be very different. It is the choices made around content, execution and interaction that effectively tell an organisation's story by visual means. This image generates connections with all the company's stakeholders so that it becomes *owned* by the organisation and trusted by the viewer, just as in the case of a storyteller and listener.

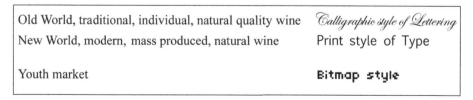

Figure 11.1   Wine label styles targeting different markets

Creating a corporate image is difficult: some projects will be based on an organisation with a strong corporate culture, values and ethos, with a long line of leaders and heritage. Others are defined as aspirational, where identities are created by the company and a designer.

PART B   CVIS Creation

11.2   Corporate Visual Identity System (CVIS) Creative Design

The CVIS has five elements – name, typography, logo and or logotype, colour and strapline. These have evolved spatially and temporally alongside technological developments and media applications. In 1995 John Balmer identified the graphic design school as one of the four approaches to corporate identity schools of thought. Figure 13.3 (Corporate Design Triangle 3) shows the CVIS elements – names, logos, colours, typography and straplines – which appeared on websites in the 1990s.

Other physical expressions of corporate design exist as illustrated in Figure 6.2 (Manufacturing, retail and distribution environments and processes). All of these physical artefacts display the CVIS on the exterior and interior of buildings, signs, vehicles, products and services, packaging, stationery, forms, publications, websites, clothing, advertising and promotions. Internally, this provides a sense of belonging to a community and pride in the organisation. Externally, it reinforces the organisation's reputation, engendering goodwill, and if that is not the case, then suitable steps can be taken to resolve the problem.

11.2.1   DESIGNER'S CREATIVE PROCESS

In a UK context, the traditional creative design approach is firstly to conduct research on the company and topic as presented in section 11.1. Concepts can be created from this work (see Figure 11.2). Then *rough* work is undertaken in the traditional mode with sketchbooks, pencil, pen and ink. It is noticeable that this facilitates a *free-flow* between cognitive, hand and eye, when a design concept is discussed, as the designer can create, alter or completely change the drawing through various iterations, letting a clear and precise sketch develop. Sketching permits development of conceptual thought, allowing ideas to be communicated and understood by others, whilst recording the iterations of the design's progress not so easily achieved digitally. Creative processes can be time-consuming, requiring real-world and online skills for drawing, colour application across numerous materials and crafting artefacts in a wide range of media. Development of samples and pieces can go through many refinements and constant crafting of the artefact until the final product is found or achieved. It has to be borne in mind that each art and designed element has to progress through a similar creative process before the final project is delivered. A key point is that the design process is path–dependent, occurring in steps where each step has to be completed before the next begins (Johnson, 2005).

Design Brief → Design Research → Market → Concept → Rough → Media → Presentation
Sector　　　　　　　　Ideas　Application

Figure 11.2 Key stages in the visual identity creative process

Once the initial concepts and ideas are composed on paper, if a digital version is necessary a handcrafted initial *mock-up* is made and then digitised in 2D or 3D, being transferred to digital media using Photoshop and/or Illustrator by a mediated mouse or e-pencil where movement allows an image to appear on the tablet or computer screen. Various refinements or streamlining occur at this stage. In the vast majority of business cases, the design has to be displayed digitally; however, the design composition itself can be in print or on computer. In the Far East, some design processes are totally digital. This said, a 3D printer has appeared on the consumer market so for some creatives, this may be the only the media and tool necessary.

11.2.2 NAMES

A name is the most recognisable feature of an artefact and the naming process is a critical decision, indicating identity, nationality, gender, age and personality.

Company name functions

A company name is a reference point to the outside world, *positioning* a business in the marketplace, so that customers will immediately identify and relate to its attributes, whilst ensuring that stakeholders are aware of its existence. Kapferer (1992) indicated the importance of company names by referring to the adage *Nome nest ome* – the name foretells. So as we walk into a shop or enter a business website URL, there are certain expectations as a name can define a business. This definition is clarified by the message communicated by the CVIS imagery so that the object or concept becomes recognisable and acceptable. Naming a company is a legal requirement and is crucial in establishing identity and in launching the organisation's unique existence. There is a whole business stream related to *naming* with legal implications through the Companies Act. Searches are undertaken to ensure that no other company exists with the same name under a country's jurisdiction. A *name* is the first of the CVIS elements, applied in image creation to differentiate a company or product in the marketplace. Whereas the other elements of the CVIS are more than likely to change, the name is unlikely to alter.

It is critical to get the name and associations correct, otherwise the strategic implications can be detrimental. On reviewing a sample of FTSE 100 companies, four business name types were recognised:

- Traditional, usually the owner's name

- Descriptive, defining what a company does, or the product or service provided

- Abstract, which has no link to the business identity, regardless of whether inspirational or aspirational

- Emotional, focusing on possibilities or emotions.

1925   *Customer delivery; Heal & Son Ltd; serif type.*

1982   *A logo for the 1980s; sans serif type with the H being adapted for a Christmas advertisement.*

2005   *A brand new identity; sans serif logotype and a wider range of products.*

So how do business names arise? In many instances they have grown from owner-managed roots; for example, Shell started trading with its pecten Shell logo within a fairly local geographical area. Those companies that have grown into worldwide operations may well have considered business expansion strategies but their names remain the same and central to the CVIS system. Names are changed if they cause offence in a country or have legal implications. The same name can be applied to both the company and its product or service; for example, Mars is a chocolate bar and also

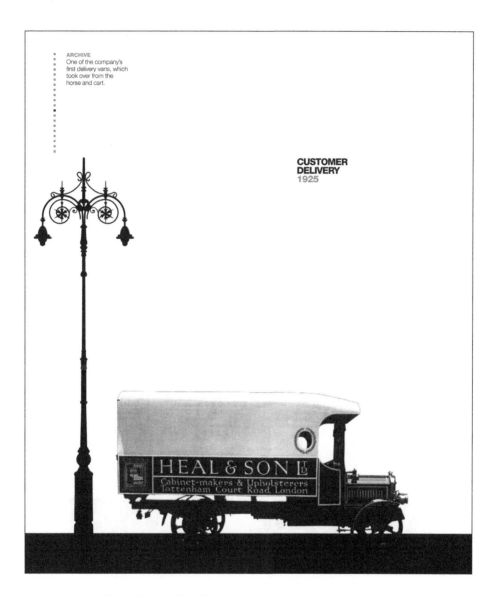

ARCHIVE
One of the company's
first delivery vans, which
took over from the
horse and cart.

CUSTOMER
DELIVERY
1925

**Plate 11.2a Heal's delivery vehicles over 80 years,
illustrating alterations to the name and logotype products
as the company diversified: 1925 – customer delivery**

Source: *Heal's 1810–2010 – 200 Years of Design & Inspiration* (2009), p. 54.
© Heal & Son Ltd. With special thanks to the V&A Archive.

MARKETING
Influential design agency Minale Tattersfield's new corporate identity for Heal's won a silver D&AD Award (regarded as the Oscars of the design industry). Applauded for its elegance and simplicity, the new identity was designed like a kit of engineered parts that could be assembled by a graphic mechanic rather than an artist.

Marcello Mario Minale, son of the agency's founding partner, Marcello Minale (senior), who worked on the rebranding, explains: "The inspiration came from the Arts and Crafts movement and Ambrose Heal. We extracted a simple element: the chequered pattern he used as his trademark. This historical element provided the foundation for translating the Heal's logo into a modern, fashionable and eye-catching icon of the 1980s."

A LOGO FOR
THE EIGHTIES
1982

BELOW
THE STYLISED 'H', TAKEN FROM THE NEW LOGO BECAME A BRANDING DEVICE THAT COULD BE ADAPTED FOR THE FESTIVE SEASON

Plate 11.2b   Heal's delivery vehicles over 80 years,
illustrating alterations to the name and logotype products
as the company diversified: 1982 – a logo for the 1980s

Source: *Heal's 1810–2010 – 200 Years of Design & Inspiration* (2009), p. 132.

**A BRAND NEW
IDENTITY**
2005

Plate 11.2c   Heal's delivery vehicles over 80 years,
illustrating alterations to the name and logotype products
as the company diversified: 2005 – a brand new identity

Source: *Heal's 1810–2010 – 200 Years of Design & Inspiration* (2009), p. 152.
© Heal & Son Ltd. With special thanks to the V&A Archive.

a company name; Hoover is a product which has a company name but in English also denotes a cleaning activity; and a more recent addition is *google* as it becomes the common name for searching the internet. Hence the naming of an object can be a noun but it can also be an activity and therefore a verb (Vaid, 2003).

> *Heal's shop name changed over time for the first 150 years, being called Heal & Son with a seriffed typography, which changed to a sans serif type thereafter. During the next ten years, the shop was called Heal and for the last 45 years has been called Heal's.*

A merger or acquisition may trigger the necessity for name renewal, as time may have dated the name as marketing approaches and technology have changed. For example, companies targeting younger age groups or fast-moving technology companies often rename and rebrand their organisations. Chelsea Girl, which was a popular young woman's dresswear shop in the 1970s–1980s, was taken over and renamed River Island. Cadbury's has had the same name since 1824, resulting in a strong brand value that creates an intangible on the balance sheet. Consideration should also be given to the organisation and its marketing identity brand structure. Virgin may be the parent name but subsidiaries known as Virgin Media, Virgin Insurance, and so on, exist. On the other hand, Ford has a separate portfolio of brand marques as it acquired different companies.

If a company changes its name, then the consumer reaction has to be considered, as well as the cost of implementing the design changes and the publicity. For example, the Royal Mail decided to change its name to Consignia; although this was praised in the design community, many people did not see the significance of the change and the name was dropped. Hence a good brand name needs to represent an identity, with perceived values and purpose – what the customer can relate to and wishes to buy from.

Domain names

Today, global communications have dramatically increased audiences, rendering greater consideration to name-giving. Online brand names require originality and are often abstract to attract attention and develop their specific brand personality, evolving online as customers begin to identify with the product or service. For example, Waitrose's online shopping business name is Ocado which has become a successful food distribution business. Domain names have a separate set of variables to consider. Many companies were late in applying for a domain name, as they had not realised how significant the internet would become as a marketing channel. A company domain name can be set up very quickly. In the short time that internet names have been in existence, these *intuitive* names have been in limited supply. Registration of two- and three-letter domain names has been almost impossible in the last 15 years – a finite entity within a complex environment. As time passes and the legal, geographical definitions have taken hold, the problem is that a user's initial reaction is to type the intuitive company URL name, expecting the company website to download.

11.2.3   TRADITIONAL TYPOGRAPHY AND FONTS

Type surrounds us in everyday life. If we look around, it is so subtle and well designed that it escapes our notice. As we read a book or website, the information is uppermost in our consciousness – indeed this is the whole objective of the written text. There are signs everywhere, on digital screens, signposts and newspaper headlines, all emitting a message by their content and *lettering*. How often do we consider the composition of the text and the layout of the page that someone has so carefully composed or designed? Typography in the design process is rarely explicitly mentioned yet it depicts the essence of an ethos by *lettering*, whether this be calligraphy, type or typography from a particular era. The following provides background and discussion on the main developments and significant aspects of typography, initially looking at print, then progressing through to digital. Whilst reading this, consider which style of typography you would use for a design project or take a close look at the texts on a webpage or book.

Writing systems

There are two systems of writing: scripts and hieroglyphs. Roman letters are scripts whereas the Egyptians used hieroglyphs (a logogram). The importance of these graphic scripts and symbols is that they are used to convey ideas and thoughts to the reader through writing. Alphabetic scripts are seen to be efficient. However, ideas can be conveyed through logograms or hieroglyphs where each one stands for a whole word (Egyptian hieroglyphs and Chinese characters). Today's laundry and motorway signage symbols fulfil a similar purpose as hieroglyphs did in the past.

Calligraphy

Scribes in monasteries, scholars and government officials wrote biblical texts, scholarly texts, proclamations and charters so that information could be conveyed to the public. Scribes in many cultures held an important position in society, usually in the higher echelons. In the fifteenth century books gave some people, those who could read, the opportunity to access information themselves. An interesting note is that scrolls were *read to* groups of people, they were not for individual reading. These were important documents, not just because they produced an artefact but also because they developed hand, eye and brain/mind co-ordination in the scribe. Through the continual development of writing texts, a system of book layouts began – thus creating a *presence* on a page.

Calligraphy receded in popularity with the development of the printing press. Edward Johnston brought it back into the arts and crafts in 1898, when he began studying some of these early manuscripts in the British Museum. Today the skills obtained and portrayed by calligraphy show individuality which does not appear in other forms of lettering. Calligraphic lettering does not necessarily follow the Old English script but can be an *abstract* form prepared by hand and traced into a digital format.

Apart from writing skills, writing tools have to fulfil calligraphy requirements, each one having been perfected by usage and design. It is important to mention these and to consider their variety and impact. Scripts using different size nibs or writing angle create an effect on the shape of a letter and indentation on the paper. This does not occur on digital prints as computer printers print the letter image, producing a different effect. Inks and paints are used with pens; in recent times biro, felt tip and gel pens have produced their own styles of lettering, most of which come in a variety of nib shapes and sizes, each one evoking an era – see Plate 6.2 (Heal's 1978 Buzz range) where the *Buzz* has a stylised font. Today there are still large calligraphy projects such as the production of a traditional calligraphic manuscript, this being a combined UK and US Millennium Project conducted in Wales and displayed in the Victoria and Albert Museum a few years ago. Here various stages of composition were shown alongside one completed Bible.

11.2.4   DIGITAL TYPE

Designers in the twentieth and twenty-first centuries have continued to create new typefaces based on historic characteristics depicted on metal type, drawings and prints. Today this type uses modern technology with a clear specification for definition and uniformity. Looking through newspapers, both titles and content will show how readily we identify copy purely by type and layout, particularly when compared with a newspaper from another country. Each language has its type idiosyncrasies noticeable when foundries made type (Spiekermann and Ginger, 2003). Universal typefaces had to be designed when business became more international. In the mid 1950s, after the war, the printing industry developed a new approach, calling printers technicians rather than craftsmen, and looked towards new technologies and a new discipline – *graphic design*, otherwise designated as design for print. Letraset also appeared, freeing the designer from the printer and allowing him to design freely.

There has been a digital typography revolution as designers can now generate digital fonts faster than previously by using a computer. This permits bespoke fonts so that today there are over 30,000 digital fonts, of which 5,000 are usable. This development has seen greater application and usage in some highly competitive business sectors where trendy new fonts are designed and used quickly for projects such as teenage magazines. This results in magazine typography producing a useful archive of social and cultural trends.

There are two methods of creating fonts: firstly, bitmap fonts from pixels, where each letter is made from a number of pixels in height and width. Bitmap fonts appear on many appliances – phone screens, microwave ovens, PDAs, iPods, TVs, car dashboards. Secondly, vectors, where letters are generated by using vector software packages such as Adobe Illustrator. Calligraphic sketches can be hand-drawn, scanned into the computer, traced and adjusted to suit requirements. The advantage of this is that if letters and logos are saved in high resolution mode they become scalable and therefore applicable to various media.

Digital graphic software

Digital graphic design began to appear in the mid 1990s as Adobe Creative Suite, that is, Photoshop and Illustrator appeared. This allowed graphic formats (.bmp, .gif, .jpeg), colour, 3D, images, icons and backgrounds to be created to portray *real-world* expressions – with designer skill and practice. Traditional media digital technology and software has allowed greater flexibility in designing and typesetting books by an author, resulting in fewer people undertaking more tasks. Anyone can use computer layout programs such as InDesign™, PageMaker™ and Quark Express™ to publish a book (Smith, 2004). On websites, with the development of *web authoring tools* such as cascading style sheets (CSS), dynamic HTML, Javascript, JavaApplets and *Flash*, designers have gained greater flexibility over their designs and how they appear on users' browsers. This allows them to create better corporate design communication, whilst attending to greater user friendliness. Designers can now create visual spaces in 3D, 4D and 5D, with movement and sound not possible with static 2D paper. This is where the creative input to the design of corporate image could be increasingly applied.

Word processing programs treat documents as a linear stream. In contrast, page layout programs such as Quark Express and Adobe InDesign use spatial arrangements whereby boxes are arranged on the *page*. Text is then inserted by allowing it to *flow* into these boxes until all the text is placed in its correct position. Images are also placed into the specified boxes – the sizes of these boxes can be altered to requirements.

Fonts for visual pacing

In oral storytelling, time and culture can be conveyed by the timbre of the voice and pace of the raconteur, providing the atmosphere and presence of a story, *painting* a picture in the mind of the listener. When print appeared in large blocks, it was difficult to read and comprehend. Through time the written word managed to produce a *visual pacing* layout and composition, by providing spaces between paragraphs, words and letters. Layouts allow the reader to quickly scan content and focus on the parts that they want to read, whilst gaining an impression on the type of product or topic subconsciously by design presentation, often regardless of what the words say.

Typographies convey distinctive messages, forming the initial impression of a company through lettering, with styles ranging from calligraphy to the latest digital typographies. Typographies are the second element in the CVIS, forming clear differentiation. In the marketplace, for example, Marks and Spencer (M&S), British Home Stores (BHS) and Morrisons (M) have logotypes registered as trademarks. A concern has been in the perceived downgrading of renowned fonts through the digital economic drive and loss of skills. For example, *The Sunday Times* newspaper, in 2006/2007, modernised its traditional typography and embellishments for a *seriffed Roman form* so that the same typography could be applied to both paper and digital media.

Letters have to work under different conditions – the *look and feel* of a typeface produces an emotional response depending on whether it is light or heavy, round or square, black on white or white on black. Through these means lettering can portray happiness, sadness, anger or elegance. As a reader, print and font size appear on a range of media and are read at varying distances. For example, in a telephone directory the clarity of names and numbers layout and print is paramount.

Backgrounds can make letters easier to read and look more dynamic or trendy; for example, psychedelic backgrounds produce a *moving image* to a typeface set in 2D. The reader registers the type in a particular manner so that the *designed* response is achieved. This is particularly evident in signage where the chosen conditions and media play an important part in type design. Some signs are read in train and bus stations, in reception areas or on the move as the journey progresses, all aspects of which have to be considered, such as reversed type looks heavier – white on a blue background – than positive type – black on yellow. Lighting effects can change the quality of definition which could be crucial in an emergency.

11.2.5   LOGOS FOR INSTANT RECOGNITION

Logos act as badges of identification and quality (Dowling, 1994), facilitating brand recognition as pictures are perceived faster than words. They serve as shorthand for the company so that its name is recalled whenever a stakeholder requires a product or service. Logos are designed to capture people's attention, evoking an emotional response, often when there is little room to place a logotype. A thorough design selection process is vital to ensure that the logo instantly attracts attention and recognition (Henderson and Cote, 1998). Any graphic representations such as a logo, for example, the Nike tick is a symbol, whereas the PwC monogram is a logotype. Plate 11.3 illustrates Heal's two logos; firstly, its name in logotype: Heal & Son Ltd; and secondly, the logo of a four-poster bed with the strapline: 'At the Sign of the Fourposter', mattresses and bedding being the origins of the company's existence and continued success.

Logos can signal a fresh output (Kapferer, 1992) on behalf of the corporate image or product branding. See the changes that have occurred to Heal's logos between the 1900s and 2005 across Plates 14.1, 7.2 and 11.3. Established organisations can draw on their emblem's historical roots and original business approaches, whereas a new company has to find or create an identity upon which a logo can be based. New designs are essential on:

PUBLISHED BY

HEAL & SON LTD

AT *THE SIGN OF THE FOURPOSTER*

From the early 20th century, Heal's was to become synonymous with the symbol of the four-poster bed, thanks to Ambrose Heal's introduction of this distinctive logo. Featuring on marketing material and around the shop, the four-poster logo appeared in many different versions, from the early 1900s through to 1984.

Plate 11.3   An early 1990s image illustrating the Heal's logotype 'Heal & Son Ltd' with the distinctive Four Poster Bed and the strapline 'At the Sign of the Four Poster'

Source: *Heal's 1810–2010 – 200 Years of Design & Inspiration* (2009), p. 8.
© Heal & Son Ltd. With special thanks to the V&A Archive.

- Start-up – Shell has maintained its red and yellow pecten shell since 1880 with subtle updated designs.

- Changes in direction – BP's environmental yellow and green heliograph took time to be accepted.

Representative emblems can also be applied, such as:

- Vodafone's apostrophe is a grammatical speech indicator.

- British American Tobacco (BAT) – three golden tobacco leaves.

- GlaxoSmithKline's triangular orange pill with abbreviation GSK is a combination of product and monogram.

A key feature in the logo design process is media application as each media has specific requirements, such as paper, card, glass, ceramic, perspex, vinyl, wood, leather or cotton fabric, where the key determinant is scalability. In recent years signwriting has declined as digital printing is faster and cheaper to make and can be applied on.

Website logos

Website logos have some standard practices and customer expectations:

- The majority of website logos appear in the top left-hand corner of the homepage.

- Most online businesses prefer a logotype as a logo style as the business name is clearly stated. Logotypes are prepared as a graphic and then placed on the relevant website layout box.

- Logotypes with *sans seriffed* typographies are frequently used in comparison with other styles as they are easier to read on a screen, cursive scripts being considered more difficult. Some well-established British companies have scripts, for example, <www.boots.com> and <www.cadburyschweppes.co.uk>.

Logo shapes are variable, with names located within shapes, or have a natural element as an emblem. Other forms include squares, ovals, circles, abstract, flowers, people, birds, coats of arms, diamonds, shells, stars and houses.

Simplification of design shapes occurred when the initial graphic interface was poor, so logos such as Barclays' spread eagle, Rolls-Royce's radiator and Shell's pecten shell have had their distinctive traditional styles adapted to technology, but still maintain their original emblem and appeal.

11.2.6 PRINTING

Printing processes developed over 500 years; casting lead for metal type was used for a considerable period of time. However, it was too soft to print large letters under pressure and, through continual usage, rounded corners often appeared, as can be seen in some of the old advertising posters. Woodcut type could be used on a much larger type size. In 1834 the pantograph revolutionised wood cuts: as a tracing tool, when connected to a carving router, it allowed an original type drawing to produce copies at differing proportions, weights and serifs.

This changed the approach to *letter making* from the calligraphic, where perfectly formed letters were sought, to the typographic, where a variable system of formal features was necessary. This resulted in the printed type that we see today with its variety of weights, serifs, angles, curves, ascenders and descenders. The relationship between letters became critical and new combinations appeared, such as ligatures where two letters were combined or moved closer. This resulted in better print clarity, allowing the reader to read easily, faster or slower as required. This was the essence of the new *print* as it was disseminated to a wider readership through newspapers and books – the ability to read type easily and quickly.

The printing press revolutionised the type process in the creation of type and the printing of books, as books are portable information which could be disseminated to a wider geographical area and across social classes, if a person could read. A whole new industry developed which continued to expand with and because of the Industrial Revolution, becoming fully mechanised by the end of the nineteenth century. Over a period of 500 years until the mid 1950s, the world of the typographer and printer held supreme, producing posters, books and signs, much of which portrayed early corporate design. In a parallel world this technological innovation could be applied to the present digital world.

Paper

Paper, the media upon which letters are displayed, can have an impact on people's perception of an organisation's market position and ethos. Animal skins were originally used for books and charters, being durable and flexible once scraped and cleaned. Vellum from cow hides is still available but it is expensive and paper substitutes are often seen in craft shops. Today, acid-free paper is preferred for calligraphy. There are three categories:

- Machine-made paper – continuous lengths of paper made by machine and cut into sheets

- Mould-made paper – individual sheets made by machines

- Handmade paper – individual sheets made by hand.

In Europe good quality paper was traditionally made from cotton, silk and linen fibres rejected by the textile industry. A pulp was made from the fibres so that they were suspended in a large vat. Size was added to allow the paper to be written on and colour added. A flat, rectangular mould was dipped into the vat so that the pulp collected in a layer on top of a mesh in the mould. The water then drained to leave a sheet of wet paper which was sandwiched between woollen felt blankets and pressed to remove excess water. The surface of the paper was affected by how it was dried:

- Rough surface – when it was removed from the blankets

- Slightly rough surface – piled sheets of paper, pressed

- Smooth hot pressed – paper sheets pressed between heated metal rollers.

Paper weight is measured in grams per square metre (gsm). The smaller the number, the lighter the weight of the paper.

11.3 Website Layout

Digital layout in websites operates differently from print as it presents data in 2D and 3D. The method of visual and hand spatial navigation impacts the manner in which the content is designed. There are numerous books on website design and content. The main points to note here are:

1. Websites are controlled by hierarchies in an even more systematic way than print documents so that navigation is more accessible. A site's file structure proceeds from a root down to directories holding

various levels of content. An HTML page contains a hierarchy of elements that can be nested one inside the other. The site's organisation is reflected in its interface – from navigation to the formatting of content. Typography helps elucidate the hierarchies governing all these features. Typographic style sheets are used to weigh information gathered, helping users find what they need.

2.   When a website user is searching for information through a website, then the 3D spatial aspect of digital media becomes more apparent. Search engines cut across website hierarchies, bringing in links from varying levels and content. Databases are information space structures rather than sequential.

3.   Cascading style sheets (CSS) allow designers to plan alternate layouts depending on the user's software and hardware, for example, mobile phones in text and image formats. Some users have outdated browsers or lack the software *plug-ins* necessary for displaying certain types of files. Style sheets can be used to design print-friendly versions of interactive documents.

11.3.1   COMPUTER SCREENS

Initially computer screens looked and operated like TV sets, working through cathode ray tubes (CRTs); today these screens look ridiculous. Flat LCD screens offer higher resolution and engineers have made bitmaps more acceptable. When bitmap letters are enlarged by *zooming*, the pixels become more exaggerated; some designers like to use this effect in their typography design. On old monitors, only whole pixels could be manipulated, but on digital LCD screens *anti-aliasing* can be used by projecting shades of grey to create an illusion of curvature. Adobe uses CoolType to achieve this by controlling the smaller red, green and blue sub pixels, individually adjusting their intensity. This effectively trebles the horizontal grid, achieving more precise smoothing along the edges of characters. Microsoft uses a similar technology called ClearType. When the text is small, anti-aliasing can make it legible. In recent years retina screen displays have increased the number of pixels dramatically, allowing a sharper definition.

On the Sklar Screen, the important areas for information are the centre and top. These are not necessarily the first areas to be scanned. Website visitors exhibit consistent behaviour in the way they search for information, with corners and edges being ideal locations for buttons, menus, toolbars and taskbars. Further research suggests that users do not go to the bottom of a webpage and that colour and animation attracts. Four principles are key:

- Proximity – related items should be grouped close together.

- Consider the rules of proportion.

- Alignment – each element on a page should have a visual connection with another element on the page.

- Repetition – the website should be consistent throughout: colour, shape, texture, spatial relationships, line thicknesses, sizes and so on, developing unity and organisation of the website.

- Contrast – avoid elements that are similar; contrast is often the most important visual attraction.

11.4   Colour

11.4.1   COLOUR – EARLY DEVELOPMENTS

Use of colour was a late development in corporate design as early corporate design communication was dependent on architecture, shapes, word-of-mouth descriptions and handmade banners and clothes. Early print technology used black ink, unless images were painted, for example, old *Wanted* and theatre posters (see Heal's black logotype across 200 years of trading, except in a few exceptional cases such as in Plate 4.1). As inks became more readily available and the means of adhering them to paper was achieved, coloured prints through adverts appeared, the colour yellow being applied in a 1900 product catalogue of Heal's brass bedsteads. Today, people can often recognise a brand by the colours and shades applied to an artefact but colour is carefully selected as it is easily remembered. Colour can also portray nationality, cultures, sentient expression and function. This impacts perception, interpretation and memories by psychological and physiological reactions (Funk and Ndubisi, 2006; Triedman, 2002).

11.4.2   DESIGNING WITH COLOUR

Colour is one of the most critical and trickiest design issues in multimedia and global design as identities and associations can vary over time, geography and context, being used to connote importance and emphasis, specify categories, direct the eye, reflect a mood, establish a style. These topics are covered in many colour textbooks. Here a few corporate design-related topics are included. The practical topics to consider when designing are:

- Additive primary colours – red, green and blue

- Subtractive colours – yellow, cyan and magenta

- Hue, saturation and brightness – perceptual attributes

- Visual illusions – tricks played in the process of visual perception

- The impact of colour blindness

- After-effects – after exposure to areas of colour.

> *In 1900 Heal's product catalogue introduced the colour yellow for their bedstead advertisement. This highlighted the product previously printed in black.*

Designers are limited in their colour choices for a range of reasons:

a) There is only a limited range of colours that look different from each other, hence colour is a key design constraint.

b) Some colour shades have to be avoided because of their similarity to other brands; for example, red is applied to *The Economist*, Virgin Group and Vodafone. Being a fast colour, red attracts the eye quickly and is often used by marketing companies.

c) Cost constraints may limit the quality and number of colour applications; for example, in print, a high-gloss, colour brochure will indicate quality, whereas cheaper colour applications on newsprint appear as lower quality. Onscreen quality differentiation is achieved by aesthetics rather than visual expressions.

d) Function can represent a particular activity or era, helping the audience to recognise a company's sector or product, especially when a logo is used. Table 11.2 illustrates the positive and negative colour associations and the sector where they are used. Representation is also applied in packaging to depict flavours, such as red – strawberry, yellow – banana; or temperature strengths of hot and cold: red – hot, blue – cold.

Table 11.2   Colour associations

Positive associations	Colour	Negative associations	Market, products and services
energy, strength, heat, passion, aggression	**Red**	blood, war, danger, stop, financial loss, anger	newspapers, mobile phone
warmth, confidence	**Orange**		supermarkets, entertainment, hospitality
summer, gold, sun, harvest, optimism	**Yellow**	cowardice, treason, hazard, illness, folly	holiday
fresh, environment, nature, relaxing, ecology	**Green**	inexperience, envy, misfortune	dairy, government, tourism, sustainable
sky, stability, peace, trust, sea, dependable, coolness, creative, imaginative	**Blue**	depression, sorrow, passivity	professional, banks, utility, healthcare, IT, dental
simplicity, purity, peace, cleanliness, innocence	**White**	simplicity, sterility, banality	
power, formality, precise, depth, solidarity, style	**Black**	fear, void, night, secrecy, evil, death, anonymity	fashion, luxury, mining, oil, financial
intelligence, calm, dignity, restraint, maturity	**Grey**	shadow, concrete, drabness, boredom	builders

11.4.3   COLOUR IMPLICATION ON CORPORATE DESIGN

Creating a corporate design requires knowledge of colour and how it transfers from one media to another. In digital media, RGB is applied through pixels, as opposed to CMYK, which is applied by ink in print. Website visitors are instinctively aware that something is not quite what they expected if the wrong colour or shade is observed, thereby arousing suspicions that the website is not the company they wished to view.

Today digital media does not have the same barriers to entry as colours are projected onto a screen. As technology progresses and the graphic interface develops, designers are experimenting with digital colour techniques. Primary colours cannot be mixed from other colours and are therefore strong. In print these are known as CMYK, while digitally they are known as RGB. Artistically they are associated with minimalist or Bauhaus design and the paintings of Mondrian and Kandinsky. Designers have to understand the implications of colour in local, national and global contexts as it impacts on customers' perception of a business. Within a commercial market, strong colours are used on children's sweets, toys and clothes, comics, Batman and Spiderman – to attract their attention. Cheap printing systems are used for red, blue, yellow and black – black elegant type on a box of chocolates. Colour can suggest an *era/period in time*: black and white classic Hollywood films – 1940s; 1960s – lime green, purple and orange; 1980s – designer matt black. *Colour coding* by grouping colour can create an order or system when visually presenting information. Signage often uses colour to make sense of different departments in a building or it can make different types of a product clearer; for example, maps, fire extinguishers and electrical wiring all use colour to create a visual system to make divisions between different elements. *Subversive colour* – sometimes designers use surprising colours that go against expectations to create visual impact. Often, changing the context within which the colour is seen is enough. Fluorescent colours began as high visibility for safety in factories and on railways, and on cheap sales tickets in bargain shops. Designers used them in punk rock graphics for tastelessness. *Neutral colours* are often used in medicine packets to avoid negative associations, camouflage to blend in with the surroundings, non-political applications or designs requiring quietness or understatement, whereas *political colours* can be provocative, such as political parties: Conservative – blue, Labour – red and Liberal Democrats – yellow.

11.5   Verbal Identity – Straplines and Jingles

Straplines and jingles sometimes appear alongside the name and logo; to many people this company slogan is very important as it can remind people of the corporate vision and mission. Ruth Finnegan's book, *Communication: The Multiple Modes of Interconnection* (2002), describes each of the following in more detail. Through text or sound – both language used and editorial tone affect the user's perception. What will the language style and word choice tell you about the company and its market position? Do they have to project a friendly, informative tone satisfying user requirements or a rigid, disciplined, off-putting tone which is indifferent to users' requirements? Examples of the verbal and text impact are:

- Evolution and fusion of language straplines – *Persil washes whiter*

- McDonald's has a restricted vocabulary which is probably a strength in a fast food outlet.

- Over time, language changes – in 30 years' time, English will be different.

- There are also the various styles of business writing – reports, brochures, website commentary and so on.

11.6   Other Sentient Identity Features

11.6.1   SOUND-AUDITORY IDENTITY

Hearing permits us to differentiate the numerous noises that make up our environments: birdsong, animal noises, cars, trains and so on, all of which we take for granted, as well as the noises we make ourselves – whether this be footsteps, breathing, clapping hands – which we may not be so aware of. Sound travels distance and round corners where visibility is impossible. Pictures can occur simultaneously and there can be many pictures on one screen; however, to hear a message there can only be one dominant sound occurring in sequence.

Sound recognition

Sound recognition has many properties – volume, pitch, rhythm, intensity, speed, tone, cadence or timbre – which the ear differentiates. *Soundscapes* are references to cultural experiences which we recognise again. An example of this can be seen in the British Library's *Turning Pages* Exhibition where the male, low monastic tone and rhythm helps to set the context in which the Bible would have been read; similarly with the Buddhist *Diamond Sutra* where the Tibetan chant is sung as the scroll unfurls, again adding context. These are available online at the British Library's website.

Auditory communication, in digital terms a voxel, is often regarded as secondary to the cognitive input, that is, the written musical score rather than the sung version, the written text rather than the spoken word. The former through the centuries are seen as having a higher cognitive faculty. We often listen to sounds to signal specific events such as fire engines or police cars to alert us that something is happening and to be vigilant.

11.6.2 TOUCH – TACTILE IDENTITY

Touch is a direct communication sense by which we interact with computers. This tactile channel is complex and often empathises with other senses, such as hearing and vibration – an undulating movement and noise through feeling – being very specific and able to work in many environments: noisy, smelly and in the dark where the other senses may not be so effective. It allows us to identify shapes, temperatures, movement and texture and yet it is momentary. Touch is immediately engaging and involves a very participatory form of communication and connection, providing a very distinct message. Touch is a key sense in human–computer interaction (HCI), usually by a keyboard which has been with us for decades in content design, but the interface artefacts are changing. The mouse has a particular significance, with many design changes.

Tactile identity occurs through the undulating surface of a fabric or artefact. Vibrating identity occurs through undulating movement and noise detected by touch.

11.6.3 SMELL – OLFACTORY IDENTITY

Taste is largely derived from smell, the latter being the most powerful of the senses, evoking the strongest and most distinctive memory. Scents are omnipresent in the environment; for example, Lush and Body Shop scent their shops, making them instantly recognisable on entering the premises. Aromas can cover a wide spectrum, from minty and floral to musky and acrid – some appeal whilst others repulse, and females react differently to scents than men.

To sum up this complicated chapter, a verse from Ruth Finnegan's book captures many of the design questions that are asked when considering the various sources in creating an organisation's image, both in the real world and online:

> *Shape by size, colour, height, texture, materials, details, decorations;*
> *Spaces by size, shape, barriers, entrances, enclosing elements, links;*
> *Colour by hue, saturation, brightness, shade;*
> *Period and artistic styles as modern, traditional, retro, Victorian;*
> *Quality by noisy, quiet, dead, reverberant;*
> *Human made by music, talk, laughter, traffic, industry;*
> *Natural by birds, animals, water, trees, wind, rain.*

(Finnegan, 2002)

11.7   Style Manual

After the final design is chosen from a selection of designs, a style manual is compiled, this being necessary for future reproduction and design changes. Style manuals manage *coherence* of the CVIS elements in traditional media. In the real world, style manuals ensure repeat order consistency applied to printed material and artefacts, ensuring that the visual identity elements, logos, colour and typography are scalable and appropriate to the media. Cascading style sheets perform a similar role for website designs. Some companies keep a strict style guide to which every building and product has to adhere and others maintain the essential design. The overall appearance has to be recognisable – Table 11.3 illustrates the standard requirements. There are many ways in which this can be compiled: hard copy or website – an electronic book where text, images (both still and video), sound (both background and music) and web links for further information can be collated; or a website designed specifically for the purpose, with key excerpts. However, as this is a key reference point for the company and its CVIS, it is often kept under lock and key.

Table 11.3   An illustration of the standard style manual requirements

Element	Example
Company information	Description of the company and its business sector, contact details, history, size, products, services, ethos and philosophy, distinguishing features – alternative, specialist, friendly
Logo	What it represents, the message being communicated and how this meets the design brief; Name, typefaces, corporate colour with Pantone; Example of logo in corporate colours, black and white and reversal, Smallest possible scale size in dpi, and further logo guidelines
Colour	Mood and atmosphere that the colour section creates, Pantone colours to be applied in print, interiors and exteriors
CVIS	How this is to be applied on artefacts, signs, vehicles and uniforms
Stationery	Letterheads, compliment slips, business cards, envelope design; font for text and type of paper
Website	Layout, colours and tone for logos and corporate branding of homepage and content webpages
Corporate communications	Annual reports, videos for digital displays and website

Conclusion

Within business there are many situations where visual identity has to be considered strategically and operationally. Strategically the corporate visual identity system (CVIS) creates a unique image that clearly distinguishes the business's existence and its position in the marketplace. There are key business change situations when a new identity has to be created: firstly, on its initial formation – the business owner/CEO and designer have a blank piece of paper to work on, this being the preferred work approach for designers as they can use their distinctive intelligence and skills in the creation of a new company and its image; secondly, when a merger and acquisition occurs and a new business entity has to be created; thirdly, when a new identity or brand may be required resulting from technological advances or legal requirements, whereupon a company and/or its products and services have to be repositioned in the marketplace.

The creative process has to source a relevant story from the company archive and create an identity around this to communicate the new market position and the message to be communicated, based on the CEO's vision and mission for the company. Some companies have a long history upon which to base or retrieve relevant information for the designer; other businesses are new or have a previously unrecognised aspiration. In the latter case, a story can be created. Based on this material, themewords are selected and agreed upon by the designer and CEO. These themewords facilitate the creation of a creative style which is a key market discriminator, such as: is the theme establishment or alternative? Then an artistic style has to be found, for example, minimalist or flamboyant.

It is against this backdrop that the CVIS is formed. Consideration of the environments and artefacts upon which the CVIS has to be put then occurs as this can impact the design specification and output. The CVIS elements of name, logo, fonts, colour and straplines are then cogitated and concepts sketched. Discussions are based on these sketches, the latter forming a record of the CVIS's design development. Mock-ups are then prepared. Then individual CVIS elements have to be formed and legally registered. The CVIS elements being:

- Names are critical as it can say much about the organisation. Often the company name and product are the same, such as in Mars chocolate bars and company. Particular care is required in the creation of domain names as they have wider geographical implications.

- Typography, fonts and colour are key style indicators, defining the market sector and often an era by the type of writing instrument used and by the lettering style, such as calligraphy or digital print. Digital type is created by digital graphic software and can be used to create logotypes, hierarchical content and visual pacing.

- Logos are a badge of identification and quality that facilitate an observer's recognition of the business. Logos can indicate a fresh start or change in direction for a company, such as BP's heliograph. Scaling logos is important as they have to be fixed to a wide range of media, including websites. If the logo is small, type may not be legible. Online screen display technology has dramatically improved, particularly with retina screen where pixilation is invisible to the naked eye.

- straplines may not be necessary but are useful in communicating the company's goals or ethos.

The final image is what you see at numerous direct and incidental touchpoints, each time reinforcing the company's continued existence and how it is adapting to trends and locations.

What should the business look like?

Once the business idea is established – market position, location and how the business organisation is going to operate – and you have the finances in place, the CVIS can be allocated a budget and the creative design process begins. The CVIS name, logo, colour, fonts and slogan are designed to ensure that the business has a unique presence in the market; then prospective customers will immediately recognise and relate to the business values. Today this is called brand as businesses move online. The combination of various elements – an abstract or descriptive name, distinctive logo, fonts for posters and stationery, clear representative colours and slogan if appropriate – provides an interesting focus for all the business activities, defining its function, aesthetic and atmosphere.

Chapter 12

Symbolism –
Organisational Behaviour

*What personality should the business
project and how should it feel?*

Introduction

Corporate identity's symbolic organisational behaviour looks internally at the organisation's distinctive ethos and way of working, separate from the common understanding of corporate identity as visual identity that communicates through graphic design. This chapter looks at what contributes to organisational behaviour – its personality, then the components that contribute to the creation of a corporate culture, proceeding on to the changing nature of business, through its organisation and networks. Thereafter we consider the necessity for having a cultural thread running through the business operations as employees have differing views on what work is and should be across all age groups. Finally, we address how digital communication is impacting culture and how organisational behaviour is developing online, especially through social media communication.

12.1 Business Personality and Process

Organisational behaviour gained increasing recognition in the mid 1980s as the design and public relations industries began to use communication and behavioural techniques. Organisational behaviour is defined as the organisation's essence and central characteristic that builds distinctiveness over time (Albert and Whetten, 1985). Business and academic research established how organisations communicate internally and externally and now encompasses an ever-increasing range of topics. Initially the personality of the founder or the CEO would define the cultural characteristics, creating a personality for the organisation. Recruitment was often based on congruence between the organisation's values and those being employed. Today there are a range of engagement criteria in the wider sense of the word, with an explosion of subjects related to cultural development and communications systems, each having their own authoritative experts and authors, as the organisation evolves and adapts to competitive environmental events.

12.1.1 CORPORATE PERSONALITY REVELATION

The *essence* can be construed as the cultural thread running through an organisation – its personality. This impacts all its business functions and processes (see Figure 6.2), including: visual identity communication; ergonomic design of the working environment; comfortable uniforms suitable for the task; streamlined production and service designed to meet employee and customer satisfaction; inspection of products so that the friction of returns does not arise; recruitment of staff who align with the corporate ethos, being well versed in how the company operates, in particular conversing with people at all levels of the organisation, customers and suppliers; CEOs and boards who know how the internet and social media are impacting their business and can connect with staff, customers and suppliers with intelligence and eloquence, both in real life and online. The list is endless.

A corporate personality is revealed when all of these features arise. Wally Olins (1978) first recognised this analogy and practitioners have used it ever since. This organisational persona can best be illustrated by human identity metaphors related to business settings and situations. For example:

- Personality provides distinctiveness, connecting an organisation's attitudes and beliefs with its internal organisational identity to the concept of corporate culture (Balmer, 2001; Balmer and Wilson, 1998; Van Riel and Balmer, 1997).

- Soul is subjective elements comprising business identity and personnel values that find expression in organisational cultures and identity types (Balmer and Soenen, 1999).

- Spirit is the organisation's values and spirit, mind and body responses it evokes from key stakeholder groups (Steidl and Emory, 1997).

- Mind is the conscious decisions made by an organisation supported by its ethos, vision, strategy and product performance. Another version is how the organisation's philosophy and strategy secures customer support.

- Voice is the organisation's communication channel internally and externally to stakeholder groups and networks. This voice now has a range of channels that can converse with many audiences simultaneously and temporally.

- Body is the infrastructure necessary to operate the business, the physical environment and the communication and people networks that develop and sustain the business.

12.2   Corporate Cultural Analysis and Recognition

12.2.1   CORPORATE CULTURE THROUGH STORIES

Corporate culture – through rituals, stories and history – characterises how company activities are achieved and recorded for the group's experience and learning as they adapt to external and internal environmental conditions. The interactions that happen during storytelling and rituals can highlight differing identity traits, depending on who is speaking and who is listening. Tonal voice inclinations and body language can add so much more to a message, usually only recognisable to the same cultural members (Czarniawska-Joerges, 1994). Through the passage of time, this builds up the organisation's cultural identity which evolved around socio-economic, political and technological events.

12.2.2   IDENTITY AND INDIVIDUALITY

Identity has become a subject in itself (see sections 5.1, 5.2 and 5.3), as the internet develops and where countries, companies and products are required to differentiate themselves. Companies have to understand how to create their individual identity, by capturing stories that express the business's purpose and strengths (see Chapter 5). Olins (1989) suggested that, if a company begins to lose its sense of identity and individuality, then mistakes occur which could result in deviations from the corporate strategy. Commercial success is therefore based on corporate culture, its organisational leadership, values and sub-cultural groups (Melewar and Karaosmanoglu, 2006).

Corporate culture is fundamental to a company's organisational behaviour – a major part of Balmer's *Actual* identity (see Figure 2.2). An organisation can have multiple identities: Balmer's 1994 study at the BBC found that a cohesive corporate identity was not achieved easily, despite organisational commitment to the subject. At one time differing ideologies within an organisation could be managed. Railway companies introduced corporate livery and employee conduct codes in the nineteenth century, not just to differentiate themselves in the marketplace but to form a cohesive cultural entity that employees were proud to work for, thereby contributing to the organisation's success.

12.2.3   ORGANISATIONAL FUNCTION AND NETWORKS

Communication of a company's culture is often determined by the manner in which the organisation functions. According to Deleuze's theory (Deleuze and Guattari, 1988), the term *machinism* addresses where the organisation is seen as a set of potential connections between elements and the environment. He proposed two analogies relevant to organisations: trees and rhizomes. Trees are the traditional hierarchical mode with a vertical, hierarchical structure: root, trunk and branches. This tree structure still exists in many corporate organisations. Rhizomes are fluid structures similar to modern organisations, operating in a different milieu of nodes and networks, where growth occurs in a horizontal, decentralised network capable of growth from a node without a central trunk. This is similar to the internet, which has been developing as a social structure by Web 2.0 communication. This fluid social structure can be applied to the creation of corporate design where practitioners with particular skillsets are employed on a project basis. Bennet (2002) demonstrated this by her network of designers located globally, who commented on whether a design was culturally acceptable to a particular location. Today this method of collaborative working has become commonplace.

12.3   Fluid Business Networks

As communication and business networks become more fluid, so identity evolves to accommodate technological and the resultant socio-economic and political events. Stories are told, blogs written and Twitter messages, TV programmes and films made. Managing a single company voice or multiple company voices is a difficult job as social media communication *spreads the word*. There is such a load of data and information that identity sociologists and anthropologists of the digital future will be swamped, that is, unless they develop another technology that can cope with it. Back to humans, it is the subtleties and inflections that adapt identity features as they evolve (Gioia, Schultz and Corley, 2000; Balmer and Greyser, 2003), regardless of whether this communication network is a market stall or a multinational/global company.

A change of emphasis from product brands to services and experience marketing has encouraged further development of organisational behaviour. In the 1970s Dame Anita Roddick of Body Shop and Sir Richard Branson of Virgin, and in the 1990s Innocent, established their businesses with a *good story* as their marketing thread. What they had identified was that, apart from the product and perhaps some added value with packaging, there was more to shopping for toiletries, flying and fruit drinks. Customers wanted a service and to feel that they were contributing to society. Body Shop introduced refills if you brought in your old bottles; Virgin launched subsidiary companies in a range of sectors: banking, bridal wear, cosmetics, new media communications; and Innocent started to hold competitions to knit hats for their fruit drink bottles, with contributions going to *Help the Aged*. So the identity of these three businesses was evolving with the times. Subsequently, in the new millennium customers wanted to know more about the company and *experience* how their product was made, see the factory, have their hair cut or get a manicure in flight.

This opened up more business opportunities as the organisation and its behaviour interacted with the evolving business environments. Customers wanted to experience and know what these organisations looked like, how they operated, how products were made and services provided. So Bodyshop, now with its worldwide shops and franchises, maintained its corporate identity and image, yet still had to adapt to the local geographical cultures and its identity characteristics – while maintaining the brand personality – each of which had the potential to provide stories and information on new product sources that customers would buy. Increasing travel meant that tourists could buy their familiar toiletries and cosmetics, knowing the brand values. Back in the UK, a showroom opened explaining the processes and distribution network. So from a shop in Brighton a global brand emerged, with its image and behavioural features based on an environmental identity.

Virgin expanded in a similar manner but here each company had its own visual identity, albeit with the same corporate shade of red but differing fonts and additions to the name related to the new business function. The business started in the media sector and diversified into a wide range of businesses, from airlines to cosmetics. When the internet appeared, Virgin became and remains one of the UK's key players, keeping their website design within the business so that they controlled the corporate *heart and face* of their business. Virgin

Airlines has the flexibility to be innovative, for example, introducing one of the first flat beds for long-haul flights and Virgin lounges, where travellers could relax whilst waiting or between flights. Although the company has invested in and divested a wide range of businesses, it has still maintained a casual, yet forward-thinking theme, with new ideas and innovative approaches being a key instrument in their successful business enterprises.

As the healthy drink company Innocent expanded and employed more people, the Woolly Hat event continues annually, with the knitting pattern on the internet. New marketing ploys appeared as they tackled larger ventures to bring in further brand affiliation to the business through an identity they knew and understood: the English village fair. The experiential event for Innocent was taking the village fair into the centre of London through the annual Regent's Park Village Fair event, with stalls of healthy food, drink and entertainment.

12.4   An Intellectual Property Company

Each of these three businesses – Bodyshop, Virgin and Innocent – have an original identity created around a story and theme, ensuring that all its internal and external stakeholders know the story and why the business is distinctive, enduring and full of character, changing with the times and market requirements – a psychological thread and purpose that engages both staff and customers. As the second decade of the twenty-first century advances, it is this engagement and retention of staff that has cultural implications. Deleuze's trees and rhizomes corporate structures exist but it is the demographics and ways of working that are changing organisational behaviour. Today there has to be a meeting of minds on the creation of the corporate brand which includes recruitment criteria, induction to the company and required expectations, training course specifications and delivery, and appraisals through to exit interview. Today there is an increasing likelihood that potential employees and companies negotiate employment contracts and conditions, in particular where skills are in short supply in fast-moving sectors. Additionally, attitudes to work have altered within various age groups, where over 55-year-olds still want or need to work as the average lifespan increases, and the young wish to be treated as equals or have flexible working, and if they are not happy, they leave (Rosethorn and Contributors, 2009).

Today a website is often the first impression of an organisation that a prospective customer will have, so design of the website homepage aesthetic and overall functionality is paramount. Organisational behaviour is different in this domain, mediated by technological filters and legal territories that set the standard on what is acceptable and unacceptable within a society or company. The brand experience begins with the first click on the homepage, followed by the user's experience whilst conducting a search or transaction on a well laid-out gestalt and aesthically pleasing image. Comparison with further branded products and service websites is inevitable, so it is important to recognise organisational behaviour as it crosses from the online experience to the real world, with order selection and delivery to the home or office, and the occasional shop visit which in itself is becoming the *shopping experience*. Every event and occurrence can be recorded in text or film, elaborating the circumstances and telling stories. Increasingly social media has a plethora of stories and anecdotes that are creating the organisation's digital identity. So the online presence now matters just as much as the real world as stories garnered from social media have to be carefully screened for reliability.

Conclusion

To conclude, regardless of the corporate communication medium, the business organisational behaviour has to run through all its networks to ensure that it functions effectively and is recognised by stakeholders. Having a strong company personality and story allows staff to understand their roles, and the standard and attitude that they are expected to maintain at work. As companies now have to operate across wide geographical areas and have employees of varying ages and cultures, these rituals and guidelines become even more important. These features ensure that the business maintains its identity and individuality which differentiates its operations in the marketplace.

What personality should the business project and how should it feel?

A business should have a core *personality* that pervades its operations, making it clearly distinctive in the marketplace and through time. This can be accomplished by training through stories and ensuring that company rituals and routines are maintained. By ensuring that everyone knows and adheres to the business standards and ethos, this effectively allows the business to operate successfully. Customers and stakeholders will then understand how the business works and identify with its operations. Today, through social media, when customers like the business they can become advocates, thereby advertising the business and its personality.

Part IV Summary
Navigating Symbolic Practice

What Has Happened So Far?

In Part IV we looked at the symbols applied through visual identity and organisational behaviour with the intention of creating an image that differentiates a business in its marketplace. Chapter 10 explained the importance of communicating the required aesthetic and the necessity of having the AC²ID identity terms in alignment. Thereafter the designer selection and website gestalt were introduced to ensure that the corporate story was clearly depicted and communicated, this being of increasing relevance within the developing digital environment. In Chapter 11 the creative process was considered, from the initial point of receiving the design brief and having it approved, to ensuring that the designer had been given all the necessary background information and *themewords* that inform a design *style* selection or creation. The next step is the CVIS creation by way of its five elements: name, logo, typography, colours and straplines. Chapter 12 considered the organisation's personality and culture with 'organisational behaviour being the essence and central characteristic that distinguishes an organisation through time' (Albert and Whetten, 1985).

What Have We Learnt in this Section?

The visual aesthetic and gestalt communicate a corporate image and message. It is important that the message received by a prospective customer is instantly recognisable so that its significance registers with the viewer. If dissonance occurs between the customer's conceived image and the business's actual image, in that case there is misalignment which has to be rectified. This is why visual communication design is important. Symbolic communication includes both visual identity and organisational behaviour, as it provides an indication of the market positioning, company structure and branded products. To start the creative design process, the corporate ethos and philosophy provide an indication of the organisation's values, beliefs and attitudes and how staff are expected to behave, internally and externally, whilst conducting their business roles and duties. Throughout, stories and historical accounts that characterise how the company's activities exist become a key source of the organisation's identity.

Visual communication through designed elements finds or creates a *design style* that communicates the market *position*. *Themewords* provide foci for image creation through *visual identity* elements; for example, a name is selected or formulated, fonts are formed, logos are created, a colour is chosen, and sometimes a strapline is added. This creates a unique identity in business and design terms, applicable to both websites and traditional media. One constraint to market differentiation is that often the first thought that springs to mind is stereotypical, instantaneously categorising people and groups. This should be avoided as the organisation itself has to convey a unique image so that it is instantly recognisable both offline and online.

Consequently, on observing an organisation, a visitor is assimilating a wide range of static and dynamic features that corporate design creates through images and other sentient features. Traditionally, in the real world, observers perceive corporate image slowly through discrete mechanisms, such as print, buildings or on TV, each having their own design process, media, tools and skills with specific features. Online a website has a screen with an arranged gestalt of text and imagery, and now access points to social media conversations. How the aesthetic appears – that is, how beautiful this image is – depends on the artistic and creative abilities of the design team.

Having a strong company story and personality ensures that its identity and differential characteristics are formulated and maintained through time. Today these features are becoming even more important as businesses increase in geographical extent and have wide networks of business connections through social media. Hence organisational behaviour has to be instilled and reinforced through induction and training programmes that highlight the necessity of staff rituals, attitudes and approaches to work by employees from all the various cultures and backgrounds that comprise a business organisation.

What Will Part V Encapsulate?

Up to this point we have recognised the necessity to communicate an image for the market position within which the CEO wishes the company and/

or its products and services to be placed, this being achieved by defining corporate and design strategies that create the corporate identity: image and/or brand. Identity is created by storytelling and, through various perceptions and perspectives, an image is created that communicates a coherent message by symbolic visual identity and organisational behaviour elements. So this appears to cover the subject – or so it would seem.

In the early 1990s this would have been the case. Regardless of the CEO's PEEST factors, the designer's STEEP factors or organisational SWOT analyses, few would have recognised the rapid development of the internet – nationally, internationally or globally – and the world's acceptance of websites as a necessary business communication medium. Part V investigates the impact of the internet and of business being conducted through websites that have to be designed.

Part V

Digital Corporate Design

Websites have become the first point of contact for prospective customers and clients. Digital advances and social acceptance of them have become part of daily life, with all generations browsing, googling, twittering, facebooking and blogging. Having a digital design strategy became a corporate necessity as technology advanced during the last decade and became firmly accepted.

Part V will look at the design inputs to a website primarily from the gestalt and aesthetic viewpoint. Much is written about functionality, social implications and legal cases; here the subject is the website contribution to a company's corporate design strategy, communicating its digital marketplace. Three topics are considered:

1. What value a website will bring to a business by its content and devices This addresses: strategic position of the business brand and brands online; the website value exchange between customers and the business; how a website is initiated by the website design brief and designer selection; and finally, the evolution of digital technology and devices enabling better communication platforms.

2. The image created by the homepage aesthetic and gestalt by looking at how a real-world corporate design *look, feel* and *attitude* is created online. This takes time strategically and operationally to create the CVIS that digitally positions a business through online visual identity and organisational behaviour elements that appear on the homepage.

3. Social media has dramatically increased two-way communication and advocacy of companies and products. As these platforms have developed, their most effective and efficient usage is emerging and

is now a key communication channel for business and personal use. Here six popular social media platforms are discussed: Facebook – a college project which expanded worldwide, used by artists and designer businesses; Twitter – commentaries, alerts, general information in 140 characters; blogs – web diaries of events and other occurrences and information; LinkedIn – a professional business network; YouTube – videos; and Pinterest – to gather ideas and suggestions for storyboards and moodboards. They appear on most websites, with some becoming key business communication channels.

Part V of the book includes:

Chapter 13   Digital Branding Strategy

Chapter 14   Designed Website Content

Chapter 15   The Social Business

Chapter 13
Digital Branding Strategy

*Do I need a website and what does
it contribute to the business?*

Introduction

This chapter on digital branding strategy considers online strategic positioning of a business, the strategic value exchange and how corporate design has progressed from the real-world corporate identity version to the online corporate brand approach. Next we look at how brand messages are perceived and how online marketing has become consumer-centric. Thereafter we consider the business's main driver for having a website and homepage content requirements that position a business in its online market. Finally we look at how digital device developments are currently impacting corporate design.

13.1   Strategic Positioning Online

When a website downloads, viewers instantly gain an impression of the company, its market *position* and segment, this being perceived by the website aesthetic quality. Additionally, the quality and reliability of products, services and distribution can similarly be perceived by innovative and intuitive website design. Designers aggregate content to promote the organisation's brands or the corporate brand *positioning* online by three mechanisms: download speed; applications that ease navigation, accessibility and information searches; and the designed gestalt and aesthetic by text and imagery. For example, <www.mercedes.com> indicates its market *position* through these techniques. Clear informative homepage design, created by relevant imagery, menus and linkage to pertinent information, convey an impression on one computer screen. Mercedes' real-world showroom at Brookwood, near Weybridge, UK, is in a location with strong historical technology links and high personal wealth. When the website and showroom are compared, the website *reveals* online a similar market *position* as its offline presence, thereby providing a consistent and coherent corporate design image and message that ultimately impacts on the company's reputation and financial market position.

13.1.1   STRATEGIC VALUE EXCHANGE

In the digital world the value exchange is satisfying the organisation's goals by driving visitors to the website through supplying content that clearly differentiates the business online. Here the emphasis is changing to corporate and product or service brands where online differentiation is achieved by answering the questions: *Who are you? What do you require?* and *Why is this product important to you*? Referring back to corporate identity, remember that the essential questions were: Who are you? What do you do? How do you do it? And where do you want to go? (Olins, 1995). These questions relate to the overall personality of the organisation – the *self*. A website that achieves the customer goals and the company's expectations is important, so that viewers know that they have accessed the required company's website and homepage, whether this be on a laptop, tablet or mobile device.

The organisation's branded message must project four aspects:

1.   *Position* in the marketplace by differential concept and strategy by PEEST, STEEP and SWOT analyses.

2.   *Coherent* communication of the corporate message strategically and operationally across all media platforms by symbolic representation.

3.   *Coherent* ethos, spirit and attitude, with staff working to the same shared standard.

4.   Attractive and informative *content* that is current and relevant to the customer's requirement.

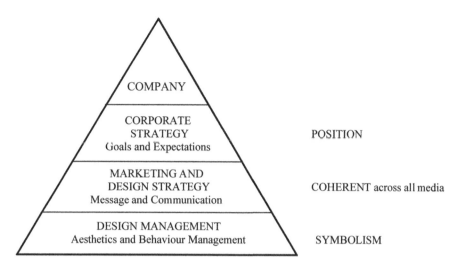

Figure 13.1   Corporate design pyramid across corporate design and creative strategy and management

13.1.2   A UNIQUE CONCEPT AND IMAGE

As each new company now has to differentiate itself online by creating a branded product or service, the image that appears online is vital. A brand concept that clearly differentiates the business and has an aesthetically designed website that communicates and engages with stakeholders will attract business, regardless of whether this is in the real-world operation or its online counterpart. If there is a lot of competition in the sector then the brand will have to find its niche by focusing on a particular or special product or aspect. When you look at a website, is it captivating, attractive, appealing, frightening, fascinating, pleasant? All of these adjectives can be applied to the website design strategy and process. There are various strategies in developing a brand but the outcome is the same – to be the most sought after brand, so that you can charge a premium for your products and services. Brand extension can be applied to strengthen a brand in its market but this has to be part of a clearly defined objective to ensure that the extension will perform over the long term and increasingly add value; otherwise it can devalue the original brand. Brand value is created when the market price is over and above the cost of making and servicing the product and normal profit margins for the sector.

Heal's homepage and website content is minimal to display products to their best advantage.

Harry Potter may have started as a book but marketing and branding has produced many market extensions all the way through, with digital spin-offs – films, websites, theme tunes, mobile phone jingles and *howling* sounds, and of course computer games – not to mention the conversion of an old film studio for the Harry Potter *real-world* experience. Then there is all the hardware necessary to view this media: smartphones, tablets, PCs, Nintendo, and gameboxes. Branding also impacts suppliers to the company. Do links take users to sites that they would associate with that product or service's market sector's quality and reliability?

13.1.3   MEANING IN BRAND MESSAGES

On viewing a website, the user applies a meaning and value system to the content. Memory and cognitive processes influence the person's psyche where meaning is communicated by cognitive triggers based on the viewer's experience, knowledge, societal and cultural values. Essentially the cognitive process triggers a signification system by interaction of the subject (user) and the object (website) (see Figure 13.2).

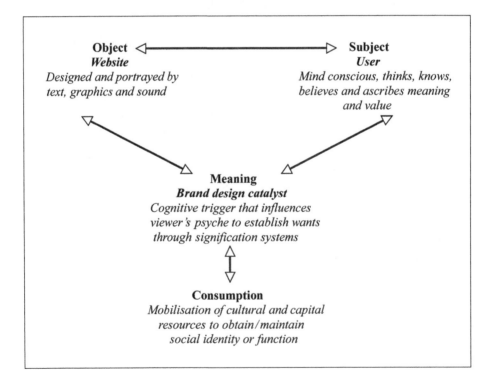

Figure 13.2   Marketing brand meaning

Baudrillard showed that semiological analysis could reveal a system of signs that permits users to differentiate populations and cultures. Hence a website design strategy has to ensure that the appropriate meaning is communicated, as this varies across individuals and groups spatially, contextually and temporally, and cannot be taken for granted.

13.2   Consumer-Centric Branding Online

Online marketing has now moved towards becoming more consumer-centric through *what you feel* the product or service can provide you, allowing the individual to define *who they are*, as opposed to what a product or service features are and what it does; hence the emphasis on branding online. Previously a brand's *unique selling proposition* was the general marketing approach. Today Edward de Bono has suggested that attention ought to be placed on the customer and their *unique buying state*. By this approach the consumer can be attached to a group of people that they wish to be a part of; for example, sporting brands such as Nike and Adidas that many athletes use and therefore many young people, a prospective market, aspire to buying. Depending on your lifestyle activities, the mood you are in or the situation you find yourself in, there is a brand (Neumeier, 2006). To ensure a unique differential impact, there has to be a clear focus on what the brand stands for and why you will want to buy its products or services. Today branding is customer-centric and what the customer thinks and says about the brand – both offline and online through social media – matters. Customers can now be brand advocates advertising products and services by commentary – essentially free advertising for the company – partially taking on the company's marketing role.

13.2.1   PERCEPTION AND MEANING IN BRAND MESSAGES

Perception of a business is now immediate on a computer display screen through sight, sound and brain. Both sight and brain perceive the differences that appear on the website homepage gestalt – that is, the relationship between text and image. Sight recognises the aesthetics – that is, how beautiful something looks – and provides a feeling about the organisation which can be of greater value than text; a picture paints a thousand words still applies. The brain makes meaning by cognition of what is relevant and irrelevant. Often when something seems to be out of place or character, whether visually or behaviourally, we become suspicious.

13.2.2 WEBSITE GRAPHIC DESIGN, AESTHETICS AND GESTALT

Digital aesthetics emerged as a humanities research field when it became apparent that new web technology was being applied to display non-informational work, for example, digital art, literature and games. Then a number of researchers started to address interactive behaviour to progress the subject beyond usability (Blythe et al., 2003; Norman, 2004; Enghom, 2002b), while Udsen and Jorgensen (2005) called this research *the aesthetic turn.*

Udsen and Jorgensen (2005) identified four key aesthetic approaches in digital media: cultural, functionalist, experience-based and techno-futurist. The cultural and functionalist approaches are important to corporate website design. Engholm's classification suggests a non-informational tradition within humanities. On the other hand, it could be argued that the term *non-informational* is a misnomer as, whatever the interface, a website visitor will still perceive some *information* regardless of whether the image is in textual or image format.

Quantifying user experience and analysing aesthetics on the basis of beauty, emotion and taste is subjective. Urmson (1957) suggested that evaluations could be made based on how an object looks or sounds – the audiovisual aesthetic – rather than on how it is constructed, similar to the Kantian idea of aesthetic judgment which is concerned with appearance. Desmet (2004) and Norman (2004) applied the term *emotional design.* To show this progression through time and design theory developments, the following example of *pats or packs of butter* is applied. In the late 1950s/early 1960s, a large *round* of butter would be for sale in the grocery and customers would request a quantity, which would be cut from the *butter round* by wooden spatulas and covered by paper or a bag that might have a grocer's name on it – a purely *functional* approach. Then in the 1960s and 1970s, *form* became important and oblong butter packs appeared that could be stored on a shop shelf. Today a product designer focuses on pleasurable and meaningful *experiences.* So butter can now be bought as a *pat,* denoting a premier traditional and natural product, or an *oblong pack,* denoting value for money. In both products the visual identity by text and imagery provides a wide range of marketing and food nutritional information which relates to people on a personal level. Here an interaction occurs between the object – that is, butter – and a customer's personal goals, attitudes and standards.

Digital aesthetic is becoming an increasingly competitive tool for CEOs as they look beyond having a website presence (Foo, 2006) to something that actively engages and evokes emotional responses from website visitors, not just by the website aesthetic but also through social communication and a strong presence on the internet. Chajet (1989) indicated that, in the late 1980s, constructing an identity meant keeping the identity solid and stable. Today the situation is completely different, where the problem of identity is how to avoid being fixed by keeping options open – a mask that can change according to context or whim; essentially what happens with many websites and their designs.

Communicating a digital gestalt (a visual combination of text and image) requires greater collaborative effort. Traditionally, graphic designers used culturally derived signs, symbols and texts that were culturally appropriate to the audience. With a global audience, these could be misinterpreted, hence an interim stage occurs where a suggested imagery is scrutinised for problematic occurrences which are then removed/altered, sometimes called usability tests. From conceptual ideas to production design, decisions can be made in virtual space by the design team through mark-up electronic documents and social media. Hence key to this new design process is that the client and audience contribute to the design gestalt and aesthetic early in the design process.

13.3   Website Design Considerations

13.3.1   WEBSITE BUSINESS DRIVER

The website business driver is a key business driver within a company's corporate strategy. This driver has to fulfil a goal, for example, to provide company information, e-commerce, news or financial information (see Figure 13.3). To convey their business activities online, companies employ a range of website design approaches. There may be one URL for the whole company with a series of tabs and menus for all the content on their operations, products, services, history, finance and recruitment. A company may have one URL with links to further branded websites, as in <www.diageo.com>, within the strategic brand link. News and media organisations use social media platforms; for example, the journalist Andrew Sullivan wrote one of the first blogs and continues to blog. E-commerce shopping began in earnest in Christmas 2007 when the under 30-year-old age group, those in remote areas and those incapacitated realised that they could buy and have presents delivered. Four of the most popular websites at that time were <www.boots.com>, <www.next.co.uk>, <www.marksandspencers.com> and <www.kingfisher.com>. Companies then had to build integrated offline back offices and vehicular distribution systems with new branding, for example, Ocado online food shopping associated with Waitrose. Tesco retained their corporate visual identity system (CVIS) in their offline distribution system. Throughout,

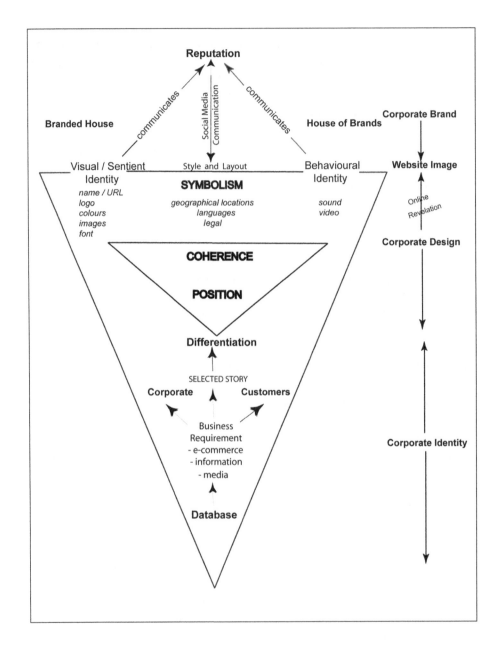

Figure 13.3   Corporate Design Triangle 3 – website business terms
and drivers with CVIS elements flows and linkages

the key design features of each organisation's market position and expected lifestyle requirement had to be conveyed by their website's quality, reliability and innovativeness.

Heal's e-commerce is part of the website, being used as a mechanism to drive sales into the store and through the website.

13.3.2 WEBSITE OBJECTIVES

Before looking at homepage content, a number of key points apply to all websites' requirements:

1. Suitable content scope by breadth and depth of website architecture.

2. Context-specific information in the relevant language and tone.

3. Intuitive navigation with information displayed by levels of importance and necessary action.

4. Actively managed content with timely relevant updates on what is happening that day.

5. Quick graphic download; minimal sound and video; small chunk of information with minimal distractions.

6. Clear social media icons to encourage comment and response.

7. Relevant legal and regulatory information.

8. Innovative concepts that drive people to the website and linger, so that they become familiar with its content.

9. What are the contingencies for future developments?

13.4 Website Designers and Developments

13.4.1 WEBSITE DESIGN BRIEF

A website design brief starts a project by establishing the themed message or thread that runs through all the organisation's corporate communications. Website design lifecycles follow a similar evolution as other services and have to be included in design change programmes, whether this be repositioning the business in a different market sector or segment, or change of design style after a merger or takeover. As with any design project, suitable website designers need to be selected; communication is key, hence all website design team members have to converse continuously; essential skillsets and knowledge have to be current, so training is important; clear management lines and well-organised information systems are required; and as website projects become more complicated, with more collaborative efforts, there have to be shared goals and commitment to resolve problems quickly.

13.4.2 DESIGNER SELECTION

Website designers can be split into three groups:

1. Cognitive designers who work on the human–computer interface, studying attention, behaviour and interface, similar to industrial designers. These humanists provide overall website and digital media usability and ergonomics, researching and implementing the information and entertainment requirements. Their backgrounds can include psychology, human factors, marketing and anthropology.

2. Artists who provide the personality and voice, branding and aesthetic images, their backgrounds being in industrial design, visual communications, computer graphics, photography, literature, communications and fine art.

3. Structural designers and technologists who provide the information architecture and functionality by translating engineering into design terms, prototyping and providing specifications as they do with the functional aspects of any other product. Their backgrounds can be in mechanics, electronics-, CAD engineering and computer science.

What to reveal and how to reveal? Website content is often dependent on advances in the designer skillset, perception and ability to transfer a concept into a digital format. Viewers perceive the quality, reliability and innovativeness of a company and its products by the completed gestalt and aesthetic. Figure 13.4 illustrates the development of a corporate identity and image by its ethos and corporate story, to enable the business to be differentiated in the marketplace by market *positioning*, designed *symbolism*, and *coherence* applied across all the media applications.

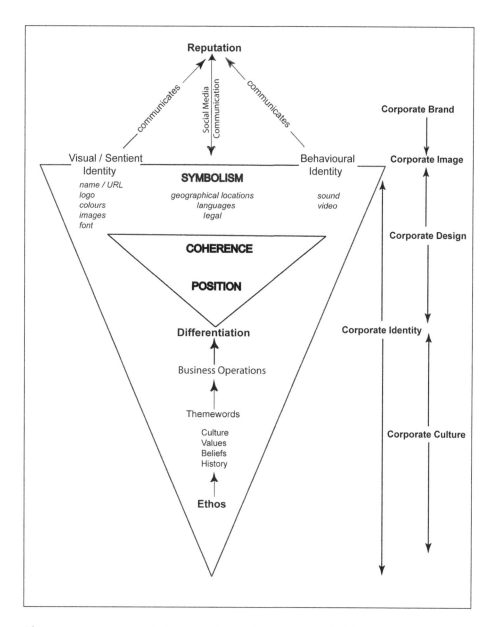

Figure 13.4   Corporate Design Triangle 4 – corporate identity/brand
image sourced through business ethos and stories

13.5   Digital Devices Hardware

There is a wide range of digital devices that act as the interface between digital content and content users. The pace of change in this technology has advanced amazingly quickly: in the 1990s Web 1.0 computers and the internet were developing; in the 2000s Web 2.0 social media communication appeared; and now in the 2010s Web 3.0 is likely to appear.

13.5.1   COMMUNICATION DEVICES

Communication between hardware designers, software designers, manufacturers and early adopters of technology has progressed transmission and presentation devices used to transmit information between sender and receiver to responsive artefacts with the ability to interact with systems. Initially these conversations began with newsgroups and emails, then texts and recently social media groups, which allows groups to be formed for specific developmental projects. There may be many fads with early adopter gadgets falling by the wayside. Yet in the last ten years we have seen mobile phones – integrated with texts, video clips and cameras – becoming smartphones with applications on every conceivable subject that can also be downloaded onto PCs, Macs and tablets such as the iPad. Head and eye movement or sound can also activate these devices, this being predominantly useful to people who are incapacitated. Today the majority of people use tablets and mobile devices on a daily basis, with smartphone communications being the most popular communication method, and a digital communication watch now being the current fashion accessory.

Of course there is other hardware that shows digital content, such as information and advertising boards in bus and railway stations and airports, and car dashboards have a wide range of digital devices, with integrated communication device and mobile phone attachments. Each of these designed devices has to be accepted in the marketplace and targeted to a relevant demographic in the market sector. If mobile phone retailers are taken as an example, the range of phones and their functionality is incredible, but one of the main problems with many of these phones is *feature creep* – a manufacturer's problem where more functions are loaded onto gadgets. Consumers then have a learning process of menus, windows, clicking, dragging, pinching and swiping, or whatever other action or gesture is required to establish which function is relevant and useful to their lifestyle.

13.5.2 DISPLAY SCREENS

Computer and telephone screens display content by form and colours, the clarity of each image being displayed though resolution and colour. Resolution is the number of slots within which pixels – these being dots of colour – are displayed. If there are 300 slots per inch, then the screen is said to have 300 dpi. Colour is created by red, green and blue light discharged at various intensities into the square pixel. If none of these colours is discharged, then the resultant effect is black. If all three appear, then the effect is white. About 16 million colour combinations, created by the 256 levels of red, green and blue light intensity, are possible. To create one colour, 256 intensity levels × three colours are required, that being 24 bits in total.

Computer screens have advanced in recent years, with the Mac Professional providing good quality image, video, sound and tactile properties favoured by designers and artists. PCs are favoured by businesses as their functionality and cost are more acceptable to them. Recently the retina display screen appeared, this being the brand name of an Apple LCD high-definition screen where the human eye is unable to notice pixilation at a typical viewing distance relative to the size of the device, for instance, iPhone, iPod Touch, iPad and MacBookPro. Smaller displays have higher 326ppi, whereas larger devices have 220ppi. These displays are manufactured by different suppliers.

13.5.3 SOUND

The interface between digital sound and the ear has been in existence for 60 years, when the first sound bite was transmitted by a computer. Today we can download music from the internet and listen to music on all the devices mentioned above: desktops, tablets and smartphones. Various types of sound – for example, music, natural and vehicular – can be heard on moving imagery, videos, e-books, games, cartoons or any other digital content. Large headphones were initially used, then smaller ear inserts, popularised by Apple products. Nevertheless larger headphones have made a resurgence in recent years with streamlined design. Fashion and design trends have always been part of digital development, and increasingly so as the choice of devices, communication platforms and applications become part of daily life and lifestyles.

13.5.4 TOUCH

Interaction by touch has seen the greatest advances in recent years with the Apple iPad retina screen display and the ability to expand and flick through webpages, download applications and books, and communicate by touching website icons connecting to social media sites. Interaction still occurs by a QWERTY keyboard and mouse on desktop and laptop computers. Again the tablet technology has integrated a pop-up QWERTY keyboard to be released and retracted at the touch of the graphic button on the tablet screen. Wireless drawing and painting pens are available – a development on earlier graphic tablets.

Conclusion

To conclude this chapter, the fast pace of digital and website design has necessitated constant vigilance by both company strategists and consumers alike. The value exchange has become an increasingly two-way process through social media, impacting all levels of the corporate design pyramid consisting of corporate strategy, corporate design strategy and design management. Yet the organisation branded message still has to be correctly *positioned, coherently* communicated through the corporate *visual identity* system (CVIS) and with attractive relevant content. Through these elements, the brand message and consumer perception converge. Webpages, in particular homepages, have to be aesthetically pleasing as they become the first impression of the business. Initially on Web 1.0, the text and imagery gestalt was the prime consideration. As corporate strategists began to understand the benefits of having a website and where they added value to the company, they began to realise that a website was a marketing and communication necessity where the aesthetic communicated gave the first impression of their business online. Hence the choice of website designers, whether cognitive, structural or digital artists and creative technologists, is paramount to ensuring a unique image that clearly communicates the corporate message and online market position. Web 2.0 social communication media now allows conversation with clear screen definition on an increasing range of tablets and smartphones.

Do I need a website and what does it contribute to the business?

In the business world, having a company website is expected. It has become the focus of internet communication, whether for displaying information or conducting e-commerce or social media conversations with two-way video. Websites have added another layer of business activity above the real world – or below (whichever manner you wish to view it). The dynamics between the two environments vary from one business to another. Some businesses prefer the real world with a small online presence while others prefer to conduct essentially all their work online. Other businesses have to use both, probably in equal measure; for example, Amazon may have a large website complex database, but it still has to have another real-world complex storage and distribution system for its books and other products that are distributed in the UK and worldwide.

Chapter 14
Designed Website Content

How is the business 'look and feel'
projected online?

Introduction

A website homepage provides the first impression of a company online and illustrates the website navigational structure and available information. This chapter looks at the website authoring software that is in popular usage. Then the page design gestalt of text and imagery selected to reflect the corporate brand's philosophy and message. Followed by a more detailed look at the tools that create an aesthetic, including styles and effects and the online CVIS elements of typeface and imagery. Finally, geographical social, cultural, political and physical aspects are addressed.

14.1   The Homepage: The Front Entrance

The homepage is the front entrance to a company online, providing a visitor's first impression, and can range in size from one page to complicated structures and databases. Every website has a homepage, regardless of the company or its size, which acts as an introduction to a company and its brand. A homepage summary approach is not new to information design, as analogies can be drawn between conventional narrative discourses and websites. Conventional summaries, for example, exordium and newspaper front pages, exist (Askehave and Nielsen, 2005). An exordium introduces a speech, signifying its structure and content, whilst identifying and promoting the speaker and the speech. Newspaper front pages and website homepage formats appear to have the same design elements – a CVIS, fonts and imagery that display columns of hierarchical content – but

Plate 14.1   Heal's homepage

differences do occur between content, form and layout. 'The homepage also displays an interesting mixture of promotional features intertwined with content information where for example pictures, sound, music and animation are combined with enticing summaries of web contents to make the user stay and explore the site' (Askehave and Nielsen, 2005). The second reason for addressing homepages is that they came into existence as a result of the World Wide Web, creating their own web-generated genre, quite distinct from any other offline applications, such as annual reports and corporate brochures. The key distinction is that website homepages are accessible by most people, in any location, at anytime, so long as they have the company URL or a search engine.

14.1.1 HOMEPAGE DESIGN DEVELOPMENT ISSUES

Three homepage design developments and issues should be mentioned to illustrate the complexity in creating one homepage. Firstly, whilst visualising (Tufte, 1997, 2005) and drawing the website design process for Corporate Design Triangles, it became apparent that in reality homepage designs were a pick and mix of text and image, both static and dynamic, selected by the designer to communicate a corporate story. Digital media creates a wide range of content possibilities – logos, text, photographs, videos, clip art, sketches, icons and sound (see Plate 14.1). These design elements are constantly being improved. Images, text and sound were and remain rendered through a range of software, for example, Adobe Creative Suite, that is, Photoshop, Illustrator, whereby graphic formats (.tiff, .jpeg, .gif and .bmp) create real-world expressions. The development of web authoring tools – for example, CSS, dynamic HTML, JavaScript, Flash – gave designers greater image flexibility by determining how designs appeared in browser software packages, for example, Adobe Dreamweaver.

Secondly, expert digital skillsets that cater for technical knowledge, cultural awareness and legal implications require a wide network of designers, whilst answering the questions: Does the design evoke the similar *look and feel* to entering the company shop or office? Does it need to? Does the company wish the website to be totally different from its real-world operations designed to cater for another part of their business operations? It is this knowledge and ability to select relevant design elements that test a designer's skill. Ultimately the image created has to engage with the target audience, clearly differentiating the brand in competitive markets.

Thirdly, problems do arise in digital expression, as the free flow of hand and mind that are part of conventional design are not so clear in the digital mode. A narrowing of the gap has occurred where interdisciplinary design training is happening. Art and design students, by virtue of their skills, focus on the aesthetics and on the act of creating a design, often forgetting that the design has to be applied to a web environment. IT students focus on functionality and take aesthetics to be secondary, as the latter is not taught on computing courses or in business schools. This could be a result of left brain–right brain approaches to work and life but the final result impacts what we all experience in daily life.

14.1.2 WEBSITE GRAPHIC DESIGN

A website as a designed communication of corporate brand requires selection of the best graphic design elements and assembling them so that the resultant emergent impression meets the company's specification and the stakeholders' and users' requirements. Usability, download speeds, accessibility and technical requirements for image optimisation and video clips have to be met. Only user testing can really determine if user specification fulfils stakeholder aims. There are two aspects to this. Firstly, assessments have to be made to determine whether the website is meeting users' needs on an ongoing basis:

- Where will users be accessing the website – at home, when mobile or at work?

- User ability and disabilities

- Different levels of web experience and education

- Relevant attitudes of the audience as a result of their age range, gender ratio, culture/social grouping and profession

- Relationship with the organisation; information they need and that which they might want.

A website designer has to take all these features into account; for example, a website targeted at children, such as <www.bbc.co.uk/cbbc>, has cartoons. Booksellers and supermarkets require realistic product imagery, for example, <www.waterstones.com> and <www.morrisons.co.uk>. Elderly and visually impaired people require readable text, with clear information on how to achieve this. A website designed to the user's preferred working methods facilitates working efficiently.

Secondly, it must be determined whether the aims of the stakeholders have been achieved by identifying:

- how the website integrates with other corporate communications

- those who control the budget, purpose and vision for the website

- what the website's primary and secondary objectives are – investor relations or products and services

- who the intended users are

- those stakeholders affected by the website

- how the website will be integrated with other channels, for example, mobile services.

14.1.3   WEB AUTHORING TOOLS AND DESIGN SOFTWARE

In designing a website, aside from creative design elements, there are many other terms that appear and disappear, leading to relevant, irrelevant and outdated definitions. To overcome these issues, the following section provides an indication of how the internet operates and the most popular software being used by designers and website developers.

For any design to be displayed, the website graphic design has to interact with a browser and HTML language. Since the early 1990s, website design development has been reliant on HTML as the mechanism for publishing hypertext, enabling the transmission of text, sound, images and graphics. Browsers read the HTML code, which determines the text architecture and location of graphics and images, alongside the functionality of hypertext. In many respects HTML is the constraint in the development of websites, but it is so integral to the system that developments have occurred primarily through website designers requesting further functionality, which in turn has been integrated into the browsers. Databases provide dynamic content, cutting across website hierarchies to the company and outside sources where the appropriate authority has been given to capture links from various levels within these websites.

Creative expressions began to appear in the mid 1990s as graphic features were prepared by Adobe Creative Suite, that is, Photoshop, Illustrator and InDesign. This allowed graphic formats (.bmp, .gif, .jpeg), colour, 3D, images, icons and backgrounds to be created to portray *real-world* expressions – with designer skill and practice.

With the development of web authoring tools, cascading style sheets (CSS), dynamic HTML (DHTML), Javascript, JavaApplets and Flash, designers have gained greater flexibility over their designs and how they appear on users' browsers. This permits them to create better corporate design communication, whilst attending to increased user friendliness. CSS, developed by Haken Wium Lie and Bert Bos of WWW Consortium (W3C), offers powerful and manageable ways for artists, typographers and authors to create visual effects, resulting in the current design terminology that puts aesthetics at the forefront of the web. CSS allows the designer to control the rendering of fonts, colours, leading, margins, typefaces and other aspects of a webpage's style without compromising its structure. As a simple style sheet mechanism, it allows authors and readers to attach style to HTML documents using common desktop publishing terminology. Hence, visual design issues such as page layout can be addressed separately from the webpage logical structure.

In the web authoring package Dreamweaver, a *style* can be set for all the headings, giving colour and size. Therefore all information is in the one place, separate from the content files; for example, when a takeover occurs, the *style* and/or the *content* can be changed. DHTML refers to webpages generated at a time when a user requests a page. Knowledge of CSS greatly facilitates the use of DHTML. Dynamic pages are compiled by the server using one or more pre-existing templates to combine with user input and other elements to the final page. *Flat* page is one that exists on the server in its finished complete form and is simply delivered to the browser when it is complete.

14.1.4   INTERACTIVE WEBSITES

In 1996 hyperfunctionality appeared, this being one of the web's first design ideologies. This enabled web structures access to information, leading to the development of e-commerce through form-filling, searches, anthropomorphic (that is, emulating human behaviour) search engines and direct communication – chats, webcams and now social media.

Virtual

Virtual content is essentially information based in a graphic format. Virtual activities require the simulation of action rather than purely information. It is useful for education and entertainment, for example, to:

- display a shop, building or exhibition space

- illustrate or simulate movement, such as a moving car

- provide dynamic feedback, for example, that a program is loading

- attract attention – a flashing button to show the user where to press

- show how something works, demonstrating activities.

In designing virtual activities, there are a series of features to be considered:

- User interface design – usability, navigation and aesthetics

- Conveying instructions about how the activity works

- Creating images and software which download quickly and do not overload a computer's memory.

The design must also take into account hardware and software – some designers do this so that they can work within known constraints – computer configurations, memory size, modems, networks and different internet browsers, with various plug-ins and functions.

Virtual programs require programs beyond HTML:

- Adobe Flash is applied as another way of creating interactive websites. Flash is a sophisticated graphics program which generates its own code and is often used to create animations. The visitor has to have a browser that can read the code.

- Plug-ins are a software application used with web browsers to view or display certain file types in a webpage. Adobe Shockwave is a plug-in that allows the browser to display interactive media.

- JAVA is used to write applets which run on the computing operating system; JAVAScript, a simple scripting program language, is used to create interactive elements. This differs from JAVA program language as some syntax is shared. It can be read from HTML source. JAVA and JavaScript work together.

- PERL Process and Experiment Automation Real-time Language is a general purpose programming language used to bind software together.

Video

Videos are currently a popular website element. As technology and communications advance through faster downloading, imagery can appear quicker and with sharper images, resulting from higher pixel counts on retina screens. The cost of filming and uploading to the internet has reduced considerably and therefore videos are now appearing more frequently on homepages. Software such as Final Cut Express makes it possible for the video to be edited.

Sound

Sound provides aural effects appropriate to the activity and aural feedback and cues, such as:

- Warning, by the sound of a siren

- Attracting attention, such as when mail arrives

- Background music or sounds.

Other internet subjects

As website and technology requirements in both software and hardware are ever increasing, there are technical and business topics which can be found in other literature, such as: e-commerce and security; software browsers; servers; editors; XML; Open Source; UNIX; protocols; caching; and history.

Web 2.0 technology introduced social media which has facilitated collaborative design practice and presentation – particularly relevant in the following two sections on the website gestalt and aesthetic. Additionally, once the website is uploaded to the internet, customers can comment on the website and, apart from the business operations, ensure that the content is truly what they require or would like to see included. Web 3.0 is presently in development, with the key aspects of its operations being discussed on the web. Chapter 15 introduces this development.

14.1.5 WEBSITE MAINTENANCE

Throughout all of these website design activities, it has to be remembered that a website has to be maintained, reviewed and updated with relevant information. Often when a website does not appear or is evidently out of date, prospective customers can become disillusioned and move on to another company website at a *click's notice*. Hence it is crucial that the website is maintained, otherwise a business can lose customers and market position. Ensuring that the corporate design ethos is conveyed is crucial online as an image on a display screen is the only means by which the customers communicate and have an impression of the business. Therefore it is important to ensure that attention is paid to what is to be *revealed* online and where the company's unique *symbols* are applied. This, in conjunction with a *coherent*, well-designed website architecture and navigation system, can provide the business environment or be another branch of the organisation's activities – not forgetting the continuous updating as change occurs in users' needs and stakeholder goals, whilst attending to new technological, legal and regulatory developments. Ultimately a coherent message with relevant and current content impacts a company's reputation.

14.2 Gestalt of Text and Imagery

The gestalt created by the composition of the text and image is the key objective in design communication. The aesthetic is how beautiful this looks. The following groupings provide an indication of the extent of website content elements, with commentary on various aspects. This has been included as we often view websites without actually realising how much information is displayed.

14.2.1 WEBSITE ARCHITECTURE AND LAYOUT PATTERNS

Architecture

Website architecture is the map for all the directions that a user could take to achieve his or her objectives by providing impact and immediate textual and visual content. Over centuries maps have been produced for real-world journeys, for example, Mercator's maps and Turgot's plans of Paris. Each site map represents a different strategy for altering a real-world situation on to a 2D printed surface or a computer screen – usually 2D but it can be 3D – so that the text and visual content has impact and is seen immediately. Conventions have built up as tacit agreement between the designer and users has evolved on the abstract topography of a homepage. To engage a user's attention on printed media, a hierarchy of layout and format (Johnson, 2005) by typographic size, style, italic and bold fonts on a front page has been the traditional graphic design approach. On a website homepage structure a similar hierarchical approach by hypertext is used, where text and image can be interrogated to many sub-levels. Again typographic size, style, italic and bold fonts are necessary.

Website genres developed slowly as the technology evolved and as experts began to discuss the genre rationale on what was shaping and influencing website design style and content (Swales, 1990). Style occurs from comparison and the effectiveness of the results. For example, three contributions to style are considered here: layout formats; homepage position on the computer screen; and number of screen rolls. Each one, and together, provides an initial impression of the company and its efficiency in achieving a user's goals, whilst concurrently communicating a corporate image that could be damaged if the homepage is too long or time-consuming to download.

Website layout patterns

Website layout patterns arose, perpetuating the original inverted *U* and *L* forms, primarily applied as navigation structures, and have now become the conventional approach (Askehave and Nielsen, 2005). Throughout history, civilisations and philosophies have manifested their way of thinking by a diagram or pattern combining textual, visual and numerical functions and relationships. Most people respond directly and unconsciously to patterns in a manner different from other visual arts, possibly explaining why there is a reluctance to change current webpage *patterns*. Homepage patterns and menu formations generate eight generic layout formats based on the *U* and *L* formats, these being the inverted *U* and *L*; the latter had four displays, described here as standard *L*, backward *L*, inverted *L* and diagonal *L*. Three further focal, band and panel formats are used.

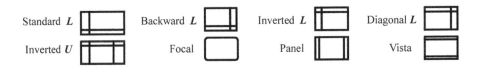

Figure 14.1   Webpage layout formats

Although companies generally retain a specific homepage format, this can change as the corporate design strategy alters; for example, Vodafone had a focal in 2009 which then changed to a catalogue e-commerce format on promoting new mobile phones. British Telecom has retained their focal homepage image for at least the last five years. In recent years the panel format has gained precedence.

Homepage position on the computer screen

Homepage position on the computer screen when it downloads has little consistency but most homepages download in a columnar format, then focal formats and then the remainder have a range of locations. The vast majority of homepages appear on the computer screen without having to screen role. There are specific instances where this does occur, for example, newpapers: <www.mirror.co.uk>. In recent years, the panel format has been increasingly prevalent.

Busyness represented by homepage elements

Homepage *busyness* is defined as the number of design elements applied to communicate the corporate image. In roughly 75 per cent of websites, viewers have to scan or read more than four boxes of textual and image content. This is in addition to recognising corporate visual identity (CVIS) elements and URL. So skim-reading webpages does mean that much information can be overlooked. The usefulness of this statistic is that it indicates the number of conjoined elements forming a gestalt that a viewer has to scan and interpret. In webpage composition, decisions have to be made on the relative importance and information values of design elements, text, image and videos. This is created by spacing, typographic size and colour to convey pacing of the website story or urgency in choosing from a selection of website options. The aim of most homepages is to ensure recognition of a company's quality and reliability.

14.3 Aesthetics

14.3.1 AESTHETICS HIERARCHY

Within the aesthetics hierarchy, the cultural perception of pattern varies across societies, social classes and wealth. At the higher end, quality products have intricate patterns and sometimes tactile properties applied to plaster, wood, fabrics and metals, with further decorations using expensive paints, threads and gilts. In other cultures, pattern is considered a lower member of the aesthetic hierarchy, regardless of the material quality. When this pattern approach is applied to websites there is a process of website classification that frequently determines a company's market position. For example, <www.rolls-royce.com> displays a more artistic, yet functional aesthetic acceptable to its quality position in the market. For oil companies, generally managed by engineers, functionality is of higher relevance than aesthetics. In recent years the aesthetic of the homepage has been improving as the technology has advanced.

14.3.2 AESTHETIC TOOLS

Cognitive designers, digital artists and creative technologists decide from their toolkits and illustrative techniques which are the most appropriate tools to create the required company image and message, this being the *style* created from the *themewords* selected by the CEO and corporate designer to depict the image that the company would like to create by way of the creative design process. There are five elements to consider:

- Ethos – the prevalent tone expressed by the organisation's values, beliefs and spirit, for example, the *Financial Times* has a gravitas tone.

- Personality – distinctive behavioural characteristics similar to editorial tone, for example, business-like, playful. Sub-sites may be different, reflecting specific characteristics or editorial tone of the business. Blogs increasingly present personality as opposed to the necessary corporate functions.

- Information content – tabs and menus are used to access and display types of information also accessible through indexes, hypertexts, audio and video.

- Interactive – for discussions and learning, whether through groups, communities of practices or games.

- Social media – for example, LinkedIn and Facebook for contacts, Twitter for commentary and YouTube for videos.

14.3.3 AESTHETIC STYLES AND EFFECTS

Aesthetic style can range from elegance and simplicity in a *cool*-coloured, streamlined style – for example, <www.joshuadavis.com> – or a colourful, busy, eclectic style – <www.cartoonnetwork.com> or <www.amazon.com>.

Aesthetic effects can include the use of the relationship and juxtaposition of objects to stimulate the imagination, where another concept appears by virtue of the fact that the objects are placed together, known as the Bewildering Effect, used by the Surrealist artists Rene Magritte and Saussure. Baudelaire described this concept of imagination as almost a divine faculty where perception can make connections between things, correspondences and analogies.

On entertainment websites, additional features can be used to create:

- Illusion – where the viewer knows intuitively how something works. In a cinema, viewers are absorbed in the medium as films are screened, whereas on computer screens and computer games, there is an interactive element.

- Realism – a constructed element made intelligible by culturally specific systems and meaning. Post-structuralism has to considered here. The meaning of a system never stands still and therefore has to be pinned down to a scientific context or dictionary definition, that is, looking at social practice not social meaning. The meaning is relational, the chain of meaning goes on and on, and final meanings are deferred, never to be solidified into fixed structures.

- Spectacle – designed to engage the senses by intense and instantaneous visual and interactive feeling, through various interface devices.

- Simulation – the representational copying or modeling of phenomenal reality on 2D, 3D or 4D virtual reality and how it reacts with consoles.

- Inventiveness – illustrated by new creative technologists and digital creative designers.

- Animations – the main components in games that are constantly advancing through graphics, sound and movement. Photorealism in digital graphic design is now of cinematic quality.

- Avatars – interactive animations answer questions from large database programs.

- Images – these can have a practical application, for example, in architecture, where a series of photographs can illustrate the construction stages of a project.

14.3.4   CURRENT SITUATION

As the internet has become an integral part of daily life, download speeds, intuitive devices and content design are more sophisticated and diverse. Functionality and aesthetics have advanced at a fast pace in the last decade. Digital versions of the most popular and important written texts are on the web; websites and their content have become central to internet usage; and textual content is increasing further with social media commentary and information appearing on blogs, Twitter, Facebook, LinkedIn and other social media platforms. Imagery content through photographs and video content has increased dramatically, appearing on websites and on Flickr, Pinterest, Instagram, YouTube and similar platforms. Currently the vast majority of people use freely available commodity content, but in certain

– often niche – sectors, viewers pay for premium content, for example, financial analysis or academic papers.

14.4   Creative Content

As digital technology and software packages advance, creative content has improved as digital artists and creative technologists find new ways of displaying content by the manipulation of typography, imagery and sound. The following provides an indication of developments and usage as they relate to the creative design process of a branding exercise.

14.4.1   TYPEFACES

The development of *letters* has had a wide timespan within which to develop, from chiseled letters, penned calligraphy – ranging from nibs and ink to fountain pens, biros, felt and gel pens – and printed wood-block typefaces, to the printing press and now computer-generated digital fonts. For business communication typefaces, these letter forms have been designed for specific technologies, for example, typewriter fonts, optical character recognition and digital type, these being the technological constraints of their period and therefore used to evoke a specific time period or effect. A point to note is that, over time, some typeface text may not be readable within certain cultural and social groupings as translated meaning has been lost (Spiekermann and Ginger, 2003).

With the introduction of digital printing there was a great fear that typography as a subject would become outdated. In fact the opposite has happened as software packages such as Adobe Illustrator combine design and artwork creatively and faster than at any previous time. The lettering style effects mentioned above – stone carving, etched glass, chiseled wood – can all be produced by these packages and a proficient designer. To illustrate these points, if a business wished to convey a Roman bathhouse atmosphere, then a chiseled Roman typeface would be used. Posters in bold block printing fonts can be applied for early poster adverts.

Fonts for visual pacing

Fonts convey distinctive messages, forming the initial impression of a company through lettering, with styles ranging from calligraphy to the latest digital fonts (see Plate 14.1). There has been an explosion of fonts available through the internet, opening up the subject to many people. The main concerns have been in the perceived downgrading of renowned fonts by the economic drive and skills being lost. For example, the traditional, elaborate script of *The Times* newspaper was considerably changed in 2006/2007 to a simple seriffed text now applied to both paper and digital media.

In oral storytelling, time and culture can be conveyed by the timbre of the voice and pace of the raconteur, providing the atmosphere and presence of a story, painting a picture in the mind of the listener. When print appeared in large blocks, there was difficulty in conveying atmosphere. Through time the written word managed to produce a visual pacing by layout and composition, with spaces between paragraphs, words and letters. Layouts allow the reader to quickly scan content and focus on the parts that they want to read, whilst gaining an impression on the type of product or topic subconsciously by design presentation, often regardless of what the words say. The French philosopher Jacques Derrida, who devised the theory of deconstruction in the 1960s, wrote that:

> ... *although the alphabet represents sound, it cannot function without silent marks and spaces. Typography manipulates the silent dimensions of the alphabet, employing habits and techniques – such as spacing and punctuation – that are seen but not heard. The alphabet, rather than evolve into a transparent code for recording speech, developed its own visual resources, becoming a more powerful technology as it left behind its connections to the spoken word.* (Lupton, 2004)

Website layout conveys the visual pacing of company information by 2D and 3D spatial navigation. The file structure and navigation progress from a root – that is, the homepage – down to directories holding various levels of content. Typography primarily elucidates the information structure by a variety of fonts which, through size, weight, leading, kerning and use of space, enables the designer to give the story or text a voice and emotional response through emphasis, in a similar manner to the rhythm, pitch and volume of the storyteller. Blank spaces create pauses, with colour and weight creating various levels or characteristics that elicit the emotional responses of happiness, sadness, anger or elegance.

The history of typography is marked by the increasingly sophisticated use of space. In the digital age, where characters are accessed by keystroke and mouse, not gathered from heavy drawers of manufactured units, space has become more liquid than concrete, and typography has evolved from a stable body of objects to a flexible system of attributes (Goveia and Hatmaker, 2003).

14.4.2   LANGUAGE

Language is an important feature of website communication, both in written and spoken formats. There are often further design considerations; for example, in names, should the first name or the surname be presented first? Does the reader read the page from right to left or left to right? These could have a corporate design impact and the perception of the viewer could be skewed. Generally speaking, international companies use English conventions and business language.

14.4.3   IMAGERY

Homepage imagery is increasingly applied to communicate website corporate branding. To date most imagery has been static, through photographs, sketches and clip art, and moving and dynamic, through video and animations, all of which have been under the website designer's control, created by, for example, Adobe Creative Suite or other similar creative applications. These have been the primary applications used, with social media providing further static imagery and video.

Static imagery

Static imagery is one of the key reference points for stakeholders, setting context and communicating company image. Through this representation, the company conveys its approach to the innovation, quality and reliability of its operations. The image selection, whether this be photograph, sketch or clip art, reinforces a corporate message or weakens it. Hence the background, cropping and silhouette have to be carefully attended to; for example, if a cutting-edge image is necessary, then a softly focused photograph communicates the wrong message. In 2007, compelling photographic imagery representative of the business was conveyed by applying a vista format on <www.angofagasta.com>. To keep colour continuity, the menu bar was the same colour tone as the photograph, thus ensuring the same style and visual impact.

This visual information can have a democratising impact on website design as anyone in the organisation can take photographs and have the image uploaded, after obtaining the right authority. There is a downside to this, that is, some controls have to be placed to ensure that the corporate reputation is not damaged, as the image chosen may not reflect the true situation. Multiple imagery on one homepage can be confusing.

Dynamic imagery

Animated images attract the eye but dynamic logos are rarely seen online. Animations are prepared on Flash software and similar applications, with animations formed by a series of renditions:

- Headline animations primarily highlighting company projects.

- Events occurring within the organisation.

Rotating background photographs often appear on a homepage, illustrating various aspects of a business's operation; for example, <www.heals.co.uk> illustrates this point.

Video clips

Video has seen rapid development in recent years and many websites now have a video somewhere on them, if not on the homepage. Social media has increased this video availability as the social media icons appear on the homepage, facilitating access to content. YouTube is a website devoted to video.

14.5   Social, Cultural, Political and Physical Geography Content

Cultural identity features on homepages enable a viewer to recognise a company and its business's geographical operations. These can be local, UK national, world region or worldwide audiences. Designing for these cultural groupings is complex where competition and co-operation occur on local and worldwide stages. Countries and companies are in competition for business and, as global economies develop, they are equally dependent on one another and need to co-operate.

Social, cultural and economic contributions are often achieved through social and economic *shakedowns* of what is considered acceptable practice. Eventually, and increasingly so, this is cast in legislation or accessibility restrictions. Political and physical geography can determine this cross-border accessibility; for example, politically China and Iran block some websites by means of firewalls. Commercially, businesses block websites to ensure that employees are working, not watching or listening to recreational websites. Physical terrain is often overlooked as it is assumed that satellites can access all locations. This is not always the case, such as in hilly regions. On the other hand, technology can be an added advantage; for example, telegraph poles are not necessary for mobile phones. Essentially homepage and website content differentiation can only be achieved if all these features are attended to within the corporate design strategy and processes.

Menu lists are frequently useful to list countries, various locations and languages, such as:

- Drop-down menus – countries and locations within

- Icons for geographical regions

- By moving a cursor over a map

- Flags.

One of the beguiling features of domain names is that a viewer expects to see the country URL suffixes – for example, .co.uk, .de or .fr – downloading, regardless of whether an image relating to a country of origin appears on the homepage.

Legislation is continually being passed on internet-related subjects, this being a new legal area within all countries' jurisdiction. A company website's legal jurisdiction is determined by the country of registration and it is upon this legislation that its internet business is conducted. Currently America and Europe are leaders in this legal field, but China and India are also legislating as the internet and related subjects have to be considered, and laws and regulations put in place. Overall, as the internet develops, companies and countries realise its advantages and disadvantages. Constant vigilance, re-examination, change and acceptance are essential as events occur.

Conclusion

To conclude, homepages provide the first impression of a company online and have created their own design genre. They act as an introduction to a company in the same way as the front page of a newspaper or the exordium of a speech. As technology has advanced, the gestalt remains similar, with necessary emphasis on a panel format, but with a clearer sense of purpose. Navigation is more precise as attention has been paid to layout hierarchies, fonts and imagery. The aesthetic produced has seen a larger step change as screen display and website communication has improved. Currently videos are increasingly appearing on homepages as social media, presented in the next chapter, moves websites into another stage of their development. All of these features do have to consider a wide range of geographical, social, cultural, political and physical aspects, as websites as a technological development have to operate within a human milieu, with all its complexities.

How is the business 'look and feel' projected online?

Originally digital content was a copy of a business's offline marketing literature. For many businesses, this continued until the second decade of the twenty-first century. As web technology has advanced, there have been significant changes in this approach as entrepreneurs have greater access to the internet and website graphic design information sources. Faster download speeds, screen definition and digital graphic design improvements have enabled the CVIS and image formats to display the required business image or 'look', with the required 'feel' being communicated by social media such as a blog, where the business personality can be displayed alongside Twitter and other social media platforms.

Chapter 15
The Social Business

Do I need to have wider

digital conversations?

Introduction

This chapter on social media introduces another communication channel into business marketing and advertising, explaining the benefits that it contributes by engaging, informing and educating customers and stakeholders, and discussing where social media is useful to small to medium sized enterprises (SME). Following this, consideration is given to how social media platforms integrate with corporate and design strategies and the necessity of implementing a business-relevant social media strategy. Thereafter the most popular social media platforms, and their relevance to content input, are described, with useful metrics at the end. Finally a short explanation is given of the next stage in digital development thought: Web 3.0.

15.1   Social Media Communication

15.1.1   ENGAGEMENT, INFORMATION AND EDUCATION

Social business through social media networks encourages engagement with and information between businesses, customers and the wider business community by two-way recursive communication. With thousands of social media platforms in existence, there is a wide choice to suit business operations or entertainment requirements. The website homepage currently provides the initial access point with the additional objective of driving prospective customers to the website, where a company provides its version of the products and services that it sells. After – and even before – a customer buys a product, he or she can hold an open conversation with the company and the wider world, providing further commentary. This becomes part of the conversation on product branding and prospective development. By opening this new business channel, an additional dimension has been introduced, dramatically altering traditional business processes in marketing and public relations roles and content. Social media is useful for four reasons:

- Business brand personality can be established and developed over a period of time.

- Being a low-cost platform, careful selection ensures that relevant channels are chosen for the business needs.

- Technical restrictions call for precise messages to be formed that engage and can be transmitted quickly to the recipient.

- It allows you to tell the world about your business – then the recipient can reply quickly or at their convenience.

Social media has become a popular communication channel, with icons for each platform appearing on public relations material, adverts, websites and corporate emails, soliciting commentary on any aspect of the company's business and its products. Generally social media platforms have facilitated conversations and collaborations by creating an enormous database of data, information and knowledge on every conceivable subject, thereby providing ideas and inspiration for new, innovative products and services. This has resulted in a wider range of contributors to design project collaboration, by skillset and geographical reach. From a business viewpoint, these platforms can:

- Launch new brands, products and services

- Progress prospective new client leads

- Strengthen client relationships

- Boost sales.

Thus, the success of a new business or product sales lead can be measured.

It has to be remembered that these platforms are aimed at being social and part of people's daily life in all its variety, as this is where products and services are consumed. Therefore prospective new products and markets can be recognised when content is analysed. Any message that you send on social media to the outside world, or a specific person, will be responded to in a particular manner, some of which will be useful and relevant but for the most part will be irrelevant. There are filters that facilitate the recognition of useful data so that you can attend to relevant business content. However, key to this is ensuring that your message is truly focused.

15.1.2   SOCIAL MEDIA AS MARKETING AND ADVERTISING

In marketing, social media communicates with people, who contribute commentary on what is and is not required of the company, its products and services; this changes the business relationship to one that is consumer-centric. So having an effective and concise message is crucial. Advertising is gaining social media momentum with five phone calls being replaced by 50 social media contacts. There are a few caveats to this: a company's social media business network has to be relevant to its operations and can take years to build. However, loyal customers will have collected the relevant information they require, having previously purchased the product, used it and probably compared notes with others on social media. There is the high-risk factor that they will go elsewhere to buy the same product. If they continue to buy, then they may advocate for your business through electronic word-of-mouth as they now trust the company and its products. This volume of data and information that streams into your business and elsewhere has to be monitored. Reply to what is being said as soon as possible as timing is clearly important. Hence why, as explained in Chapter 3, companies ought to maintain their reputation offline and online. Remember that what goes online stays digital forever.

As a result of social media activities, the competitive business environment has widened and introduced previously unlikely players such as SMEs that now have access to formerly unreachable markets. This is not to say that larger organisations do not use social media as part of their business, marketing and communication strategies, but social media is only part of their business and communication. For SMEs, these cheaper digital word-of-mouth social media channels enable engagement with designers and customers, keeping them regularly informed. Additionally there is the potential for brand conversations to reach larger companies and markets as far afield as China, India and the Americas. It has been said that Google now has a strong competitor with the increase in social media platforms. On the other hand, businesses find that customers still use the search engine to find information they require through Google.

Effective branding can be achieved by access to an increasing number of social media platforms, with a few falling by the wayside, such as MySpace. In this chapter, the most popular ones will be concentrated on:

- Blogs are web logs – diaries of projects and events with serial updates. Advertising products and services.

- Facebook has evolved as a business and social contact network.

- Twitter solicits information, reactions and discussions.

- LinkedIn is a professional network where each person or business can have their own branded page.

- YouTube uploads video content.

- Pinterest, Instagram and Flickr allow photographs to be uploaded.

With so many platforms, their usage is becoming defined and refined through time.

15.1.3   SOCIAL MEDIA STRATEGY

During the last decade companies have had to adapt to this new communication channel and establish which platforms are most suitable for their needs and how they will implement the systems into their corporate and marketing strategies. Where does a social media strategy fit within a corporate strategy?

a) Social media is consumer-centric as customers respond to the company's products and services, often described on the website as well as other promotional material.

b) The company has to be honest and realistic in the entries and comments they provide.

c) Consumers have input to decisions and therefore this information has leverage.

d) As a learning tool, feedback on strategic plans gets everyone on board and clears the implementation path.

e) Organisational relationships and roles may have to be redefined and resources reallocated.

Determining a social media strategy often occurs by trial and error, with a key consideration being that many platforms have been transient in nature. It is not a communication channel that works wonders overnight; rather it builds up a rapport with clients, customers and the general public which can take months, even years. The social media audience is key and an important consideration in how a social media platform is introduced to the market and how companies will use it. If the service is accepted, a business model develops. Initially all of the platforms started as *social* networks rather than business networks, with the common denominator being people communicating with one another.

Some platforms such as LinkedIn and Facebook were initially restricted to professional colleagues in the former and friends and family in the latter. As the practicalities were observed and likely problems found across social, technological, political and legal concerns, then users and developers decided to have both business and social versions on LinkedIn and Facebook, so that private and public lives could be separated. On the other hand, Twitter and blog (web log) accounts are specific, with wider unrestricted audiences. Everything that is typed in will be viewed by everyone unless defined otherwise.

A debate is still being conducted on whether social media is a useful marketing tool. Many early adopters are fascinated by its capabilities and see it as the future of websites and business communication, with everyone having a say (Surowiecki, 2004). Others consider it a step too far as the implications of everyone having a say can make decision-making difficult. However, the impact and vicissitudes of social media on society, cultures and the historical development of geographical and political intent are still occurring and having ramifications, with positive and negative impacts.

15.1.4   SOCIAL MEDIA STRATEGY QUESTIONS

Defining a social media strategy is fluid, with many contributors who provide input for specific products and markets. A social media strategy has to employ creative tactics in the use of this technology. The following is a list of factors that should be considered:

- What are the company's SMART goals and target audience for social media?

- Is the platform for publishing information or generating income?

- What platforms are customers using?

- What products or services are selling and how are you going to sell these on social media?

- Identify relevant return on investment (ROI) measurements at the start so that success can be measured at the end of a period.

- Does the company have a strong visual identity?

- Does the corporate message sound authentic and appropriate for the audience?

- How much time do you have to spend on social media?

- Keep private information private – what you say online does not get erased.

- Measure the result – brand profile online, presence on social networks and impact being made.

15.2   Social Media and Corporate Strategy

In the business environment, social media creates a marketing network, allowing brand development by engaging with customers and colleagues so that a corporate strategy or product sales can progress. The consumer has greater input to this strategy by providing a running commentary on their thoughts and suggestions, ultimately becoming advocates of the company and its operations. Marketing therefore becomes a far more engaging and dynamic activity as services and products are crafted by all interested parties. This first stage of social media is transactional, often taking a long time communicating and forming a relationship every time a message is reacted to.

Senior executives can converse with a wide range of contacts and customers to solicit responses to queries, reflect on results and strengthen customer relationships. Collaboration has been a buzzword for a number of years and is inherent to many art and design activities. Here collaboration allows a suggestion or request to be made to a wide audience whose differing contributions enable a corporate strategy to be thought through, a particular problem to be addressed or a product/service development to be advanced. It becomes a free-flowing information stream, sharpening corporate, design and marketing strategies, making them pertinent to the corporate goals and direct communication through the social media *voice*. All of these factors reduce the risk of failures and financial losses.

15.2.1   OTHER CONSIDERATIONS

Current homepages

Website designers and social media strategists should work together to ensure that the selected platforms are relevant to their audiences. Website homepages and blogs increasingly have to be more engaging and clearly visible across a range of devices such as tablets and smartphones. Questions have to be asked why people would want to return to your website.

Audience

There are four types of audience:

a) *Creators* create content by writing articles and stories and posting photographs and videos online by social media and other platforms.

b) *Spectators* read, watch and listen to content created by others and provide reviews and ratings.

c) *Critics* post ratings and reviews of products and services, contributing and editing online content where permissions are allowed.

d) *Joiners* visit and maintain profiles on social media networking sites (Forrester Groundswell Report, 2012).

Online image

A clearly unique image is important online as consumers now purchase by website comparison and social media commentary. This, in conjunction with functionality, aesthetic and communication technology (FACT), has to convey the brand message and product effectively. A brand's reputation is built on the success of these three elements.

Brand voice

Who should go on social media? Some companies have the CEO, others the brand manager or someone who brings to mind the brand values and *voice* through the type of content and its quality. As this is a new medium, roles are just emerging. Brand negotiations occur over time so it is worthwhile empowering some of the sales force to become a product category *voice*, once their skills are recognised, by giving them branding material and notices upon which they can pitch future discussions. One of the most important points to remember throughout social media is that it is a social medium and therefore the tone should be *informal professional* by including commentary on unrelated topics such as musical taste and hobbies, as well as more serious business topics. This said, it can depend on the topic discussed. Crucial to this *voice* is the online negotiations that build up customer relationships and social capital for the business.

15.3   Social Media Platforms

The following is a list of current social media platforms that have found a popular usage and become useful business tools. These platforms are web logs (Blogs), Facebook, Twitter, LinkedIn, Flickr, YouTube, Pinterest and Instagram.

15.3.1   BLOGS

Blogs started in the late 1990s as web logs and diaries. This was the first Web 2.0 development where the blogosphere arrived, with authors of all types finding it a useful medium for their scripts. It opened up new communication and marketing channels, with the added advantage that *conversations* and *commentaries* could be undertaken with readers on a continuous basis. Illustration, animations and small videos progressively appeared, becoming a useful archive of an author's work and discussion medium with readers. Blog search engines, such as Technorati, Blogdigger and Feedster, provide blog-genres on a variety of subjects – such as travel, fashion, politics, law, and so on – that allow wider publication.

With increasing bandwidth, media content expanded to include: vlog (videos); photoblog (photos); linklog (links), sketchblog (sketches); and moblog (device using mobile phone blog composition). Hence almost any type of content can be blogged, adding a wider design potential and personal touch. Blogs, as well as being stand-alone websites, can also be integrated with a blog on the company website. Blogs aid a website's search engine optimisation (SEO) as Google indexes every new blog post; therefore a website page will be indexed and thereby update the website.

Blogs are used in brand development to create *personality*, rather than the corporate faces of LinkedIn. Within a business it has to be decided where a blog is most suitable within the website and social media strategy. Some companies have one blog that appears on the website, usually the homepage, with subdivided content. Others have a separate blog on particular topics, thereby creating the company's personality informally. Rather than selling a product or service directly, it can provide information indirectly, such as the best conditions for growing plants and trees, with suggestions for the most suitable plants/trees for certain locations and conditions. Of course, company events past and future, new personnel and anything else that contributes to the brand image online can be shown. A few useful points:

- Define your target audience for the blog.

- Create a memorable blog brand by having a unique name and aesthetic style for easy recognition.

- Wordpress is the most used application for blogs, with content being transferable to websites.

- Have a clearly defined blog policy regarding the type of content topics to be included.

- Select someone within the organisation to blog. Rotating this role can provide a variety of insights to the business and there are many bloggers online who can be asked to contribute.

Social media can track traits and trends, establishing how a trend forms, operates and affects the marketplace (Christakis, 2013). Do the traits pass from one person to another? Do like-minded people group together? Or is distribution scattered, flowing and morphing over time and location? If the latter is the case, it can have a dramatic impact on a company, its product and service sales as it is difficult to keep track of what is happening, whereas in the former elements, through induction and groupings, it is easier to keep track.

According to Christakis' analysis, the benefits of being connected on social media outweigh not being connected. However, to overcome security risks, processes and policies have to be well tested, with pilot tests and working practices written down.

15.3.2 FACEBOOK

Facebook arrived in 2004, having initially started as a means of student communication at Harvard University, expanding locally within the Boston area to include the Ivy League and Stanford University. This platform grew quickly as young people found a means of communicating with one another, *Liking* information, photographs and videos that they posted online. Facebook became part of their daily life as the phrase *I'm posting and checking Facebook* became a common expression. As this group aged, Facebook became an obvious business communication platform, particularly used by the art and design SME community. Today Facebook has over one billion active users, with the over 45-year-olds being the main users as younger age groups find newer platforms. In early 2012 Facebook became a limited company, with the ability to differentiate between business and personal usage appearing in September 2012. Individuals generally react differently to their company persona. Facebook is still one of the key social media platforms, although recent comments suggest that it has reached its peak in UK and Europe, with Latin America and India still in the development stage.

Facebook provides a wide network of potential consumers who stay ten times longer on Facebook than any other platform. You can create a business community of people who previously you would not have met, and promote other business contents such as your blog, webinars and videos; so larger brands currently prefer to use this platform. Content, regardless of whether it is text, image or video, has to stay relevant on the fan page. Pictures rank highest and require a high level of curatorship. Since video costs have dropped, there has been an increase in its appearance on all social media platforms. Beware granting everyone in a group administration rights; instead have one person or a few people allocated with the role. Facebook has further useful integrated tools that let people know where your office is located, opening times and contact details.

Business relationships can be built by asking questions on the business Facebook page to start a conversation; then, by facilitating the conversation, the solution you are looking for may appear.

Some points on a business Facebook page:

- Pages represent a business, not a person; apply a business logo, not a picture of yourself.

- A cover image can be used to explain what the business does and its products.

- Pages have fans – with no limit on numbers and likes – not friends.

- Pages are seen globally by fans; some countries have restrictions.

- Pages send updates rather than messages.

- Updates provide information from the business; it is not a discussion forum.

- Facebook has to be answered, and answered honestly, without giving irrelevant information.

- Do not sell; Facebook is for connecting with customers.

- Establish a routine for replying by letting people know when they will receive a reply.

- Privacy settings allow personal and business information to be kept separate.

- Twitter can pull updates from your Facebook account and publish them as Twitter tweets.

- Do you want Facebook updates to be tweeted? Are they cross-platform relevant?

- Applications can place your blog on to your Facebook page.

- Taking spam out of feeds is important.

- Remember that information cannot be backed up on Facebook.

- Terms and conditions should be read frequently as they are often changed.

- Follow the rules and shares.

As there is a huge amount of information online, targeted marketing is required based on profiles. Facebook is very big in India amongst 24 to 34-year-olds where there is great social status attached. A few years ago a car advert was initiated on Facebook with online self-promotion submissions. After filtering to the top 100, a final was held live for the final 20 actors, with voting then occurring online. The final trailer was launched on Facebook.

15.3.3 TWITTER

Twitter arrived in 2006 with social networking and micro-blogging capability that facilitates electronic word-of-mouth communication by *tweets* – text-based focused messages of 140 characters. Twitter is not confined to groups or professional networks and has become one of the top ten most visited websites. Registered users can post *tweets* with 1.3 B registered accounts confirmed in 2013. Comments, images and votes are *tweeted* with links to images, to the world. Twitter can be integrated into websites and other social media platforms.

Engagement with people in the public sphere has meant that Twitter users can have direct contact with a cross-section of society. A *follower* is someone who subscribes to your feed. All types of artists can have followings on Twitter with a wider fan base geographically and demographically. You have to set the frequency of your tweets and say the number of times it will be displayed. On the other side of the conversation, tweets must be replied to *in person* and bad comments cannot be ignored but replied to quickly. A number of social media companies provide a social media service providing commentary and replies. Remember, tweets cannot be deleted, only the Twitter.

Twitter builds brand credibility and makes the world aware of the business's services and products, event information, promotions, links to related information and stories. Through tweeting, people begin to recognise the company and then, when they require a product or service, they know who to contact. If problems occur, they have to be replied to quickly. *Hashtag* is another new media word now in popular usage, being a way to categorise social media content, allowing users to monitor and search for relevant conversations. Use hashtag events, names, themes or trends by keyword or phrases such as # bread. This links your business into the *bread* community and can be used as a promotional tool, with the key objective being to have repeat customers. Key information points:

- Determine the frequency and tweet a timetable.

- Integrate the Twitter feed onto your website.

- *Retweet* – so that followers know they have been heard.

- A URL shortener such as bitly makes a difference.

- Keep brand-relevant.

15.3.4   LINKEDIN

LinkedIn was launched in 2003 as a social networking website for people in professional roles. Initially academics predominated by networking with other academics and engaging with other professionals. Short business profiles are entered on the webpage with the person's business role, summary and photograph inserted into a proforma and accessible by the wider LinkedIn community. Through time the system advanced and subscription tiers of accessibility, free emails and other add-ons became available. The company was floated in early 2011 and LinkedIn now has company and personal pages which still have a corporate feel. In mid 2013 there were 225 million members in about 200 countries.

Individuals and companies can find jobs and business opportunities through the individual's or company's contact network. Businesses can list jobs for potential candidates and job seekers can follow the company, looking for job opportunities; then before the interview, the interviewee can review the interviewer's profile. User groups are communities that specialise in an interest, which users can join, thereby getting exposure to people in the same sector, similar fields or who have a shared interest.

A LinkedIn user can decide what type of user they wish to be, such as a *LION*, that is, a LinkedIn Open Networker, who openly connects by sending out and accepting invitations from everyone, thereby achieving a larger network and greater opportunities. A *Turtle* connects only with highly trusted individuals who they know well. *Hound dogs* connect with those they know and those they would like to know, accepting invitations that are beneficial to their business or job opportunities. *Alley cats* accept invitations from almost everyone. A useful promotional feature of LinkedIn is the *Answers* feature for asking questions or to provide information on a particular topic.

15.3.5   FLICKR

Flickr appeared in 2005 as an image and video hosting website. Flickr is popular with bloggers and photograph researchers as they can embed images in blogs and other social media. Photos and videos can be uploaded to showcase to a wider audience without being registered, but registration is required if the image is uploaded to a website. A useful Twitter hashtag is when image curation is required: #curatorgeneration, that is, the ratio 30:70 for creation:curation rule.

15.3.6   YOUTUBE

YouTube began uploading videos to the internet in 2005 and then home enthusiasts and professionals began uploading their videos, movie clips and music videos. Various professions and amateurs found YouTube to be a source of inspiration for numerous projects. Professional advertising companies upload and source ideas for commercials; actors upload videos of their acting abilities and CVs for casting companies, advertisers, and programme and film-makers. Amateur singers, musicians, comedians, crafters and wildlife cameramen could show their abilities online.

Video is becoming more important as costs decrease. Once customers engage with video content, this can increase the likelihood of a sale by 85 per cent.

15.3.7   PINTEREST

Pinterest appeared in 2010, being a social image book-marking system – essentially a pinboard photosharing website by which users create imagery on a topic. Pinterest has achieved a number of landmarks: being the third most popular social media network; being the quickest to reach the ten million visitors mark; and having the highest rate of turning users into customers. It is a very good research and marketing tool, being very popular for home decoration, fashion, recipes and hobbies (see Plate 15.1 which illustrates a business use of Pinterest and Instagram). It is often considered to be Facebook's photo album. Pinning can be undertaken from a business website if you have a board, and images can be uploaded on a theme related to your business, this being particularly useful for physical products; for example, a restaurant may pin recipes and photographs of meals. These social media images can be

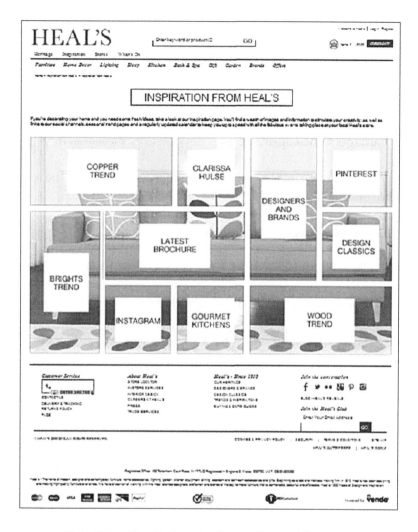

**Plate 15.1   Heal's Inspiration webpage illustrates
a successful use of Pinterest and Instagram**

pinned and you can re-pin other people's images, which makes the company known and followed. You can follow other businesses and people. On creating a business page, verify it as there is a useful analytics feature enabling you to improve content.

15.3.8   INSTAGRAM

Instagram appeared online in 2010. This is a mobile experience that focuses on live events, travel and design. It shares photos and videos and is a social networking website which, by using filters, allows content to be shared with other social media platforms such as Twitter, Facebook and Tumblr. One distinctive feature is that the image is confined to a square, as opposed to a rectangular mobile phone shape.

15.4   Management Operations

Remembering that the aim is to drive information to the website, the following should be considered:

- To start, have a few key messages. Send and talk.

- Timetable when content is going to be available for each platform.

- Check that material is copyright cleared.

- Bitly can be used to shorten URLs.

15.4.1   CONTROL AND MEASUREMENT

How do organisations control this multi-channelled two-way recursive communication channel? Some organisations control and plan their tweets, blogs, videos, postings and reviews. Others do not. By measuring results, a useful contribution can be made, identifying which platforms are truly relevant to the business and those that are not. This can only be established by trial and error at this point in time. If your message is not getting across, then perhaps this has to be revised and the audience carefully selected. Even a small targeted audience can create a widely relevant network through their contacts. A similar approach can be taken to test a new product or service, resolving any problems. Two types of tools exist:

- Measuring and monitoring brand feelgood factors, as social media is about perception, engagement and emotions. Some tools are: Social Mention, BrandsEye (protecting your online reputation), Google Alerts.

- Listening – these tools enable you to listen to conversations that your target market is having. Use keywords related to your brand. Some tools are: Twitter Search, Technorati, Google Blog Search, NMA SocialBusinessGuides.

15.4.2 EFFECTIVENESS OF SOCIAL MEDIA – METRICS

The following is a list of metrics that are useful in controlling the effectiveness of social media:

1. Have your business goals been reached?

Engagement

2. Ratio of posts to comments in a time period

3. Percentage of returning customers and visitors

4. Is customer retention increasing?

5. Are you engaging with followers and information effectively?

Cost savings

6. By how much did costs reduce or increase (noting fixed and variable costs)?

7. Cost per message sent

8. Cost per new contacts and continual communications over a period of time

9. Are sales increasing or decreasing?

10. Are there correlations with cash flow?

Brand awareness

11. Brand awareness through social media word-of-mouth and viral videos

12. How quick is the brand recall and favourability?

13. What is the search engine optimisation ranking?

Content

14. How many ideas or inspirations do you have in a time period?

15. Have you effectively managed the content?

16.   How quickly do you reply, especially if there is a problem?

17.   How useful is social media to your business use analytical tools in measuring the success of selected goals?

In conclusion, what does social media contribute to a business?

- Increases in brand equity.

- Increases in intellectual capital through the content generated.

- Consumers have a greater input to product and service creation and innovation.

15.5   Developing Digital

15.5.1   REAL LIFE–MOBILE–ONLINE LIFE

The convergence of the digital world with the real world is becoming a seamless experience as various platforms and technologies become *invisible*. Three environments are appearing: real life, mobile and online life. Questions are still asked about how businesses should approach their online and offline worlds. Currently the standard approach is to: plan the business and platforms; then create content; select media; and finally execute. In the future this is expected to change, with a business being influenced by an audience.

At the 2013 Digital Shoreditch Conference, Matt Teeman of *Metro* newspaper provided a good example of this interaction. This explanation was based on the newspaper's own experience, when the mobile format and other more familiar formats and elements were applicable at a particular time and place. The newspaper's audience is busy professional people and fast early adopters of technology. In its experience, people use the offline–mobile–online media at various times of the day:

- Print in the early morning

- Online website in the middle of the day

- Tablet in the early morning and evening

- Mobile smartphone throughout the day.

Further expectations were that, this year, more people will be using tablet and smartphones than any other devices, including desktops. The latter could be doubtful as many people use a desktop for business work. A second forecast was that mobile browser users will increase from 25 to 50 per cent as *swipers* consume five times more content.

15.5.2   COLLABORATION AND NETWORKS

Content strategies which facilitate *flow* will encourage collaboration, as opposed to *stock* that concentrates on products and consumers. Again there appears to be a need to break or reduce the silo functional mentality that occurs in many projects where managers and designers are concerned, the former working within the silos and the latter across them. So communication and collaboration is key to ensure success in any project, whether technology-related or not. This includes working with a wide range of business partners, some with left brain predominance, others with right brain predominance, and some who can work with both sides. Who are the influencers? Build relationships with them. Often it is the biggest *voice* online that is heard, not the one with the authority – but both have to be listened to, regardless of the network size.

15.5.3   CONTENT

The key term relating to content is *added value* by engaging, relevant, concise and precise content, otherwise it will not spread through social media channels. Again the biggest *voice* will be heard, or the one which appears to project the company *voice* well. Social media tracking tools may find what people want to buy by analysing the brand conversations that are occurring (Earles, 2013). You should filter data from social technology into your organisation and identify branded content so that the company *cash cow* is recognised.

Web 3.0 is in its early days but it is proposed by Steve Seager and other writers in the field that searching will be faster and easier; for example, searches could be conducted by complex sentences rather than multiple keywords. Artificial intelligence techniques will mine human behaviour, with the outcome being to provide a guide rather than a catalogue approach. The more the web learns about *you/the consumer*, the less specific you will have to be; therefore more open questions can be asked, such as: What films can I see this evening? So the next Facebook will probably be *what you like* rather than *who you are*. Web 3.0 concentrates more on the right side of the brain rather than the left side which is where Web 2.0 currently operates, the former being more subjective, intuitive and synthesising rather than objective and analysing. All the media will flow in and out of virtual worlds so that any media, anywhere, at anytime reinforces the offline–mobile–online life triumvirate.

15.5.4 DATA

A new role is likely to appear, this being the Chief Data Officer who will provide leadership and business strategy as *data* becomes the raw material of business, on a par with capital and labour. Understanding who stores this raw data material, who writes the programs and who records the imagery within the business will become relevant. There are a number of debates on the subject of *Big Data*, but there is a strong argument that there is and will be so much *data* that no one will know what to do with it, never mind analyse it.

Conclusion

To conclude, as with all innovative digital platforms, there is an evolution in their benefits and application to organisations and their strategies. In the last two decades there has been a paradigm shift as social media platforms alter the consumer relationship to consumer-centric. Working methods, communication channels, business practices and the creation of products and services have all been impacted. The platforms mentioned in this chapter – blogs, LinkedIn, Facebook, Twitter, YouTube, Flickr, Pinterest and Instagram – all started in the *playful* mode as digital technologists created better two-way communications and technological aesthetics advanced. The range of social media applications has mushroomed where people have found a constant communication mode between interested parties beneficial to their objectives. In a review of social media published articles, seven clusters were found: education, business, lifestyle, entertainment, politics, causes and protest. In education, Twitter is used to converse with and between students to inform them about academic and social events. Blogs provide information on a wide range of subjects, from lifestyle information and cookery recipes to plumbing. In business, customisation of products, rather than mass production, has been progressed as co-creation occurs between the consumer and the manufacturer, which has revolutionised sales and buying techniques. Now the consumer can compare product and service prices, function, aesthetic and delivery times whilst sitting at home with a PC and internet connection, or with a smartphone and Wi-Fi whilst waiting or travelling. Hence corporate strategy development and design strategies have changed tack again as companies define which social media platforms fulfil their business communication and marketing requirements. The knock-on effect is that today product development strategies include a wide range of consumer networks that provide digital social contacts and networks that establish businesses and contact designers, manufacturers, marketers and potential consumers to make and sell a product.

Do I need to have wider digital conversations?

Social media had a rapid impact on business communications and has been found to be particularly useful in marketing SME businesses, their products and services. There is a caveat: research is necessary to determine which social media platform is the most relevant to the business. Thereafter *who*, *when* and *how* have to be considered: *who* is the best person to communicate the business's *voice* and message? *When* should the conversations occur and what should be their frequency? (These can be timetabled over a period of time, perhaps a week across selected platforms.) And *how* will the content be created? This depends on the platform – text being scripted and uploaded onto a blog or LinkedIn, as required. On the other hand, Twitter requires a social, professional, conversational tone and often the company *voice* will undertake this, as it is a dedicated role best allocated to a staff member.

Part V Summary
Digital Corporate Design

What Has Happened So Far?

Websites are a key marketing communication tool which cannot be ignored as they provide a worldwide stage, communicating the business market position and potential. Part V started by looking at digital strategy in Chapter 13, considering strategic positioning through the value exchange and creation of a differential digital concept and image to communicate the brand message, then explaining the most common use of a website within a corporate strategy and how this is initiated through the design brief, selection of designers and digital hardware. As the human–computer interface of a website is through a screen display, in Chapter 14 an examination of three aspects of the website homepage and content were discussed. Initially this occured through the website graphic design, authoring tools and interactive options, then progressed to the gestalt of text and imagery, followed by the aesthetic created and the impact that creative content has on developing and evoking the corporate message for the selected market sector. At the end of this chapter the impact of geographical, social, cultural, political and physical aspects was discussed. Finally, in Chapter 15 the impact of social media through the most popular platforms was presented. The benefits of social media as an advertising tool in the increasingly competitive business environment were explained, along with the key points in creating a social media strategy that links with the business's corporate and design strategy. This was followed by a précis of the key points of the most popular platforms. Then social media metrics were presented that establish which platforms can be most effective for your business. Finally, mobile marketing and the key points of impact of Web 3.0 were discussed.

What Have We Learnt in this Section?

The fast pace of digital development, both in communication and design potential, has required constant attention by both company strategists and designers as websites have become ubiquitous throughout the world, now being the centre of a company's communications. Homepages often determine what drives usage with many retail businesses applying their websites as the front entrance to their online e-commerce. Hence the initial gestalt of text and imagery and how attractive the website appears through aesthetics have to be thought about. Content webpages display business operations such as contact details, business interests, news and corporate stories. Selection of a distinctive CVIS style is paramount to differentiate the business online, this being achieved by name selection or creation, colours, fonts and logo creation focused on the target market segment. Social media has specific communication objectives, enabling two-way recursive conversations which contribute to business strategies, operation and sales. Some platforms have grown and been captured globally as having a business function, but many businesses were unaware of its likely impact and a steep learning curve ensued.

How Will This Develop My Business Corporate Design?

Detailing to which purpose the business website should be applied requires great consideration within both the corporate and the corporate design strategy. In recent years this has become more complex as technology has advanced into social media communication, requiring precise commentary and image clarity. The CVIS still has to be applied to all corporate communications to ensure that a business is instantly recognised by the corporate message and visual and auditory styling. Similarly the content has to have the same tone of voice through editorial presentation in text, static imagery and video. The selection of social media communication platforms is also relevant, with each having a defined purpose; for example, Twitter and blogs may be highly relevant to authors of all descriptions, whereas Instagram and Pinterest are more relevant to retailers and interior designers. This is not mutually exclusive as many businesses can have four or five social media sites. Finally, there is the device by which all this communication occurs; now the tablet and smartphone have precedence as we move into another era, that of Web 3.0.

Chapter 16
Summary and Conclusions

Brand and Corporate Identity Today

To pull all of this work together over the five parts is complex so, as many designers do, two sketches are forthcoming to illustrate: a) where the key terms and their activities occur and their direct linkage and relationship with one another; and b) where within the strategic and operational hierarchy they appear. Then you can read, reread or dip into the book at the relevant chapter that you are interested in:

PART I: GROUND BASE: HOW CORPORATE DESIGN STARTED AND EVOLVED

Chapter 1   Corporate Identity and Image Development

Chapter 2   Corporate Identity and Branding Debate

Chapter 3   New Media, Communication and Reputation

PART II: SETTING THE STRATEGY

Chapter 4   Corporate Strategy

Chapter 5   Storytelling and Identity

Chapter 6   Corporate Design Strategy

Chapter 7   Perception and Perspectives

PART III: COHESIVE DESIGN MANAGEMENT

PART IV: NAVIGATING SYMBOLIC PRACTICE

PART V: DIGITAL CORPORATE DESIGN

Corporate design encompasses a wide array of subjects, skills, expertise and daily contributions as we observe what is happening around us on a daily basis. When a company is defining its corporate strategy in today's highly competitive marketplace, there are a host of environmental and organisational factors to consider. Apart from the CEO or business owner's instincts, a political, economic, environmental, sociological and technological (PEEST) environmental analysis can be conducted. Then internal factors can be assessed by a strengths, weaknesses, opportunities and threats (SWOT) analysis. However, the company's objective is to make a profit and maintain and display its unique market position, whilst maintaining the company ethos and philosophy in conducting the business operations. Customers then become familiar with a business's reputation, and if the company products are *as described on the packet*, to use a familiar phrase, then the customer is happy and willing to pay for the convenience and fact that they intuitively understand and can work with the business. This happens both online and in the real world. As technology advances into Web 3.0 and digital media merges seamlessly with daily life, introducing the offline–mobile–online experience, then understanding the key components of corporate design through a company's identity and branding facilitates the creation of a company's position in this marketplace and the communication of its existence.

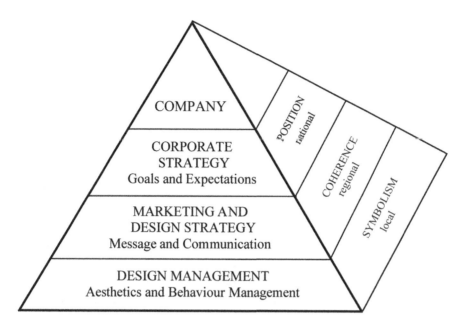

Figure 16.1 **Corporate design pyramid – corporate, marketing and design strategy with management across local, regional and national geographical areas**

Corporate design strategy addresses this aspect of placing a company in the marketplace by the creation of a coherent, symbolic image and message communicated through and by its existence online and in the real world's wider environmental extent. Some businesses are local, others national, international or global. A clearly defined corporate design strategy that works hand in hand with the corporate strategy allows the webpage gestalt, manufacturing and shop spatial layout, and overall aesthetic to work together in communicating the necessary corporate image. This time a sociological, technological, economic, environmental and political (STEEP) environmental analysis is undertaken. Designers look at businesses from a different angle; instead of working functionally and down silos, they work with people and processes across the functions and silos. Sometimes this causes friction but again, communication is key. Once both the CEO and corporate design strategist agree on the position of the company in the marketplace, they can select a relevant identity story, themewords and style appropriate to the market *position*. Then the designers can create an image from this information.

Design projects have many contributions, whether this be for website content or a retail park. Design managers have to recognise the design policy that expresses the strategy and apply this thinking to the practicalities of design management. Design is a part of life so most artefacts that exist in a home or working environment are designed; often *silent design* is not recognised. There are many skillsets, media, tools and expertise essential to make one item. This book has concentrated on corporate design from the viewpoint of a changing world as businesses move into the online world. Here and in the real world, having a unique differential existence and brand attracts viewers and customers. So a second corporate design term, *symbolism*, created by visual identity elements and organisational behaviour, was discussed, this combination being called the corporate visual identity system (CVIS).

To create the *symbolic* visual identity, five elements are considered: the creation or selection of a name, font, logo, colours and straplines. Corporate designers create a corporate image for the business so that it stands out amongst its competitors in the marketplace. This image, usually a logo, has to be applied to a wide range of artefacts in extra large, large, small and minute sizes. Now this is the crux of where the understanding of corporate identity is commonly misconstrued – visual identity is part of a corporate identity or brand. There are many other contributions. Within the symbolic heading, organisational behaviour is included, this being the aspects of the culture and the business personality which make it unique. This is achieved by recruitment, training and working to standards, whilst observing those little rituals and ways of working which make that business distinctive – working environment, buildings, interiors and exteriors, and the aggregation of content such as text, video and music – the quality, finish and render all expressing the business position in the marketplace. There are many aspects to the creation of a corporate design and this is why the third corporate design term, *coherence*, is necessary.

As many people are involved in a design project, collaborative working has been at the forefront in recent years, although it has existed by other terms in the past. Here planning and management of all the skillsets over a period of time require commitment and enduring spirit to ensure that the corporate image is *positioned* correctly in the marketplace. In addition, all the necessary legal regulations and standards have to be complied with. Figure 16.2 illustrates the key corporate design terms, their linkage and relationship with one another, as discussed above. So the next time you walk into a shop or view a website, think of all the work that has been put into creating that entity; the skills that have been developed over years, some based in a millennia of evolution and understanding; the materials sourced; the plans and strategies that have had to be formed so that the business exists and functions.

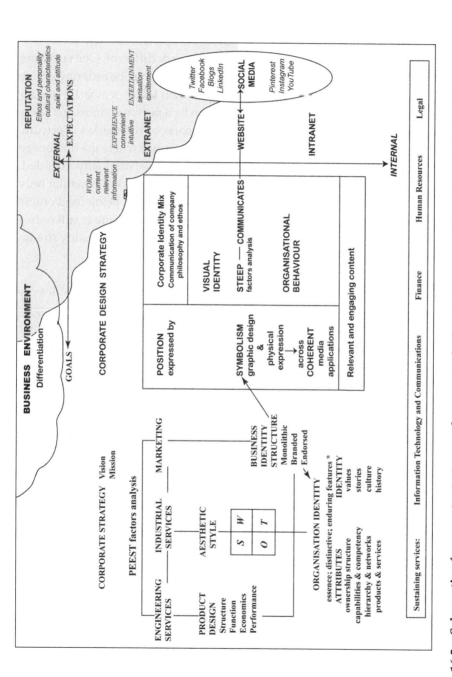

Figure 16.2   Schematic of corporate strategy and corporate design strategy terms linkage and relationship with one another

To end, in an increasing number of situations, websites are the first point of entry to the user's experience of the business. That first click on entering the website to the final exit, whether in the real world or online, matters and therefore has to be carefully managed. Most companies use the same logo offline and online but the customer experience is very different. One customer may walk through the front door of the shop; a second may be ordering online at a desktop PC; and a third may be browsing on their tablet or smartphone for future purchases. The electronic device itself can be a personal status. Yet users can access online shops at any time and in all parts of the market spectrum. The term corporate branding is applied to this occurrence where the homepage is for viewing and purchasing – the bottom line as it was originally intended. SMEs and branded products can be put online with a market potential only dreamt of in the past. Increasingly the term *corporate brand* is being used online as products, services and experiences are branded, but a website is still only a marketing channel, albeit that social media may be adding a personality stream to the corporate image.

Corporate identity appears to be dead or expensive. In fact it is still very much alive as global organisations maintain their initial corporate philosophy by subtle changes, using website technology in a manner conducive to their business ethos. The corporate brand and its image is still sourced in an identity story, with an aesthetic being created by a theme and style, and communicated by relevant technology.

A few points to be made here are that the ramifications of a corporate design are now worldwide, being transmitted across vast distances, countries and cultures. As website technology and digital devices have evolved, both static and dynamic imagery have improved, but as always the image taken is also a reflection of the photographer and film-maker as well as the subject. Hence it is useful to have context comments and the photographer's name. Some would say that the organisational behaviour online is being achieved by social communication. This is true up to a point, but someone has to be employed who has the relevant personality and ability to communicate the idea in the first place.

This takes me back to organisational behaviour in the real world. On entering a shop or themepark, how are customers and visitors welcomed? Are they given a sticker or stamped? A pamphlet or a map? Although many people, including CEOs, associate corporate identity and branding design with visual identity, they are overlooking the impact that the retail, working or themepark's buildings and environs have on customers and visitors, including how well the staff are trained and behave when they are working. Organisational behaviour is about staff attitudes, service and company rituals that instil a sense of belonging to that organisation. Customers go elsewhere if both visual identity and organisational behaviour features are not well attended to, in a similar manner to a website e-commerce site being overcrowded with content, with an architecture that does not aid navigation. Essentially every individual element matters in the cohesive expression of the company identity, brand and image communication – from the first to the last, from the first click to the final exit, both in the real world and online.

Bibliography

Aaker, D.A. (1996). *Building on Brands*. New York, NY: The Free Press.

Abratt, A. (1989). A new approach to the corporate image management process. *Journal of Marketing Management*, 15 (1), pp. 63–76.

Abratt, R. (1995). Role of the market maven in retailing: a general marketplace influencer. *Journal of Business and Psychology*, 10 (1), Fall, pp. 31–55.

Ackerman, L.D. (1988). Identity strategies that make a difference. *The Journal of Business Strategy*, 9 (3), May/June, pp. 28–32.

Addis, M. (2005). New technologies and cultural consumption – edutainment is born. *European Journal of Marketing*, 39 (7/8), pp. 729–736.

Airey, D. (2010). *Logo Design Love*. Berkeley: New Riders.

Albert, S. and Whetten, D.A. (1985). Organizational identity. In Cummings, L.L. and Straw, M.M. (eds), *Research in Organizational Behaviour*, 7. Greenwich, CT: JAI Press, pp. 263–295.

Alvesson, M. (1994). Talking in organizations: managing identity and impressions in an advertising agency. *Organizational Studies*, 15 (4), pp. 535–563.

Appadurai, A. (1986). *The Social Life of Things – Commodities in Cultural Perspective*. Cambridge: Cambridge University Press.

Appleyard, S. (1991). *The Storytellers*. Cheltenham: This England.

Argenti, P.A. (1998). *Corporate Communication*. 2nd edn. New York: Irwin/ McGraw-Hill.

Askehave, I. and Nielsen, A.E. (2005). Digital genres: a challenge to traditional genre theory. *Information Technology and People*, 18 (2), pp. 120–141.

Baines, P. and Haslam, A. (2005). *Type and Typography*. London: Laurence King.

Baker, M.J. and Balmer, J.M.T. (1997). Visual identity: trappings or substance? *European Journal of Marketing*, Bradford, 31 (5), pp. 366–382.

Balmer, J.M.T. (1994). The BBC's corporate identity: myth, paradox and reality. *Journal of General Management*, 19 (3), pp. 33–49.

Balmer, J.M.T. (1995). Corporate branding and connoisseurship. *Journal of General Management*, 21 (1), pp. 22–46.

Balmer, J.M.T. (1997). Corporate identity: the concept, its measurement and management. *European Journal of Marketing*, 31 (5), pp. 340–355.

Balmer, J.M.T. (1998). Corporate identity and the advent of corporate marketing. *Journal of Marketing Management*, 14 (8), pp. 963–996.

Balmer, J.M.T. (2000). *Applying the AC²ID Test of CIM*. April, University of Bradford.

Balmer, J.M.T. (2001). Corporate identity, corporate branding and corporate marketing – seeing through the fog. *European Journal of Marketing*, Bradford, 35 (3/4), pp. 248–291.

Balmer, J.M.T. (2002). Of identities lost and found. *International Studies of Management and Organization*, 32 (3), Fall, pp. 10–27.

Balmer, J.M.T. and Greyser, S.A. (2002). Managing the multiple identities of the corporation. *Californian Management Review*, 44 (3), pp. 72–86.

Balmer, J.M.T. and Greyser, S.A. (2003) (reprinted 2004). *Revealing the Corporation*. London: Routledge.

Balmer, J.M.T. and Greyser, S.A. (2006). Corporate marketing – integrating corporate identity, corporate branding, corporate communications, corporate image and corporate reputation. *European Journal of Marketing*, 40 (7/8), pp. 730–741.

Balmer, J.M.T. and Soenen, G.M. (1999). The AC²ID test of corporate identity management. *Journal of Marketing Management*, 15 (1/3), pp. 69–92.

Balmer, J.M.T. and Wilson, A. (1998). Corporate identity: there is more to this than meets the eye (corporate image and identity management). *International Studies of Management and Organization*, 28 (3), pp. 12–31.

Barich, H. and Kotler, P. (1991). A framework for marketing image management. *Sloan Management Review*, pp. 94–104.

Barthes, R. (1977a). *Image Music Text.* London: Fontana Press.

Barthes, R. (1977b). *Elements of Semiology.* New York: Hill and Wang.

Bar-Yam, Y. (2004). *Making Things Work – Solving Complex Problems in a Complex World.* US NECSI: Knowledge Press.

Baudrillard, J. (1983). The precession of simulacra. In Baudrillard, J., *Simulations.* New York: Semiotext(e).

Bauer, M.W. and Gaskell, G. (2005). *Qualitative Researching; with Text, Image and Sound.* London, Thousand Oaks and New Delhi: Sage Publications.

Baumgarten, A. (1735). *Aesthetica.* In Levinson, J. (ed.) (2005), *The Oxford Handbook of Aesthetic.* Oxford: Oxford University Press, pp. 3–24.

Beal, A. and Strauss, J. (2008). *Radically Transparent Monitoring and Managing Reputations Online.* Indianapolis: Wiley Publishing.

Bennet, A. (2002). Interactive aesthetic. *Design Issues*, 18 (3), Summer, pp. 62–69.

Benjamin, W. (1999). *Illuminations.* London: Pimlico.

Bernstein, D. (1984). *Company Image and Reality: A Critique of Corporate Communications.* Eastbourne, UK: Holt, Rinehart and Winston.

Bernstein, D. (1986). *Company Image and Reality: A Critique of Corporate Communications.* London: Cassell Ltd.

Bernstein, D. (1989). Corporate void. *International Journal of Advertising*, 8, pp. 315–320.

Best, K. (2006). *Design Management: Managing Design Strategy, Process and Implementation.* Lausanne, Switzerland: AVA Publishing SA.

Best, K. (2010). *The Fundamentals of Design Management.* Lausanne, Switzerland: AVA Publishing SA.

Bickerton, D. (2000). Corporate reputation versus corporate branding: the realist debate. *Corporate Communications*, Bradford, 5 (1), pp. 42–48.

Black, M. (1975). The designers and manager syndrome. In Cooper, R., Junginger, S. and Lockwood, T., *The Handbook of Design Management*. Oxford: Berg, pp. 64–73.

Blythe, M., Overbeeke, K., Monk, A.F. and Wright, P.C. (eds) (2003). *Funology: From Usability to Enjoyment*. Dordrecht: Kluwer Academic Publishers.

Boulding, K.E. (1956). *The Image*. Ann Arbour: The University of Michigan Press.

Branigan, J., Robbies, R. and Wolfreyo, J. (1992). *Applying to Derrida*. London: Palgrave Macmillan.

Bruce, M. (2011). Connecting marketing and design. In Cooper, R., Junginger, S. and Lockwood, T., *The Handbook of Design Management*. Oxford: Berg, pp. 331–346.

Budelmann, K., Kim, Y. and Wozniak, C. (2010). *Brand Identity Essentials*. Beverly: Rockport.

Burawoy, M., Blum, J.A., George, S., Gille, Z., Gowan, T., Haney, L., Klawiter, M., Lopez, S.H., Riain, S.O. and Thayer, M. (2000). *Global Ethnography: Forces, Connections and Imaginations in a Post Modern World*. Berkeley, CA: University of California Press.

Caves, R.E. (2002). *Creative Industries: Contracts between Art and Commerce*. Cambridge, MA: Harvard University Press.

Chajet, C. (1989). The making of a new corporate image. *The Journal of Business Strategy*, May/June, pp. 18–20.

Chajet, C. (1997). Corporate reputation and the bottom line. *Corporate Reputation Review*, 11 (2), pp. 19–23.

Cheney, G. and Christensen, L.T. (1999). Identity at issue: linkages between internal and external organizational communication. In Jablin, F.M. and Putname, L.L., *New Handbook of Organizational Communication*. Thousand Oaks, CA: Sage.

Cheyne, T.N. and Ritter, F.E. (2001). Targeting audiences on the internet. *Communications of the ACM*, 44 (4), pp. 94–98.

Christakis, N. (2010). The hidden influence of social networks. Available from: <www.youtube.com/watch?v=2U-tOghblfE>. Sourced from <http://www.newmediaangels.com>.

Clark, H., Chandler, J. and Barry, J. (1994). *Organisation and Identities*. London: Chapman and Hall.

Cloninger, C. (2002). *Fresh Styles for Web Designers: Eye Candy from the Underground*. Indiana: New Riders Publishing. In Engholm, I. (2002), Digital style history: the development of graphic design on the internet. *Digital Creativity*, 13 (1), pp. 193 211.

Cooper, R., Junginger, S. and Lockwood, T. (2011). *The Handbook of Design Management*. Oxford: Berg.

Cooper, R. and Press, M. (1997). *The Design Agenda: A Guide to Successful Design Management*. Chichester: Wiley.

Cornelissen, J.P. and Elving, W.J. (2003). Managing corporate identity: an integrative framework of dimensions and determinants. *Corporate Communications*, Bradford, 8 (2), pp. 114–121.

Coupland, K. (2000). *Webworks: Navigation*. Gloucester, MA: Rockport Publishers Inc.

Creelman, J. (1998). *Building and Implementing a Balanced Scorecard*. London: Business Intelligence Ltd.

Cross, N. (1984). *Developments in Design Methodology*. Chichester: John Wiley & Sons Ltd.

Czarniawska-Joerges, B. (1994). Narratives of individual and organizational identities. In Deetz, S.A. (ed.), *Communication Yearbook*. Thousand Oaks, CA: Sage.

Davidow, A. (2002). Computer screens are not like paper: typography on the web. In Sassoon, R. (ed.), *Computers and Typography 2*. Bristol: Intellect Books, pp. 21–39.

De Bono, E. (1998). *Simplicity*. London: Viking Penguin.

De Brabandere, L. (2005). *The Forgotten Half of Change: Achieving Greater Creativity Through Changes in Perception*. Chicago: Dearborn Trade Publishing.

De Chernatony, L. (2001). Succeeding with brands on the internet. *Brand Management*, 8 (3) February, pp. 186–195.

De Large, C. (2004). Storytelling as a critical success factor in design processes and outcomes. *Design Management Review*, Summer.

Deleuze, G. and Guattari, F. (1988). Introduction: rhizome. In Deleuze G. and Guattari, F., *A Thousand Plateaus*. London: The Athlone Press, pp. 3–28.

De Saussure, F. (1966). *Course in General Linguistics*. New York: McGraw Hill.

Desmet, P. (2004). From disgust to desire: how products elicit emotions. In McDonagh, D., Hekkert, D., Gyi, D. and van Erp, J. (eds), *Proceedings of the 3rd International Conference on Design and Emotion*. Loughborough University, Loughborough, England.

Devereaux, L. and Hillman, R. (1995). *Fields of Vision: Essays in Film Studies, Visual Anthropology and Photography*. Berkeley, CA: University of California Press.

D'Orazio, F. (2013). *The Brand Gap, FACE*. Digital Shoreditch Conference and Exhibition.

Dolphin, R.R. (2004). Corporate reputation: a value creating strategy. *Corporate Governance*, 4 (3) pp. 77–92.

Dormer, P. (ed.) (1997). *The Culture of Craft*. Manchester: Manchester University Press.

Dowdy, C. (2002). Bonjour. Hello again. Who am I? *Print*, 56 (2), May–June, pp. 114–119.

Dowling, G.R. (1994). *Corporate Reputations: Strategies for Developing the Corporate Brand*. London: Kogan Page.

Dowling, G.R. (2004). Corporate reputations: should you compete on yours? *Californian Management Review*, Spring.

Dumas, A. and Whitfield, A. (1989). Why design is difficult to manage: a survey of attitudes and practices in British industry. *European Journal of Management*, 7 (1), pp. 50–56.

Duncan, T.R. and Everett, S.E. (1993). Client perceptions of integrated marketing communications. *Journal of Advertising Research*, May–June, pp. 30–39.

Dutta, S. (2010). What's your personal social media strategy. *Harvard Business Review*, November, pp. 1–5.

Earles, M. (2013). *Mapping Social Behaviour.* Digital Shoreditch Conference and Exhibition.

Edelman, D.C. (2010). Branding in the digital age: you're spending your money in all the wrong places. *Harvard Business Review,* December, pp. 65–69.

Edgar, A. and Sedgwick, P. (2002). *Cultural Theory: The Key Thinkers.* London: Routledge.

Engholm, I. (2002a). Digital style history: the development of graphic design on the internet. *Digital Creativity,* 13 (4), pp. 193–211.

Engholm, I. (2002b). Digital art history? Exploring practice in a network society. Genre and style as a classification method. The graphic design development of the WWW from the perspective of genre and style history. Available from: *<http://www.chart.ac.uk/chart2002/papers/noframes/engholm.html>* [Accessed: 31 May 2007].

Feisner, E.A. (2014). *Color Studies.* London: Bloombury Publishing Inc.

Finnegan, R. (2002). *Communication: The Multiple Modes of Interconnection.* London: Routledge.

Fletcher, A. (1994). *The Art of Looking Sideways.* Oxford: Phaidon.

Fombrun, C.J. (1996). *Reputation: Realizing Value from the Corporate Image.* Cambridge, MA: Harvard Business School Press.

Fombrun, C.J. and Rindova, V.P. (2000). The road to transparency: reputation management at Royal Dutch/Shell. In Schultz, M., Hatch, M.J. and Larsen, M. (eds), *The Expressive Organization.* Oxford: Oxford University Press, pp. 77–96.

Fombrun, C.J. and Shanley, M. (1990). What's in a name? Reputation building and corporate strategy. *Academy of Management Journal,* 33, pp. 233–258.

Fombrun, C.J and Van Riel, C.B.M. (1998). The reputational landscape. *Corporate Reputation Review,* 1 (1), pp. 5–13.

Fombrun, C.J and Van Riel, C.B.M. (2004). *Fame and Fortune: How Successful Companies Build Winning Reputations.* Upper Saddle River, NJ: Financial Times Prentice Hall.

Foo, C-T. (2001). Designing e-logos in corporate identity strategy. *Brand Management*, 8 (4 and 5), May, pp. 334–345.

Foo, C-T. (2003). Visualizing complexity in corporate identity on the internet: an empirical investigation. *Corporate Communications: An International Journal*, 8 (1), pp. 11–17.

Foo, C-T. (2006). Competitive aesthetics, semiotics, chaos and leadership: corporate photography strategy for the CEO. *Corporate Communications: An International Journal*, 11 (2), pp. 109–125.

Forrester Groundswell Report (2012). In Harris, C., *Surviving Social Media*. New Media Angels SocialBusinessGuides.com.

Fraser, M. and Dutta, S. (2008). *Throwing Sheep in the Boardroom: How Online Social Networking Will Transform Your Life, Work and World*. Chichester: Wiley.

Fry, T. (2000). *A New Design Philosophy: An Introduction to Defuturing*. Sydney: University of New South Wales Press.

Funk, D. and Ndubisi, N.O. (2006). Colour and product choice: a study of gender roles. *Management Research News*, 29 (1/2), pp. 41–52.

Gaines-Ross, L. (2008). *Corporate Reputation*. Hoboken, NJ: Wiley and Sons.

Gardener, H. (1983). *Frames of Mind: The Theory of Multiple Intelligences*. New York: Basic Books.

Garmann Johnsen, H.C. and Ennals, R. (2012). *Creating Collaborative Advantage*. Farnham: Gower.

Genosko, G. (1994). *Baudrillard and Signs*. London: Routledge.

Giaccardi, E. (2006). Collective storytelling and social creativity in the virtual museum: a case study. *Design Issues*, 22, Summer, pp. 29–40.

Gioia, D.A. (1998). From individual to organizational identity. In Whetten, D.A. and Godfrey, P.C. (eds), *Identity in Organizations*. London: Sage.

Gioia, D.A., Schultz, M. and Corley, K.G. (2000). Organizational identity, image and adaptive instability. *Academy of Management Review*, 25 (1), pp. 63–81.

Gorb, P. (1988). What is design management? *Design Management Seminar Papers*. London Business School.

Gorb, P. and Dumas, A. (1987). Silent design. In Cooper, R., Junginger, S. and Lockwood, T., *The Handbook of Design Management*. Oxford: Berg, pp. 52–63.

Goveia, C. and Hatmaker (2003). *Visual Thesaurus: A Quick Flip Brainstorming Tool for Graphic Designers*. Gloucester, MA: Rockport Publishers.

Grant, D. and Oswick, C. (eds) (1996). *Metaphor and Organizations*. London: Sage.

Gray, E.R. and Balmer J.M.T. (1998). Managing corporate image and reputation. *Long Range Planning*, 31 (5), pp. 695–702.

Gray, E.R. and Smeltzer, L.R. (1985). Corporate image: an integral part of strategy. *Sloan Management Review*, 26 (4), pp. 73–78.

Greyser, S.A. (1999). Advancing and enhancing corporate reputation. *Corporate Communications: An International Journal*, 4 (4), pp. 177–181.

Grunig, J. (ed.) (1992). *Excellence in Public Relations and Communication Management*. Hillsdale, NJ: Lawrence Erlbaum.

Grunig, J. (1993). Image and substance: from symbolic to behavioural. *Public Relations Review*, 19 (2), pp. 121–139.

Guirand, P. (1975). *Semiology*. London: Routledge.

Hallam, J. (2013). *What Happened When Social Media Grew Up*. Digital Shoreditch Conference and Exhibition.

Hampden-Turner, C. and Trompenaars, F. (2004). *Building Cross-Cultural Competence*. Chichester: Wiley.

Harris, C. (2012). *Surviving Social Media*. NewMediaAngelsSocialBusinessGuides. com.

Harvey, M. (2002). Hand, eye and mind: a design trinity. In Sassoon, R. (ed.), *Computers and Typography 2*. Bristol: Intellect Books, pp. 91–97.

Hatch, M.J. and Schultz, M.(1998). The identity of organizations. In Whetten, D. and Godfrey, P. (eds), *Identity in Organizations*. Thousand Oaks: Sage.

Hatch, M.J. and Schultz, M. (2000). Scaling the Tower of Babel: relational differences between identity, image and culture in organizations. In Schultz, M., Hatch, M.J. and Larsen, M. (eds), *The Expressive Organization*. Oxford: Oxford University Press, pp. 11–35.

Held, D. and McGrew, A. (2000). *The Global Transformations Reader: An Introduction to the Globalization Debate*. Cambridge: Polity Press.

Henderson, P.M. and Cote, J.A. (1998). Guidelines for selecting or modifying logos. *The Journal of Marketing*, 62 (2), April, pp. 14–30.

Henrion, F.H.K., Ludlow, C. and Schmidt, K. (1993). *Corporate Identity in a Multicultural Marketplace*. Summary of the Third Pan-European Study on Corporate Identity. Henrion, Ludlow, and Schmidt: Consultants in Corporate Identity, London.

Hine, C. (2000). *Virtual Ethnography*. London, Thousand Oaks and New Delhi: Sage Publications.

Hollins, W.J. (2011). A prospective of service design management: past, present and future. In Cooper, R., Junginger, S. and Lockwood, T., *The Handbook of Design Management*. Oxford: Berg, pp. 214–230.

Hufton, S. (1995). *Step by Step Calligraphy: A Complete Guide with Creative Projects*. London: Phoenix Illustrated.

Ind, N. (1992). *The Corporate Image: Strategies for Effective Identity Programmes*. London: Kogan Page.

Ind, N. (1998). An integrated approach to corporate branding. *Journal of Brand Management*, 5 (5), pp. 323–329.

Introna, L.D. and Nissenbaum, H. (2000). Shaping the web: why the politics of search engines matters. *The Information Society: An International Journal*, 16 (3), July–September, pp. 169–185.

Jamieson, F. and Miyoschi, M. (eds) (1998). *The Cultures of Globalization*. London: Duke University Press.

Jevnaker, B.H. (2000). How design becomes strategic. *Design Management Journal*, Winter, pp. 41–47.

Jevnaker, B.H. (2005). Viva activa: on relationships between design(ers) and business. *Design Issues*, 21 (3), Summer.

Johnson, J. (2005). Complexity science in collaborative design. *CoDesign*, 1 (4), pp. 223–242.

Johnson, J., Petrie, M. and Sharp, H. (2006). Complexity through combination: an account of knitwear design. *Design Studies*, 27 (2), March, pp. 183–222.

Jones, P. (2010). *Communicating Strategy.* Farnham: Gower.

Jones, R. (2000). *The Big Idea.* Hammersmith: Harper Collins.

Jury, D. (1999). Craft: before, during and after graphic design. *Typographic*, 55.

Jury, D. (2002). Changes in the relationship between printer and designer: craft before, during and after graphic design. In Sassoon, R. (ed.), *Computers and Typography 2.* Bristol: Intellect Books, pp. 81–90.

Kapferer, J. (1992). *Strategic Brand Management.* London: Kogan Page.

Kaplan, R.S. and Norton, D.P. (1996). *Translating Strategy into Action: The Balanced Scorecard.* Boston: Harvard Business School Press.

Knox, S., Maklan, S. and Thompson, K.E. (2000). Building unique organization value proposition. In Schultz, M., Hatch, M.J. and Larsen, M. (eds), *The Expressive Organization.* Oxford: Oxford University Press, pp. 138–153.

Kotler, P. and Rath, G.A. (2011). Design: a powerful but neglected strategic tool. In Cooper, R., Junginger, S. and Lockwood, T., *The Handbook of Design Management.* Oxford: Berg, pp. 87–95.

Kress, G. and Van Leeuwen, T. (1996). *Reading Images: The Grammar of Visual Design.* London: Routledge.

Lane Keller, K. and Aaker, D.A. (1998). The impact of corporate marketing on a company's brand extensions. *Corporate Reputation Review*, 1 (4), pp. 344–355.

Larsen, M.H. (2000). Managing the corporate story. In Schultz, M., Hatch, M.J. and Larsen, M. (eds), *The Expressive Organization.* Oxford: Oxford University Press, pp. 196–207.

Lash, S. and Lury, C. (2007). *Global Culture Industry.* Cambridge: Polity.

Laurel, B. (1993). *Computers as Theatre.* Reading, MA: Addison Wesley Longman.

Levinson, J. (2005). Philosophical aesthetics: an overview. In Levinson, J. (ed.), *The Oxford Handbook of Aesthetic*. Oxford: Oxford University Press, pp. 3–24.

Levy, D. (2002). Slouching toward cyberspace: the place of the lettering arts in a digital era. In Sassoon, R. (ed.), *Computers and Typography 2*. Bristol: Intellect Books, pp. 75–80.

Lindstrom, M. (2001). Corporate branding and the web: a global/local challenge. *Brand Management*, 8 (4/5), May, pp. 365–368.

Lockwood, T. (2004). Integrating design into organizational culture. *Design Management Review*, 15(2), Spring, pp. 32–39.

Lopuck, L. (1996). *Designing Multimedia*. Berkeley, CA: Peachpit Press.

Luhmann, N. (2000). *Art as a Social System*. Stanford, CA: Stanford University Press.

Lupton, E. (2004). *Thinking with Type: A Critical Guide for Designers, Writers, Editors and Students*. New York: Princeton Architectural Press.

McAdams, S. and Bigand, E. (eds) (1993). *Thinking in Sound: The Cognitive Psychology of Human Audition*. Oxford: Clarendon Press; New York: Oxford University Press.

Mackenzie-Kerr, I. (2002). Book design: before and after. In Sassoon, R. (ed.), *Computers and Typography 2*. Bristol: Intellect Books, pp. 69–74.

Mahon, J.F. and Wartick, S.I. (2003). Dealing with stakeholders: how reputation, credibility and framing influence the game. *Corporate Reputation Review*, 6 (1), pp. 19–35.

Malinowski, B. (1922). *Argonauts of the Western Pacific: An Account of Native Enterprise and Adventure in the Archipelagos of Melanesian New Guinea*. London: Routledge and Sons.

Manu, A. (2012). *Behavior Space*. Farnham: Gower.

Marcus, G.E. (1986). Contemporary problems of ethnography in the modern world system. In Clifford, J. and Marcus, G.E., *Writing Culture: The Poetics and Politics of Ethnography*. Berkeley, CA: University of California Press.

Marcus, G.E. (1992). Past, present and emergent identities: requirements for ethnographies of late twentieth-century modernity worldwide. In Lash, S. and Friedman, J. (eds), *Modernity and Identity*. Oxford: Blackwell.

Marguiles, W. (1977). Making the most of your corporate identity. *Harvard Business Review*, July–August, pp. 66–77.

Martineau, P. (1958). Sharper focus for the corporate image. *Harvard Business Review*, November–December, pp. 49–58.

Marwick, N. and Fill, C. (1997). Towards a framework for managing corporate identity. *European Journal of Marketing: Special Edition on Corporate Identity*, 31 (5/6), pp. 396–409.

McLuhan, M. (1964). *Understanding Media*. London: Routledge.

McLuhan, M, Benedetti, P. and De Hart, N. (1997). *Forward Through the Rearview Mirror: Reflections on and by Marshall McLuhan*. Cambridge, MA: MIT Press.

Melewar, T.C. (2001). Measuring visual identity: a multi-construct study. *Corporate Communications*, 6, pp. 36–42.

Melewar, T.C. (2003). Determinants of the corporate identity construct: a review of the literature. *Journal of Marketing Communications*, 9 (4), pp. 195–220.

Melewar, T.C., Bassett, K. and Simoes, C. (2006). The role of communication and visual identity in modern organisations. *Corporate Communications*, 11 (2), pp. 138–147.

Melewar, T.C. and Harold, J. (1999). The role of corporate identity in merger and acquisitions activity. *Journal of General Management*, 26 (2), pp. 17–31.

Melewar, T.C. and Jenkins, E. (2002). Defining the corporate identity construct. *Corporate Reputation Review*, 5 (1), pp, 76–91.

Melewar, T.C. and Karaosmanoglu, E. (2006). Seven dimensions of corporate identity: a categorization from the practitioner's perspective. *European Journal of Marketing*, Bradford, 40 (7/8), pp. 846–869.

Melewar, T.C. and Navalekar, X. (2002). Leveraging corporate identity in the digital age. *Marketing Intelligence and Planning*, Bradford, 20 (2), pp. 96–104.

Melewar, T.C. and Saunders, J. (1998). Global corporate visual identity: standardization or localization. *International Marketing Review*, 15 (4), pp. 291–308.

Melewar, T.C., Saunders, J. and Balmer, J.M.T. (2001). Cause, effect and benefits of a standardised corporate visual identity system of UK companies operating in Malaysia. *European Journal of Marketing*, 35 (3/4), pp. 414–427.

Melewar, T.C. and Smith, N. (2003). The internet revolution: some global marketing implications. *Marketing Intelligence & Planning*, 21 (6), pp. 363–369.

Merleau-Ponty, M. (1964). Indirect language and the voices of silence. In M. Merleau-Ponty, *Signs*, Evanston, IL: Northwestern University Press. In Engholm, I. (2002), Digital style history: the development of graphic design on the internet. *Digital Creativity*, 13 (4), pp. 193–211.

Merleau-Ponty, M. (1964). *Primacy of Perception*. Northern University Studies in Phenomenology and Existential Philosophy.

Meyer, L. (1989). *Style and Music: Theory, History, and Ideology*. Philadelphia: University of Pennsylvania Press.

Mintzberg, H. (1989). *Mintzberg on Management: Inside Our Strange World of Organizations*. New York: Free Press.

Mitroff, I.I. and Kilmann, R.H. (1979). *Methodological Approaches to Social Science: Integrating Divergent Concepts and Theories*. San Francisco: Jossey-Bass.

Moingeon, B. and Ramanantsoa, B. (1997). Understanding corporate identity: the French school of thought. *European Journal of Marketing: Special Edition on Corporate Identity*, 31 (5/6), pp. 383–395.

Morley, D. (2000). *Home Territories: Media, Mobility and Identity*. London and New York: Routledge.

Napoles, V. (1988). *Corporate Identity Design*. New York, NY: Vas Nostrand Reinhold.

Neumeier, M. (2006). *The Brand Gap*. Berkeley: New Riders.

Nielsen, J. and Trias, J.M. (2000). From the times of the first scribes: innovation and technology within graphic design. *Digital Creativity*, 11 (2), pp. 89–98.

Norman, D.A. (2002). *The Design of Everyday Things*. London: The MIT Press.

Norman, D.A. (2004). *Emotional Design: Why We Love (or Hate) Everyday Things*. New York: Basic Books.

Oakley, M. (1984). Organising design activities. In Cooper, R., Junginger, S. and Lockwood, T., *The Handbook of Design Management*. Oxford: Berg, pp. 74–86.

Oakley, M. (2001). Policies, objectives and standards. In *What is Design Management?* Open University Press, pp. 106–114.

Olins, W. (1978). *The Corporate Personality: An Inquiry into the Nature of Corporate Identity*. London: The Design Council.

Olins, W. (1978–1979). Corporate identity: the myth and the reality. *Journal of the Royal Society of Arts*, 127, December 1978–November 1979, pp. 209–218.

Olins, W. (1989). *Corporate Identity: Making Business Strategy Visible Through Design*. London: Thames and Hudson.

Olins, W. (1990a). *The Wolff Olins Guide to Corporate Identity*. London: The Design Council.

Olins, W. (1990b). *Corporate Identity – Making Business Strategy Visible Through Design*. London, Thames and Hudson.

Olins, W. (1991). Corporate identity and behavioural dimension. *Design Management Journal*, Winter, pp. 42–45.

Olins, W. (1995). *The New Guide to Identity*. Aldershot: The Design Council.

Olins, W. (2000). How brands are taking over the corporation. In Schultz, M., Hatch, M.J. and Larsen, M. (eds), *The Expressive Organization*. Oxford: Oxford University Press, pp. 51–65.

Olins, W. (2003). *On B®and*. London: Thames and Hudson.

Olins, W. (2008). *The Brand Handbook*. London: Thames and Hudson.

Oxman, R. (2006). Theory and design in the first digital age. *Design Studies*, 27, pp. 229–265.

Parker, M. (2000). *Organizational Culture and Identity*. London: Sage.

Patel, M. (2005). Search for vernacular identity. *Design Issues*, 21 (4), Autumn, pp. 32–40.

Pavitt, J. (ed.) (2001). *Brand New*. London: V&A Publications.

Perrow, C. (1986). *Complex Organizations* (3rd edn). New York: Random House.

Podnar, K. (2005). Corporate identity in Slovenia. *Corporate Communications: An International Journal*, 10 (1), pp. 69–82.

Powell, W.W. (1990). Neither market nor hierarchy: network forms of an organization. *Research in Organizational Behaviour*, 12 (1), pp. 295–336.

Press, M. (2011). Working the crowd: crowdsourcing as a strategy for co-design. In Cooper, R., Junginger, S. and Lockwood, T., *The Handbook of Design Management*. Oxford: Berg, pp. 512–531.

Press, M. and Cooper, R. (2003). *The Design Experience: The Role of Design and Designers in the 21st Century*. Aldershot: Ashgate Publishing.

Preston, P. and Kerr, A. (2001). Digital media, nation states and local cultures: a case of multimedia 'content' production. *Media, Culture and Society*, 23, pp. 109–131.

Pruzan, P. (2001). Corporate reputation, image and identity. *Corporate Reputation Review*, 4 (1), pp. 50–66.

Pye, D. (1968). *The Nature and Art of Workmanship*. London: The Herbert Press.

Pye, D. (1978). *The Nature and Aesthetics of Design*. London: The Herbert Press.

Qvortrup, L. (2006). Understanding new digital media: medium theory and complexity theory. *European Journal of Communication*, 21, pp. 345–356.

Rassam, C. (1995). *Design and Corporate Success*. Aldershot: The Design Council/ Gower Publications.

Read, H. (1934). *Art and Industry: The Principles of Industrial Design*. London: Faber and Faber.

Ries, A. and Trout, J. (2001). *Positioning: The Battle for Your Mind*. New York: McGraw-Hill.

Robinson, A. (1995). *The Story of Writing: Alphabets, Hieroglyphs and Pictograms*. London: Thames and Hudson.

Rosethorn, H. and Contributors (2009). *The Employer Brand: Keeping Faith with the Deal*. Farnham, UK: Gower Publishing.

Ross, S. (2005). Style in art. In Levinson, J. (ed.), *The Oxford Handbook of Aesthetics*. Oxford: Oxford University Press, pp. 228–244.

Rowden, M. (2000). *The Art of Identity*. Aldershot: Gower.

Sametz, R. and Maydoney, A. (2003). Storytelling through design. *Design Management Journal*, Fall, pp. 10–24.

Sassoon, R. (ed.) (2002). *Computers and Typography 2*. Bristol: Intellect Books.

Schapiro, M. (1994). *Theory and Philosophy of Art: Style, Artist and Society*. New York: George Braziller.

Schmidt, C. (1995). *The Quest for Identity: Strategies, Methods and Examples*. London: Cassell.

Schmitt, B. and Simonson, A. (1997). *Marketing Aesthetics: The Strategic Management of Brands, Identity, and Image*. New York: Free Press.

Schroeder, J.E. (2000). Edouard Manet, Calvin Klein and the strategic use of scandal. In Brown, S. and Patterson, A. (eds), *Imagining Marketing: Art, Aesthetics, and the Avant Garde*. London: Routledge.

Schroeder, J.E. (2005). The artist and the brand. *European Journal of Marketing*, 39 (11), pp. 1291–1305.

Schultz, D.E., Tannenbaum, S.I. and Lauterborn, R.F. (1994). *Integrated Marketing Communication: Pulling It Together and Making It Work*. Chicago: NTC Business Books.

Schultz, M., Hatch, M.J. and Larsen, M.G. (2000). *The Expressive Organization*. Oxford: Oxford University Press.

Sebastian, R. (2005). The interface between design and management. *Design Issues*, 21 (1), Winter.

Selame, E. and Selame, J. (1995). *Developing a Corporate Identity: How to Stand Out in the Crowd*. New York: Wiley.

Shaw, G.G. (2000). Planning and communicating using stories. In Schultz, M., Hatch, M.J. and Larsen, M. (eds), *The Expressive Organization*. Oxford: Oxford University Press, pp. 182–195.

Shelton, S.T. (2012). Threats to brands from social media. *New York Law Journal*, May.

Simmons, A. (2002). *The Story Factor*. Cambridge, MA: Perseus Publishing.

Sklar, J. (2000). *Principles of Web Design*. Cambridge, MA: Thomson Learning.

Slater, D. (1998). *Consumer, Culture and Modernity*. Cambridge: Polity Press.

Smith, A.D. (1999). *Towards a Global Culture? Global Culture, Nationalism, Globalization and Modernity*. London: Sage Publications.

Smith, K.A. (2004). *Text in the Book Format*. New York: Keith Smith Books.

Sparke, P. (2004). *An Introduction to Design and Culture*. London and New York: Routledge.

Sparke, P. (2009). *The Genius of Design*. London: Quadrille Publishing.

Sparrow, J. (2012). *The Culture Builders*. Farnham: Gower.

Spiekermann, E. and Ginger, E.M. (2003). *Stop Stealing Sheep and Find Out How Type Works*. Berkeley, CA: Adobe Press.

Steidl, P. and Emory, G. (1997). *Corporate Image and Identity Studies: Designing the Corporate Future*. Warriewood, Australia: Business and Professional Publishing.

Sterling, L.C. (2012). *Confessions of a Grumpy Advertising Man: What It Really Takes to Succeed with Advertising, Branding and Social Media*. L.C. Sterling.

Stern, B.B. and Schroeder, J.E. (1994). Interpretative methodology from art and literary criticism: a humanistic approach to advertising imagery. *European Journal of Marketing*, 28 (8/9), pp. 114–132.

Stuart, H. (1998). Exploring the corporate identity–corporate image interface: an empirical study of accountancy firms. *Journal of Communications Management*, 2 (4), pp. 357–371.

Stuart, H. (1999). Towards a definitive model of the corporate identity management process. *Corporate Communications: An International Journal: Special Edition on Corporate Identity*, 4 (4), pp. 200–207.

Sturken, M. and Cartwright, L. (2001). *Practices of Looking: An Introduction to Visual Culture*. Oxford: Oxford University Press.

Surowiecki, J. (2004). *The Wisdom of Crowds: Why the Many Are Smarter Than the Few*. New York: Doubleday; London: Abacus.

Swales, J.M. (1990). *Genre Analysis: English in Academic and Research Settings*. Cambridge: Cambridge University Press. In Askehave, I. and Nielsen, A.E. (2005), Digital genres: a challenge to traditional genre theory. *Information Technology and People*, 18 (2), pp. 357–371.

Tapia, A. (2003). Graphic design in the digital era: the rhetoric of hypertext. *Design Issues*, 19 (1), Winter, pp. 5–24.

Teeman, M. (2013). *Mobile Marketing at Metro Newspaper*. Digital Shoreditch Conference and Exhibition 2013.

Topalian, A. (1984). Corporate identity: beyond the visual overstatements. *International Journal of Advertising*, 3, pp. 55–62.

Topalian, A. (2003). Experienced reality: the development of corporate identity in the digital era. *European Journal of Marketing*, Bradford, 37 (7/8), pp. 1119–1133.

Triedman, C.D. (2002). *Color Graphics: The Power of Color in Graphic Design*. Gloucester, MA: Rockport Publishers.

Tufte, E.R. (1997). *Visual Explanations: Images, Quantities, Evidence and Narrative*. Cheshire, CT: Graphics Press.

Tufte, E.R. (2001). *The Visual Display of Quantitative Information*. Cheshire, CT: Graphics Press.

Tufte, E.R. (2005). *Envisioning Information*. Cheshire, CT: Graphics Press.

Turkle, S. (1995). *Life on the Screen*. New York: Simon & Schuster.

Turkle, S. (2005). *The Second Self Computers and the Human Spirit*. London: MIT Press.

Turner, R. (2013). *Design Leadership: Securing the Strategic Value of Design*. Farnham, UK: Gower Publishing.

Udsen, L.E. and Jorgensen, A.K. (2005). The aesthetic turn: unravelling recent aesthetic approaches to human–computer interaction. *Digital Creativity*, 16 (4), pp. 205–216.

Urmson, J. (1957). What makes a situation aesthetic? *Proceedings of the Aristotelian Society*, Supplement, 31, pp. 75–92.

Vaid, H. (2003). *Branding: Brand Strategy, Design and Implementation of Corporate and Product Identity*. London: Cassell Illustrated.

Van Gelder, S. (2003). *Global Brand Strategy: Unlocking Brand Potential, Across Countries and Markets*. London: Kogan Page.

Van Rekom, J. (1993). *Corporate Identity: Its Measurement and Use in Corporate Communications*. Proceedings of the European Marketing Association Conference, pp. 1497–1514.

Van Riel, C.B.M. (1995). *Principles of Corporate Communications*. London: Prentice Hall.

Van Riel, C.B.M. (2000). Corporate communication orchestrated by a sustainable corporate story. In Schultz, M., Hatch, M.J. and Larsen, M. (eds), *The Expressive Organization*. Oxford: Oxford University Press, pp. 157–181.

Van Riel, C.B.M. and Balmer, J.M.T. (1997). Corporate identity: the concept, its management and measurement. *European Journal of Marketing: Special Edition on Corporate Identity*, 31 (5/6), pp. 340–355.

Van Riel, C.B.M. and Fombrum, C.J. (1998). The reputational landscape. *Corporate Reputation Review*, 1 (1) pp. 5–13.

Van Riel, C.B.M., Stroeker, N.E. and Maathuis, O.J.M. (1998). Measuring corporate images. *Corporate Reputation Review*, 1, pp. 313–326.

Van Riel, C.B.M., Van den Ban, A. and Heijmans, E-J. (2001). The added value of corporate logos. *European Journal of Marketing*, 35 (3/4), pp. 428–440.

Vendelo, M.T. (1998). Narrating corporate reputation. *International Studies of Management and Organization*, 28 (3), pp. 120–137.

Vergin, R.C. and Qoronfleh, M.W. (1998). Reputation. In Dolphin, R.R. (2004), Corporate reputation: a value creating strategy. *Corporate Governance*, 4 (3), pp. 77–92.

Walker, D. (2001). Managers and designers: two tribes at war? In *What is Design Management?* Open University Press, pp. 147–154.

Westcott Allesandri, S. (2001). Modelling corporate identity: a concept explanation and theoretical explanation. *Corporate Communications: An International Journal*, 6 (4), pp. 173–184.

Wheeler, A. (2009). *Designing Brand Identity*. Hoboken, NJ: Wiley.

Whetten, D.A. and Godfrey, P.C. (1998). *Identity in Organizations*. London: Sage.

Wilson, R. and Dissanayake, W. (1996). *Tracking the Global/Local*. Durham and London: Duke University Press.

Winograd, T. (1996). *Bringing Design to Software*. New York: ACM Press.

Zec, P. (2000). *Designing Success: Strategy, Concepts, Processes*. Essen: Design Zentrum Nordrhein Westfalen.

Zeldman, J. (2001). *Taking Your Talent to the Web: Making the Transition from Graphic Design to Web Design*. Indianapolis: New Riders.

Michael Wolff, Interview, 18 May 2006.

www.european-patent-office.org   European Patent Office

www.fipr.org   Foundation for Information
                                    Policy Research

www.icann.org   Internet Corporation for Assigned
                                    Names and Numbers

www.ilpf.org   Internet Law and Policy Forum

www.ipo.gov.uk   Intellectual Property Office

www.legislation.gov.uk	UK legislation
www.oii.ox.ac.uk	Oxford Internet Institute, University of Oxford
www.patent.gov.uk	UK Patent Office
www.uspto.gov	United States Patent and Trademark Office
www.w3.org	World Wide Web Consortium

Index

For Product Safety Concerns and Information please contact our EU
representative GPSR@taylorandfrancis.com Taylor & Francis Verlag GmbH,
Kaufingerstraße 24, 80331 München, Germany

Printed and bound by CPI Group (UK) Ltd, Croydon, CR0 4YY

01/05/2025

01858461-0005